KT-159-610

WOOSTER'S WORLD

Jeeves and Bertie Wooster are P. G. Wodehouse's
most celebrated characters, made famous
in print, on radio and on television. *Wooster's
World* is the indispensable companion to their
unique world, stretching over the half-century of their
life together.

Wooster's World assembles every character
from the Wooster-Jeeves series of stories from
1917 onwards. It covers also the doings and
personnel of the Drones Club, as well as such
diverse subjects as A Surging Sea of Aunts, A
Miscarriage of Justices and a useful Now We
Know Department. Hilariously funny when
encountered in the pages of Wodehouse, these
characters seem to take on an extra dimension of
hilarity, when seen here, as it were, in the
round.

'Mr Wodehouse's idyllic world can never stale.
He will continue to release future generations
from captivity that may be more irksome than
our own. He has made a world for us to live and
delight in.'

Evelyn Waugh

Wooster's World

Geoffrey Jaggard

CORONET BOOKS
Hodder and Stoughton

To A. W. 'Dusty' Rhodes,
who strove valiantly for it

Copyright © Geoffrey Jaggard, 1967

First published in Great Britain 1967
by Macdonald & Co Ltd

Coronet edition 1979

This book is sold subject to the condition that
it shall not, by way of trade or otherwise, be
lent, re-sold, hired out or otherwise circulated
without the publisher's prior consent in any
form of binding or cover other than that in
which this is published and without a similar
condition including this condition being
imposed on the subsequent purchaser.

Printed and bound in Great Britain for
Hodder and Stoughton Paperbacks, a
division of Hodder and Stoughton Ltd,
Mill Road, Dunton Green, Sevenoaks, Kent
(Editorial Office: 47 Bedford Square,
London, WC1 3DP) by William Collins
Sons & Co Ltd, Glasgow

ISBN 0 340 23680 9

INTRODUCTION BY AUBERON WAUGH

Somewhere on earth, as we know, there exists the Complete
Concordance to Wodehouse. It was the life's work of Geoffrey
Jaggard, and already extended to over 350,000 words when he
published this handbook twelve years ago – what he modestly
described as a 'smallish though (one hopes) fairly ripe and fruity
slice of the big plum cake'. One day, no doubt, some learned or
philanthropic foundation will pay to have it all printed; even
before then, it might occur to someone to produce a second handbook covering the Blandings Castle cycle of novels. One is reminded
of this aching gap in Wodehouse studies on reading the present
work, which allows itself to mention Lord Emsworth briefly and
his younger son, Freddie Threepwood, a member of the Drones,
but few others from that golden canon.

Even *Wooster's World* is incomplete. Mr Jaggard suffered from
a problem which never troubled Alexander Cruden in his work on
the Concordance of the Holy Scriptures (1737) – the Master was
still producing new Wooster novels to the very end. Two appeared
after *Wooster's World* had gone to press – 'Much Obliged Jeeves'
(1971) and 'Aunts aren't Gentlemen' (1974). These late Jeeves
books are missing from the sources, which nevertheless extend
beyond Jeeves and Wooster to include the whole world which
revolved around the Drones Club.

What we have, then, at the end of the day, is a companion
which takes in sixteen of the Jeeves books, a further twelve of the
Drones Club group and five biographical works. Its main use, I
would suggest, is not so much for a work of reference, although it is
invaluable in helping to trace names and quotations which are
only dimly remembered, as for a commonplace book or souvenir
album. More than anything else, it is a delicious reminder of past
pleasures, when few of us have time to re-read the whole canon. It
recreates the books by reminding us of names and incidents, as well
as providing an anthology of some of the most memorable writing,
the best jokes.

When the Master finally handed in his dinner pail in February 1975 at the grand old age of ninety-three, none of us could say, in our sorrow, that his death was untimely. Three years earlier, when he celebrated his ninetieth birthday, I happened to find myself at a Conservative Party Conference in Brighton and spent much of my time agitating for the Conference to send him a telegram of congratulations. It would have been a small gesture, after so many years of neglect. Several members of the Cabinet were quite enthusiastic at the time and so was the then Chairman of the Conservative Party, Mr Peter Thomas. Unfortunately nothing came of it, possibly as a result of the glacial indifference of the then Prime Minister, Mr Edward Heath. It is to the eternal credit of Sir Harold Wilson, however history may judge him in other matters, and whatever his detractors may now say against him, that he righted this historic wrong a few weeks before the old man died. It was almost as if Sir Pelham Wodehouse had been waiting all that time for some sign of recognition, some token of the enormous affection and gratitude we felt for him at home. *Wooster's World* is a memorial to two men – the comic genius who created it in the first place, and the humbler disciple who assembled and annotated this *vade mecum*. But above all, it should be seen as a memorial to the love which Wodehouse inspired and continues to inspire among those who cherish his genius.

February 1979

INTRODUCTION

In much the same way as Clarence, 9th Earl of Emsworth, was smitten by the brief pumpkin phase which preceded the more lasting pig seizure, the modest ambition to prepare a Concordance to the Blandings saga came upon me some fourteen years ago when (fitly enough) I was living in that pleasant Chelsea thoroughfare which the Master calls Budge Street, and was swiftly overtaken by the more irrational desire to cover the whole Wodehouse opus with a Complete Concordance embracing the whole of the eighty books which he had then published. This was stimulated further when I came to live in the heart of the Wodehouse country of the West Midland Marcher counties.

But, as I have pointed out in a B.B.C. broadcast talk, life, faint but pursuing, never quite catches up with Wodehouse. It echoes his most bizarre incidents, his most fantastic effects, but only after he has shown it the way. So the labourer in the Wodehouse furrow never quite catches up either. By the time I had re-read and worked upon those eighty books, I found I had five more to cope with. Those edited, four more had appeared. A delightful process, and I am all for its going on forever. The Complete Concordance, 'WODEHOUSE WORLD', now covers all of his ninety-one books published to date. But as he has so often told us, although in this life you sometimes get goose, you never get pure goose; and the fly in this all-but-Concordant ointment is that publishers—even American ones—are prone to look askance at a manuscript embodying some 350,000 words.

The present book therefore is a smallish though (one hopes) fairly ripe and fruity slice of the big plum cake. It covers the half-century cycle of the Wooster-Jeeves books together with a representative content of honey from the Drones' hive. If enough of those five-and-a-quarter million people who (the B.B.C. tells us) watched and enjoyed the recent television series are willing to invest in a permanent souvenir to it, other sections on Blandings, the Mulliners and so on, will be inflicted in due course.

I have never met the Master; but when he heard, as long ago as 1952, what I was about, he not only bore the blow with fortitude but

7

was kind enough to write, both then and through the ensuing years, with the most heartening encouragement, as well as elucidating, from time to time, such minor problems as the change in Psmith's Christian name. To him, and to all those friends and well-wishers, known and unknown, and especially to Richard Usborne, 'Dusty 'Rhodes, Lord Kilmuir, James Dowdall, Roy Plomley, Joseph Hone and Lionel Hale, who have given constant and practical encouragement, I offer my all-too-inadequate thanks. I wish also to record my thanks to Herbert Jenkins Ltd. for their co-operation and permission to quote from the opus.

1966

Brockworth,
Glos.

KEY TO THE BOOKS COVERED

For the benefit of ensuing generations, as well as for those who may wish to re-read them chronologically, these are listed in their order of publication, together with appropriate code-letters by which they are referred to in the text.

(Quotations in the text which carry no Code reference are from novels which do not strictly fall within the Wooster-Jeeves cycle.)

* published after *Wooster's World* was written

Many of Bertie's bread-throwing companions (e.g. Hugo Carmody, Ronnie Fish, Psmith, Monty Bodkin) as well as other characters who make brief appearances in Bertie's world, play leading parts elsewhere. A complete list of all known Drones is given under the Club entry.)

A

Abimelech: a remorseful Drone, drinking in the first Lesson at Evensong in a village church, contrasts his own behaviour towards Pongo Twistleton with that of, towards Jazzbo (YMS)

Abyssinia: Archie Mulliner of the Drones, mingling expansively with the masses at the Goose and Gherkin, Bottleton, E., puts a man with a broken nose right on the subject of the Apostolic Claims of the Church of, (YMS)

A FEW QUICK ONES: published 1959; a collection of ten short stories about old friends. Bertie and Jeeves figure in one (FO)

Aga Khan, H.H. the late: had the mares, and that (in Rory Carmoyle's expert view) is what counts in a breeding stable, especially when one is assessing form for the Derby (RJ); Lord Rowcester's sudden and astonishing acquisition of a butler, a housemaid and a gardener suggest to his sister the home life of, (RJ)

Agincourt, The Battle of: (Azincourt, 1415); the Earl of Rowcester remembers that a bold forebear of his held the field at, and decides to emulate him (RJ); a prudent ancestor of Clarence, 9th Earl of Emsworth, took cover at, and Clarence discreetly follows his example; the grand old Sieur de Wocestre (or Wooster) fights with vim at, (RHJ)

Albert, H.R.H. Prince, The Prince Consort: would have had a word to say about a girl like Stephanie Byng, and would infallibly have said it with her over his knee, while he laid into her with a slipper (CW)

Anatole: unparalleled, unapproached, unchallenged (see Press) French chef to Tom and Dahlia Travers at Brinkley Court, Worcs, is the only cook yet discovered who can push food into the dyspeptic

Tom without starting something like Old Home Week in Moscow under the third waistcoat button. To a woman, therefore, who periodically has to dig into that waistcoat for large slabs of the ready to finance her rocky magazine, the talents and wellbeing of Anatole are of the essence. Three factors militate against this. There is the recurrent menace of the bribes and machinations of less happier homes, ever ready to spare neither ingenuity nor treasure to acquire this jewel; there is the Provençal temperament of Anatole himself, superimposed on that of a creative genius of the first order—than which there is no whicher; and there is Dahlia's basic and fatal sporting instinct which, in pursuance of some will-o'-the-wisp dead cert, urges her recurrently to wager Anatole's services to recoup her gaming losses. The balance is redressed by Jeeves's perception and manipulation of Anatole's southern proclivities. Volatile as only a great artist can be, Anatole in moments of stress expresses himself in terms explicit only in Digne or Montélimar. Words like *marmiton de Domange, pignouf, roustisseur* and *hurluberlu* flutter from him like bats out of a barn, and once, even, a *rogommier*. Of his galaxy of masterpieces one may (with slavering jaws) single out for special devotion his *Rognans de Montagnes*, his *Selles d'Agneau laitues à la Grecque*, his *Nonats de la Méditerrannée au fenouil*, his matchless *ris de Veau à la Financière, Consommée aux Pommes d'Amour* and his *velouté aux fleurs de Courgette:*

'Ice,' Aunt Dahlia repeated, and sighed dreamily. 'I think of those prawns in iced aspic of his! That *Selle d'Agneau à la Grecque*! That *Mignonette de Poulet Rôti Petit Duc*! Those *Nonats de la Méditerrannée au Fenouil*! Sweet suffering soupspoons!' she vociferated, if that's the word, anguish written on her every feature, 'I wonder what Tom will say when he hears Anatole is leaving!' (JFS)

'Night after night,' said Gussie, 'I had to refuse Anatole's unbeatable eatables, and when I tell you that two nights in succession he gave us those *Mignonettes de Poulet Petit Duc* and on another occasion his *Timbales de Ris de Veau Toulousiane*, you'll appreciate what I went through.' (SLJ)

Uncle Tom and I sat down alone to a repast in Anatole's best vein. Over the *Suprême de Foie Gras au Champagne* and the *Neige aux Perles des Alpes* I placed him in possession of the facts (SLJ)

Some Press tributes: 'that wizard' (CW); 'that peerless disher-up (CW); 'God's gift to the gastric juices' (FO); 'suddenly developed

a cooking streak which put all his previous efforts in the shade'
(VGJ); 'the superb French chefferie of,' (HRJ); 'the gourmet's
lure, (CW); 'that superb master of the roasts and hashes' (CW);
'a hash-slinger without peer' (VGJ); 'that peerless disher-up' (CW);
'the outstanding virtuosity of' (CW); 'the middle of the pheasant
season, which this superman is at his incomparable best' (CW); 'I
would look at Aunt Dahlia, and Aunt Dahlia would look at me, and
our eyes would be full of unshed tears. . . .' (VGJ)

Annie's Night Out: A Drone orders an, (EBC)

Anstruther, Mr: a moth-eaten septuagenarian valetudinarian,
tolerated at Brinkley Court as a friend of Bertie's late grandfather.
Has a strong but misplaced faith in the policy of appeasement towards small boys, and ends even wetter than he began. 'An agreeable cove', in Bertie's view, 'but rather given to nervous breakdowns'
(VGJ)

Anstruther, Harold (Beefy): partnered Bertie Wooster at racquets at Oxford, and is now engaged to the equally beefy Hilda
Gudgeon (MS)

Archimedes: (d. 212 B.C.) Gussie Fink-Nottle stiffens his fibres at
the thought of the great mathematician's resolute end. (CW)

Argus Private Enquiry Agency, the: Hayling Court, Beeston
St., S.W. (P. Frobisher Pilbeam, Mgr.) whose boast is that it Never
Sleeps. This (feel those who know it) is, if it possesses a conscience,
not surprising. Few would be able to sleep with what the Argus
Enquiry Agency has on its mind (JO *et al.*)

Aspinalls Ltd.: the well-known jewellers in New Bond St. W.
Bertie Wooster is among their clients, as are Lord Emsworth and
Lady Worplesdon, who possibly purchases there the knives with
which she conducts human sacrifices at times of full moon (JM,
JFS *et al.*)

Astaire: Bertie Wooster, on occasion, out-Freds the nimblest (JM)

Attila and His Huns: the boys get around. They are to be seen,
e.g., planning their next campaign in the bar of the Green Pig at
Hockley-cum-Meston, where every member of the village football
team looks like the Village Blacksmith's big brother (VGJ); solo
appearances by the celebrated take-over expert (fl. *c.* A.D. 450) are
usually in potential combat with personable but dominating young
women. Bertie conjectures, e.g., that Attila is unlikely to have
possessed the stamina capable of turning on Lady Florence Craye
(q., if you must, v.) like a tiger, even at the peak of his form

A Surging Sea of Aunts

IN THIS LIFE IT IS NOT AUNTS THAT MATTER, BUT THE COURAGE THAT ONE BRINGS TO THEM (MS)

In that dining-room there would be five aunts, one of them deaf, one of them dotty, one of them Dame Daphne Winkworth, and all of them totally unfit for human consumption on an empty stomach (MS)

When Aunt is calling to Aunt like mastodons bellowing across primeval swamps and Uncle James's letter about Cousin Mabel's peculiar behaviour is being shot round the family circle ('please read this carefully and send it on to Jane') the clan has a tendency to ignore me. It's one of the advantages I get from being a bachelor and—according to my nearest and dearest, practically a half-witted bachelor at that (IJ)

My Aunt Julia lacks Aunt Agatha's punch, but in a quiet way she has always made me feel, from boyhood up, that I was a poor worm. The difference between the two is that Aunt Agatha conveys the impression that she considers me personally responsible for all the sin and sorrow in the world, while Aunt Julia's manner seems to suggest that I am more to be pitied than censured. (MT)

As far as the eye could reach, I found myself gazing on a surging sea of aunts. There were tall aunts, short aunts, stout aunts, thin aunts, and an aunt who was carrying on a conversation in a low voice to which nobody seemed to be paying the slightest attention, she being the aunt of whom Corky had spoken as the dotty one. From start to finish of every meal she soliloquised (MS)

I have an aunt, sir (said Jeeves), who a few years ago was a martyr to swollen limbs. She tried Walkinshaw's Supreme Ointment and obtained considerable relief—so much so that she sent them an unsolicited testimonial. Her pride at seeing her photograph in the daily papers, in connection with descriptions of her lower limbs before taking, which were nothing less than revolting, was so intense that it led me to believe that publicity, of whatever sort, is what everybody desires (COJ)

There are many ways of saying 'Well!' The speaker who had the floor at the moment said it rather in the manner of the prudish queen of a monarch of Babylon who has happened to wander into the banqueting hall just as the Babylonian orgy is beginning to go nicely. (MS)

Aunt Agatha is one of those strong-minded women. She has an eye like a man-eating fish, and she has got moral suasion down to a fine point. . . . If you're fond of a quiet life, you simply curl into a ball when you see her coming, and hope for the best. My experience is that when Aunt Agatha wants you to do a thing you do it, or else you find yourself wondering why those fellows in the olden days made such a fuss when they had trouble with the Spanish Inquisition (MT)

Aunt Charlotte, when the facts had been relayed to her through her ear trumpet, for she was wired for sound, had said with a short quick sniff that she supposed that they ought to consider themselves highly honoured that the piefaced young bastard condescended to sleep in the bally place, or words to that effect (MS)

'Disgustingly vulgar,' said Dame Daphne. The rest of the aunts didn't say 'You betcher', or 'You've got something, there, Daph', but their manner suggested these words. Lips were pursed and noses looked down (MS)

'If I had my life to live again, Jeeves, I would start it as an orphan without any aunts. Don't they put aunts in Turkey in sacks and drop them in the Bosphorus?'

'Odalisques, sir, I understand. Not aunts' (CW)

I had never scorned a woman myself, but Pongo Twistleton once scorned an aunt of his, flatly refusing to meet her son Gerald at Paddington and give him lunch and see him off to school at Waterloo, and he had never heard the end of it. Letters were written, he tells me, which had to be seen to be believed. Also two very strong telegrams and a bitter picture-postcard with a view of the Little Chilbury War Memorial on it (RHJ)

It has probably occurred to all thinking men that something drastic ought to be done about aunts. If someone were to come to me and say, 'Wooster, would you be interested in joining a society whose aim will be the suppression of aunts, or at least will see to it that they are kept on a short chain and not permitted to roam hither and thither at will, scattering desolation on all sides?' I would reply 'Wilbraham', if his name was Wilbraham, 'put me down as a foundation member' (FO)

'I tell you, Jeeves, behind every poor, innocent, harmless blighter who is going down for the third time in the soup, you will find, if you look carefully enough, the aunt who shoved him into it.'

'There is much in what you say, sir.'

'It is no use telling me there are good aunts and bad aunts. At the core, they are all alike. Sooner or later, out pops the cloven hoof' (CW)

Aunt Dahlia was in the drawing-room, and welcomed me with gratifying enthusiasm.

'Hello, ugly,' she said. 'So here you are.'

It was the right tone, and one I should be glad to hear in others of the family circle. (VGJ)

Awash: see **blotto**

B

Bablockhythe, Lady: sells the serial rights of her *Frank Recollections of a Long Life* to Dahlia Travers, who anticipates a *succès de scandale* for *Milady's Boudoir* (COJ)

Bacon, Sir Francis: and the Baconian 'theory'; see **Verulam** (JM et al.)

Bailey, the late Dr Cyril: Public Orator, University of Oxford, at the Encaenia, 21st June, 1939; see **Gussie Fink-Nottle**

Bailey's Granulated Breakfast Chips: a favourite with Tootles (COJ)

Bali: B. Wooster is visited by the intriguing conviction that someone has been telling Jeeves about the dancing girls of, (CW)

Ballindallochs, the: of Portknockie, N.B. the late (though, who knows?) Countess Dowager of Wivelscombe sprang from this ancient and renowned Highland family—remarkable even in a land where every castle has its doom and one clan in three, forbye, is is process of dreeing its weird. The Ballindallochs are no' juist canny. For the lady's talents, consult her shade under **Wivelscombe,** where may be discovered the source of the present Earl's half-share in the Sicht and (perhaps) his talent for perceiving pink secretaries under the breakfast-table (YMS)

Bankhead, Tallulah: Lady Wickham speaks in a hoarse, throaty voice like, after swallowing a fish-bone the wrong way (JO); Gussie Fink-Nottle would not go any too well with, (RHJ)

Banks, Isabel: s. of Rosie M. and an aunt of the infant prodigy Algernon Aubrey Little (FO)

Banks, Rosie M.: celebrated and best-selling romantic novelist, author of *All for Love, A Red, Red Summer Rose, 'Twas Once in May, Madcap Myrtle, Only a Factory Girl, Mervyn Keene, Clubman, The Courtship of Lord Strathmorlick* and other works, m. Richard (Bingo) Little, a nephew of Lord Bittlesham, q.v.; m. of Algernon Aubrey Little, q.v.; Res.; Wimbledon Common, S.W.; later Magnolia Road, St. John's Wood, N.W. She precipitates a marital crisis by writing an article on 'How I Keep the Love of my Husband-Baby' (COJ *et al.*)

Bartlett, Alexander: notable sprinter with years of experience gained in escaping the hand of the law, starts at 11–4 in the Choir-boys Handicap Race, open to all whose voices have not broken before the second Sunday in Epiphany (IJ)

Bassett, Madeline: England's premier pill, periodically engaged to Gussie Fink-Nottle, with Bertie Wooster as first reserve, is o.d. of **Sir Watkyn Bassett** q.v. In Bertie's view is, from topknot to shoe sole, The Woman Whom God Forgot:

> A far as the outer crust is concerned there is little to cavil at in this pre-eminent bit of bad news. The eyes are large and lustrous, the features delicately moulded, the hair, nose, ears and teeth well up to standard. But there is a catch. She is the sloppiest, mushiest, sentimentalest young Gawd-help-us who ever thought that the stars were God's daisy-chain and that every time a fairy hiccoughs a wee baby is born. She is squashy and soupy, and her favourite reading is Christopher Robin and Winnie the Pooh (MS)

After years of playing Bertie Wooster and Gussie Fink-Nottle, on and off the hook, always with the purest, pseudo-Arthurian intentions, Madeline seems to be committed to marriage at last with Roderick Spode, Lord Sidcup, so proving that the pure springs of justice cascade eternally in their timeless caverns close below our feet. (See **Laughing Love God, Xyrids,** etc.) (RHJ, CW, MS, SLJ *et al.*)

Bassett, Sir Watkyn, C.B.E.: resident beak at Bosher Street police court, W.C., his first meeting with Bertie is as the prisoner Wooster, on a charge of trying to separate a policeman from his helmet:

I was one of his last customers, for a couple of weeks later he inherited a pot of money from a distant relative and retired to the country. That, at least, was the story that had been put about. My own view was that he had got the stuff by sticking like glue to the fines. Five quid here, five quid there—you can see how it would mount up over a period of years (CW)

With aunts, uncles, headmasters and others vested with feudal rights over the individual, Sir Watkyn is an integral link in the chain of Authority which exerts its lifelong restraint over the fifth-form status which Bertie habitually accepts as his lot. When the chain is occasionally broken it is almost invariably through the agency of his sole (but priceless) weapon of offence, which is Jeeves:

'I was merely about to inquire if it is your intention to bring an action against Sir Watkyn for wrongful arrest and defamation of character before witnesses. You are undoubtedly in a position, sir, to mulct Sir Watkyn in heavy damages.'

'Yes, I suppose you are right. Still, I don't know that I want actually to grind the old bird into the dust.'

'I was merely thinking, sir, that were you to threaten such an action, Sir Watkyn might see his way to rectifying the betrothals of Miss Bassett and Mr Fink-Nottle and Miss Byng and the Reverend Mr Pinker.'

'Golly, Jeeves! Put the bite on him, what?'

I sprang from the bed and nipped to the door.

'Bassett!' I yelled.

The man had presumably gone to earth. But after I had persevered for some minutes . . . I heard the distant sound of pattering feet, and along he came, in a very different spirit. . . . This time it was more like some eager waiter answering a bell.

'Yes, Mr Wooster?'

I led the way back into the room, and hopped into bed again.

'There is something you wish to say to me, Mr Wooster?'

'There are about half-a-dozen things I wish to say to you, Bassett, but the one we will touch on at the moment is this. Are you aware that your headstrong conduct in sticking police officers on to pinch me and locking me in my room has laid you open to an action for—what was it, Jeeves?'

'Wrongful arrest and defamation of character before witnesses, sir.'

'That's the baby. I could soak you for millions. What are you going to do about it?'

He writhed like an electric fan.

'I'll tell you what you are going to do about it,' I proceeded. 'You are going to issue your O.K. on the union of your daughter Madeline and Augustus Fink-Nottle and also on that of your niece Stephanie and the Rev. H. P. Pinker. And you will do it now.'

A short struggle seemed to take place in him. It might have lasted longer, if he hadn't caught my eye.

'Very well, Mr Wooster.'

'And one other thing. You owe me a fiver.'

'I beg your pardon?'

'In repayment of the one you took off me at Bosher Street. I shall want that before I leave.'

'I will write you a cheque in the morning.'

'I shall expect it on the breakfast tray. Good night, Bassett.'

'Good night, Mr Wooster. Is that brandy I see over there? I think I should like a glass, if I may.'

'Jeeves, a snootful for Sir Watkyn Bassett.'

'Very good, sir.'

He drained the beaker gratefully, and tottered out. Probably quite a nice chap, if you knew him. (CW)

For the record, Sir Watkyn becomes affianced to Spode's aunt, **Mrs Wintergreen,** q.v. He res. at Totleigh Towers, Glos (CW, MS, SLJ, *et al.*)

Bassington-Bassingtons, the: of Hampshire (IJ); of Kent (IJ); of Shropshire (IJ); no imminent shortage of, (IJ)

Bassington-Bassington, Cyril: although the dish-faced Kid Blumenfeld is the actual instrument which snooters the stage ambitions of this eminent piece of bad news, the underlying strategy is the product of the Jeeves brain at its best (IJ, VGJ)

Bates: a hot entry for the jobs-one-doesn't-envy stakes, is hall porter at the Drones Club, Dover St., W. (CT)

Bates, the Rev. James: an assistant master at Eton, is locum for the Rector of Gandle-by-the-Hill, Glos, receiving 15 minutes in the Great Sermon Handicap (IJ)

Battersea Home for Lost Dogs, S.W.: Corky Pirbright acquires Sam Goldwyn at the,

> a shaggy dog with a mixed parentage and a tongue like an ant-eater. It looked like Boris Karloff made up for something (MS)

Bayard, the Chevalier: remarked (possibly) that either a chap's preux, or he isn't (JO)

Baxter, Prudence: fancied by Jeeves for the Girls Egg and Spoon Race at Twing:

> 'The daughter of his lordship's head gardener, sir. Her father assures me that she has a very steady hand. She is accustomed to bring him his mug of beer each afternoon, and he informs me she has never spilled a drop.' (IJ)

Beckley-in-the-Moor: shares with ffinch the distinction of representing Yorkshire, the most northerly county touched on in the Wodehouse opus (see **Gazetteer**). Its destinies are ordered by Miss Vera Sipperley of The Paddock:

> one of those medium-sized houses with a goodish bit of very tidy garden and a carefully-rolled gravel drive curving past a shrubbery that looked as if it had just come back from the dry-cleaner—the sort of house you take one look at and say 'Somebody's aunt lives there' (COJ)

Belfry: family name of the Earl of Rowcester, q.v.

Belfry, the Lady Agatha: after some 750 years is still a popular and respected resident of Rowcester Abbey. Early tradition suggests she was the first victim claimed by the persistent and ingrowing dampness of the venerable pile—its proto-martyr to rheumatic fever. Her well-attested return visits are believed by many to be laudable attempts to warn guests of the Abbey's inherent arthritic perils. She has, however, never been known to enter the room once occupied by the Tudor king whose name the late G. K. Chesterton would never mention in the presence of ladies (see **Rowcester Abbey**) (RJ)

Belfry, Lady Barbara: Monica Carmoyle realises that, by Rosie Spottsworth's Rotationist theory, she herself is a reincarnation of this ancestress. Her claim that Lady Barbara was the leading hussy of King Charles II's court seems, however, a little pretentious (RJ)

Belfry, Sir Caradoc: known to the castle-hopping public as Caradoc the Crusader, he did well at the battle of Joppa. He espoused the Lady Agatha, now Rowcester Abbey's ghost, and was an early ancestor of that well-known Drone, Lord Rowcester (RJ)

Belfry, the Hon. George: the acute sense of smell of, stands him in good stead (RJ)

Belfry, Lady Monica: see **Lady Monica Carmoyle**

Bellamy, the Rev. Mr: nonagenarian Vicar of Hockley-cum-Meston, a living in the gift of Major Plank. As Sir W. S. Gilbert wrote of the Vicar of Otium-cum-Dig, 'the good incumbent's ninety-five, and cannot very long survive'. He is succeeded by the Rev. H. P. (Stinker) Pinker (SLJ)

Bellamy Bros.: of Covent Garden, W.C, horticultural merchants and neighbours of the *Mayfair Gazette* (VGJ)

Bellinger, Cora: upstanding light-heavyweight with a commanding eye, square chin and coloratura soprano voice, who all but appropriates Tuppy Glossop (VGJ)

Belloc, Hilaire: (1870–1953). See **'WEEK-END WODEHOUSE'**

Bergerac, Cyrano de: see **Schnozzle Durante**

Berks and Bucks Foxhounds, the: Aunt Dahlia always vocal in the field with, (CW)

Bessemer, Clifton: pulp magnate and first husband of Rosalinda Spottsworth (née Banks) passes the veil in a head-on collision with a truck carrying a full load of empty beer bottles on the Jericho Turnpike (RJ)

Bessington-Copes, the: acquire an outstanding butler in exchange for an oviform period silver chocolate-pot on three scroll feet (CW)

Bethnal Green, E.: while professionally spreading the light in, the Rev. Harold Pinker experiences an odd, dreamy feeling on being kicked in the stomach by a costermonger (CW)

Bewdley: Worcs., a heroine of, famed in local folklore, is hymned by a guest at the annual banquet of the Loyal Sons of Worcestershire (YMS)

Bickersteth, Francis: the Duke of Chiswick's nephew is an early beneficiary of Jeeves's genius:

'I am open to correction, sir, but is not your dilemma due to the fact that you are at a loss to explain to his Grace why you are in New York instead of in Colorado?'

Biffen, Charles Edward: one time fellow-sabreur of Bertie Wooster, inherits a Herefordshire estate worth £15,000 a year and retires to the country to wear gaiters and prod cows in the ribs. Loses a newly-acquired fiancée in the New York Custom Shed, is ensnared by Honoria Glossop, rescued when sinking for the third time and weds Mabel Jeeves, q.v. (Whether this bemuddled wooer is a scion of the stock which produced Gally Threepwood's gallant fellow-boulevardier, Admiral Sir George J. (Fruity) Biffen, R.N., the chronicles do not say, but certain traits encourage the belief) (COJ)

Biggleswade: Sir Mortimer Prenderby's wristy butler at Matcham Scratchings, Oxen, is placed on sentry duty outside Freddie Widgeon's bedroom (YMS)

Bill: A disembodied voice from the flies of a Schenectady theatre (IJ)

Bingham, the Rev. 'Beefy': has a cure of souls at Bermondsey, E., where he founds a Lads' Club and runs bright, clean entertainment in the Oddfellows' Hall (VGJ)

Binghampton, the Rt. Hon. Viscount: Theodore Fotheringay-Phipps, uncle of the well-known Drone, is well known as a breeder of Siamese cats, but even better known as the Curse of the Southern Counties (VGJ)

Bingham-Reeves, Alistair: having a valet who has been known to press his trousers sideways, follows Jeeves with a glittering, hungry eye (MJ)

Bingley-on-Sea: setting for the Drones' annual golf tournament and for Bertie Wooster's embroilment with Miss Mapleton's chain-gang at St. Monica's school. It is at Bingley that the Albert Hall falls upon the Crystal Palace (VGJ, *et al.*)

Birmingham College of Veterinary Science, the: see G. Bullett (RHJ)

Birmingham Repertory Theatre, the: a production of Chekhov's *The Seagull* at, is instanced by Bobbie Wickham as an example of Phyllis Mills' spinelessness in the presence of her stepfather, the Rev. Aubrey Upjohn:

'I'd like to catch anyone trying to make me see Chekhov's *Seagull*. But Phyllis just bowed her head and said "Yes, Daddy". That'll show you how much will of her own she's got.'

It did indeed. I knew Chekhov's *Seagull*. My Aunt Agatha had once made me take her son Thos. to a performance of it at the Old Vic, and what with the strain of trying to follow the cock-eyed goings on of characters called Zarietchayna and Medvienko and having to be constantly on the alert to prevent Thos. making a sneak for the great open spaces, my suffering had been intense (JO)

Biskerton, the Viscount: Godfrey Edward Winstanley Brent (known to his fellow Drones as the Biscuit) is e.s. and heir of the Earl of Hoddesdon. He is a leading character in **'Big Money'**

bite the ear, to: to touch, get into the ribs of, and if unusually lucky, to punch in the pocket-book (*passim*)

Bittlesham, the Rt. Hon. Lord: Mortimer Little, cr. 1st. Baron, clambers to the Upper House with the aid of Little's Liniment (It Limbers Up the Legs) and is titular head of the family of which Richard (Bingo) is an outstanding member. Bertie is introduced to him as Rosie M. Banks, a writer for whom he has a profound devotion:

> 'A somewhat curious character, sir,' said Jeeves. 'Since retiring from business he has become a great recluse, and now devotes himself almost entirely to the pleasures of the table.'
> 'Greedy hog, you mean?'

A well-known racing owner, Lord Bittlesham owns the Goodwood Cup favourite Ocean Breeze. He m. his cook, Jane Watson, q.v. Res; 16 Pounceby Gardens, S.W. (IJ, COJ, FO)

Black Shorts, the: see **Saviours of Britain**; also **Spode, Roderick**

BLANDINGS CASTLE AND ELSEWHERE: published in 1922, is a collection of stories described in the author's preface as 'short snorts in between the solid orgies'. It contains the Bobbie Wickham masterpiece **'Mr. Potter Takes a Rest Cure'**

Blaye-en-Sainonge: the Sieur Geoffrey Rudel, Prince of, and *lacrymae rerum;* see **Laughing Love God** (CW)

Bleaching Court: Upper Bleaching, Hants; res. of Sir Reginald Witherspoon Bart. Opinion in the servants hall tends to the belief that Tuppy Glossop would be well advised to keep clear of the football field (VGJ)

Blenkinsop, Alderman Robert: of Liverpool City Council, achieves the honour of knighthood. The thought of his having to walk backwards in black silk knee breeches with a sword between his legs makes the day for his civic rival, Alderman L. G. Trotter, q.v. (JFS)

Blenkinsop, Mrs Robert: inveterate rival of Mrs Alderman Trotter in Liverpool's social rat race (JFS)

Blennerhasset, Sir Everard and Lady: of B.7 Berkeley Mansions, Berkeley St., W., raise the *Clameur de Haro* when Bertie starts to say it with a banjolele (TJ)

Blicester, the Rt. Hon. the Earl of: Rodney Widgeon, third of his line, is u. and guardian to Frederick Fortescue W. and, though wealthy, is a prime exponent of the one-way pocket system. Moths have nested for years in his wallet, raising large families. May be seen three-dimensionally in the Fat Uncles competition organised by Freddie at the Drones, where (despite the entry of the Duke of Dunstable) Lord Blicester disposes of all legitimate competition with ease. Res; Blicester Towers, Blicester Regis, Kent (LEO, YMS, FO *et al.*)

Bligh, Capt. William, R.N.: master of H.M.S. Bounty, later Vice-Admiral of the Blue (1754–1817), makes sporadic appearances, either solo or in association with other prototypes of severity and iron discipline, as Simon Legree, the Emperors Nero and Tiberius, Herbert Spencer, Tsar Ivan the Terrible, etc. Albert the Good, Prince Consort, makes a solo appearance, but as a disciplinarian of firm rather than of extreme measures (*passim*)

blotto: see **boiled**

Bluchers: of Burlington Arcade, W.; famous for many generations as purveyors of gentlemen's neckwear and shirtings, and as indispensable to the well-dressed Drone as, e.g. Bodmins of Vigo Street in the matter of headgear (VGJ *et al.*)

Blumenfeld, Pop: U.S. theatrical impresario whose success is partly due to his reliance on the judgment of his small son as to the likely appeal of a play or of its cast. He reasons logically that what appeals to the mentality of a child of eight must infallibly win the approval of the average modern audience (VGJ)

Blumenfeld, the Kid:

> 'Pop, that one's no good.'
> 'Which one, darling?'
> 'The one with a face like a fish.'
> 'But they all have faces like fish.'
> 'The ugly one.'
> 'Which ugly one? That one?' said old Blumenfeld, pointing to Cyril
> 'Yep, he's rotten.'
> 'Your're dead right, my boy. I've noticed it for some time.'
> (IJ)

Boat Race Night: universally conceded to be an occasion for a toot or bender, except at Bow St., Bosher St., Marlborough St., Vine St., Vinton St. and places where they sting (*passim*)

Bodmin, Jno.: of Vigo Street, W., By Appointment Hatters to the Royal Family. 'The Amazing Hat Mystery' in YMS turns upon the unchallengeable precision of a Bodmin fitting:

> 'Allow me,' said Nelson Cork, hot under the collar but still dignified, 'to tell you something about Jno. Bodmin, as the name appears new to you. Jno. is the last of a long line of Bodmins, all of whom have made hats assiduously for the nobility and gentry all their lives. Hats are in Jno. Bodmin's blood.
> ... Over the door of his emporium in Vigo Street the passers-by may read a significant legend. It runs "Bespoke Hatter to the Royal Family". That means ... that if the King wants a new topper he simply ankles round to Bodmin's and says "Good morning, Bodmin, we want a topper." He does not ask if it will fit. He takes it for granted that it will fit. He has bespoken Jno. Bodmin, and he trusts him blindly. You don't suppose his Gracious Majesty would bespeak a hatter whose hats did not fit? The whole essence of being a hatter is to make hats that fit, and it is to this end that Jno. Bodkin has strained every nerve for years. And that is why I say again—simply and without heat—this hat is a Bodmin' (YMS)

Bodsham, the Rt. Hon. the Earl of: fifth of his line, an austere, Wednesday-matinee-ish nobleman who not only shanghais his guests to church twice on Sundays, sparing neither age nor sex, but has family prayers in the dining-room at 8 a.m. on Mondays. Is a crony (not surprisingly) of Aubrey Upjohn. F. of Mavis Peasemarch, the Earl would have become Freddie Widgeon's father-in-law but for the trifling circumstance of Freddie's having been a Sugar Daddy Discovered In Love Nest as Blizzard Grips City. (NS, YMS)

Bognor Regis: Sussex resort, was (well within living memory) designated Bognor, *tout court*. The convalescence there of his late Majesty King George V earned the 'Regis'. The local authority has not yet decided what sobriquet should be added to commemorate the sojourn of Jeeves, for the shrimping season. Some consider '*et Promi*' would be suitable (JFS)

Bohea: Bertie's matutinal refreshment; orig. a black tea from the Wu-I hills of China, later used for any infusion of tea (JM)

boiled: see **fried**

Bolton, Guy: collaborator with P. G. Wodehouse in a number of successful theatrical productions. **RING FOR JEEVES** is a novel written by Wodehouse from a play by Bolton, for which Wodehouse 'lent' him the character of Jeeves the butler (WAW, PF)

Book Society, the: has not (Bertie learns) selected *Spinoza* as its Choice of the Month (JM)

Bosher, Plug: Oofy Prosser is amazed that so much human tonnage can be assembled in one all-in wrestler. He feels that, at sight of Plug, any Cannibal King would whoop for joy and reach for his knife and fork (CT)

Bosher, Major General Sir Wilfred, K.B.E.: victim of an unfortunate contretemps at a school Speech Day (RHJ)

Bosher St. Police Court: a gathering point, esp. on Boat Race Night, Founders' Day and other red-letter occasions, for Eggs, Beans and Crumpets. In its time has provided plain but wholesome fare and accommodation for about half the membership of the Drones. The presiding spirit is Sir Watkyn Bassett, q.v. (*passim*)

(Some satisfied customers see no point in waiting for the calendar. Ronald, last of the Fishes, e.g., makes an overwrought appearance there after taking on most of the staff of Mario's Restaurant singlehanded.—Ed.)

Bostock, Hermione: o.d. of Sir Aylmer and Lady Bostock, is a girl whom it is unwise to cross. The Empress Catherine, one feels, could have taken her correspondence course. She places Pongo Twistleton on matrimonial probation for a brief space:

> Her father might look like a walrus and her mother like something starting at 100–8 in the 2.30 at Catterick, but their offspring, tall, dark, with large eyes, perfect profile and equally perfect figure, was an oriental potentate's dream of what the harem needed. (UD)

Bott, Matilda: Lady Florence Craye is advised to lose no time in becoming, of 365 Churchill Avenue, East Dulwich, before being clapper-clawed by the law in a raided night-club (JFS)

Bottsworth, Elizabeth:

> 'Tell me, Percy. When do you open?'
> 'Open?' said Percy.
> 'On the halls. I thought that hat must be part of the make-up and you were trying it on the dog. I couldn't think of any other reason why you should wear one six sizes too small.' (YMS)

Bottleton, E.: Lord Blicester presides at a political rally at the Palace of Varieties here, and Freddie Widgeon, desperate to tap him for five pounds, follows him, though feeling he would much prefer to go to Whipsnade and try to take a mutton chop from a tiger (LEO, *et al.*)

Bounding Beauty: a quadruped wearing the outward guise of a racehorse, for which some unfortunates (including Bingo Little) mistake it. For Bingo, its chances seem enhanced by his dream, in which he sees his Uncle Willoughby dancing the rumba in the nude on the steps of the National Liberal Club—a piece of stable information which proves singularly unstable (COJ)

Bow, Clara: celebrated Hollywood star, is the first love of Master Sebastian Moon (VGJ)

Bowles, Jimmy: one of many Drones who are unlikely to curb their comments if they should learn that Bingo Little has been described by his wife, in a magazine article, as 'half god, half prattling, mischievous child'. (COJ)

Brabazon-Biggar, Capt. Cuthbert Gervase: leading exponent of The Code, as it is understood by those servants of Empire whose lives are equated to a timeless search for any overlooked chunks of White Man's Burden which they can add to the load. There is not

27

just one Bwana Biggar; there are three of him. Over each of his shoulders there hovers an invisible monitor, each keeping up a running admonishment as to the comportment, thoughts and conduct proper to an officer, a gentleman and a white man. Into his left ear the Subahdar pours whispered injunctions to Keep his Chin Up and Remember the Code; Tubby Frobisher the while fiercely advises his right ear to Keep a Stiff Upper Lip and to remember he is a Sahib. Such arbitrary counsel, aggravated by his persistent penury, go far to explain the Bwana's single state at the age of forty. For the rest, he has one of those Pistolian visages and small, bristly moustaches over which far-flung persons in general seem to exercise patent rights. Here (you would have said) is a man who many a time has looked his rhinoceros right in the eye; and you would have been right. Along Bubbling Well Road, and in the Long Bar at Shanghai any of the boys would tell you that Bwana Biggar has made more rhinoceri wilt than you could shake a stick at. But then, there is all the difference in the world between a wilting rhino and a well-endowed, attractive widow who (as Tubby and the Subahdar insistently hiss) is the very reverse of fair game for a penniless White Hunter, even though the said hunter played a leading part in the brief drama which culminated in her millionaire husband's going to reside with the morning stars (see **Kuala Lumpur**) (RJ)

Bradbury, Capt.: a beefy bird in tweeds, on leave from India, knows what to do about puny rivals who start hornswoggling operations in the neighbourhood of April Carroway (YMS)

Bramley-on-sea: Is So Bracing. Some would feel that three years at Aubrey Upjohn's penal establishment there was an experience bracing enough for a lifetime. Not so F. Widgeon, who follows his heart and contrives, by the light of the holy flame, to choose Upjohn's study as a crèche wherein to deposit young Algernon Aubrey Little (NS)

Brancaster, the Rt. Hon. the Earl of: former employer of Jeeves and a noted psittaphile (see **Dumbchummery**) the Earl is also keen on addressing school speech days (RHJ)

Braythwayt, Daphne: 'There is none like her, none,' said Bingo. 'We were alone in a world of music and sunshine. Bertie, you do believe in love at first sight, don't you?' (IJ)

Brent: family name of the Earl of Hoddesdon (see **Biskerton**)

Bridgnorth, the Earl of: his noble (but unspecified) parents res. in the Cadogan Square area, and his appearances are outside the

28

present saga. He writes a gossip column, and is known at the Drones as Tubby

Bridgworth, the Rt. Hon. Lord: Digby Thistleton, cr. 1st Baron, is an early employer of Jeeves, notable for his commercial resilience and enterprise. His favourite saying is that there is Always a Way:

> 'After the failure of a patent depilatory which he promoted, sir, he put it on the market again under the name of Hair-O, guaranteed to produce a full crop of hair in a few months. It was advertised, if you remember, sir, by a humorous picture of a billiard ball, before and after taking, and made such a substantial fortune that Mr Thistleton was soon afterwards elevated to the Peerage for services to his Party' (MJ)

Brief instances

THAT SCARLET WOMAN. WAS SHE SCARLET ALL OVER, OR WAS IT JUST THAT HER FACE WAS RED? (MS)

'Corky,' I said, 'I've been through hell.'
'About the only place I thought you didn't have to go through to get to King's Deverill. And how were they all?' (MS)

Mrs Trotter loomed up in the doorway.
'Oh, good evening, Mr Wooster,' she said in a distant sort of way. 'I was hoping to find you alone, Mrs Travers,' she added with the easy tact which had made her the toast of Liverpool (JFS)

I remember having seen the same defiant glitter behind the spectacles of a man I met in a country hotel once, just before he told me his name was Snodgrass (JM)

Jeeves, in speaking of this Fink-Nottle, had described him as disgruntled, and it was plain at a glance that the passage of time had done nothing to gruntle him (MS)

Nothing is more difficult than to describe a Charleston danced by, on the one hand, a woman who loves dancing Charlestons and throws herself into the spirit of them, and on the other hand, by a man desirous of leaving no stone unturned in order to dislodge from some part of his associate's anatomy a diamond pendant which has lodged there (RJ)

Blackmail, of course, but the gentler sex love blackmail. Show me a delicately nurtured female, and I will show you a ruthless Napoleon of crime prepared without turning a hair to put the screws on some unfortunate male whose services she happens to be in need of. There ought to be a law . . . (SLJ)

It was one of those jolly, bread-crumbling parties where you cough twice before you speak, and then decide not to say it after all (MJ)

That slight sheepishness which comes to married men when the names of those whom they themselves esteem highly, but of whom they are aware that their wives disapprove, crop up in the course of conversation (LEO)

Stiffy's map tends to be rather grave and dreamy, giving the impression that she is thinking deep, beautiful thoughts. Quite misleading of course. I don't suppose she would recognise a deep, beautiful thought if you handed it to her on a skewer with tartare sauce (CW)

One noticed a marked increase in the resemblance to Wallace Beery, and the thought crossed my mind that life for the unfortunate moppets who had drawn this Winkworth as a headmistress must have been like Six Weeks on Sunny Devil's Island (MS)

'We'll just loose you down on the sheet, Gussie, and drop the suitcase down after you. All set, Jeeves?'
I don't think I've ever assisted at a ceremony which gave such universal pleasure to all concerned. The sheet didn't split, which pleased Gussie. Nobody came to interrupt us, which pleased me. And when I dropped the suitcase, it hit Gussie on the head, which delighted Aunt Dahlia (CW)

'Jeeves, have you ever pondered on life?'
'From time to time, sir, in my leisure moments.'
'Grim, isn't it, what?'
'Grim, sir?'
'I mean, the difference between things as they look and things as they are?'
'The trousers perhaps half-an-inch higher, sir. A very slight adjustment of the braces will effect the necessary alteration. You were saying, sir?' (VGJ)

'We'll stifle his cries with the velours. And when he's grovelling on the ground I shall get a chance to give him a good kick in the tail-piece.'

'There is that added attraction, m'lord,' said Jeeves. 'For blessings ever wait on virtuous deeds, as the playwright Congreve reminds us' (RJ)

Brinkley: that dark and devious valet, enters Bertie Wooster's service when the banjolele outbreak compels Jeeves to take his talents elsewhere. A melancholy type, with a long, thin, pimply face and eyes that brood darkly on the coming Revolution, there are times when Bertie feels he is being mentally measured for his lamp-post:

> You never knew when you had the man. You couldn't go by the form-book. One moment he might be consenting to be kicked the length of the drive; the next, he could be chasing you up the top staircase, a short head behind you with the carving-knife (TJ)

Brinkley Court: the Worcestershire home of Tom and Dahlia Travers, a few miles from Market Snodsbury (near Droitwich) is the setting for some of Bertie's most coruscated adventures. As Blandings is to Shropshire, as Dover Street to Mayfair, so Brinkley is to Worcestershire; it seems to play its own part in ensuring that no moment there can possibly flag (*passim*, esp. RHJ, JFS, JO)

Briscoe, Angelica: d. of the Vicar of Maiden Eggesford, Somerset, and a girl so surpassingly lovely that C. (Barmy) Phipps and R. (Pongo) Twistleton, when they set eyes on her in the local grocers shop, putting in a bid for five lbs. of the best streaky, feel they have been struck by lightning. The sequel involves much church attendance, a phrenetic interest in the school treat, and a regrettable rift in the relations between the two Drones:

> 'Might I trouble you to pass the mustard, Fotheringay-Phipps,' said Pongo coldly.
> 'Certainly, Twistleton-Twistleton,' replied Barmy, with equal hauteur (YMS)

Briscoe, the Rev P. P.: vets the souls of the local peasantry at Maiden Eggesford. When his curate sprains his ankle, asks Barmy Phipps to supervise the annual outing of the Village Mothers (YMS)

Broadway Special, the: however favoured by New York's younger set, a form of headgear, in Jeeves's view, quite unsuited to an Englishman (COJ)

Brookfield: friend and confidant of Jeeves, is butler to the Earl of Wickhammersley at Twing (IJ)

Brookfield: brother of the major-domo at Twing Hall, is butler to the Vicar of Twing

Brown, Lana: nubile and shapely damsel from East Dulwich, to whom Jeeves judicially awards second prize in the Bathing Belle contest at Folkestone

Bruton Street, W.: reluctant though we are to record details of what P.c. Butt would term a private frakkus your worship, duty compels us to mention that about midway down this most respectable Mayfair street a deepish groove in the pavement bears visible proof of Diana Punter's wrath when she and Nelson Cork conducted their painful researches into each other's family backgrounds:

> Nelson uttered a nasty laugh. 'A mystery, eh? As much a mystery, I suppose, as why your Uncle George suddenly left England without stopping to pack up.'
> Diana's eyes flashed. Her foot struck the pavement another shrewd wallop. 'Uncle George,' she said, 'went abroad for his health.'
> 'You bet he did,' Nelson retorted. 'He knew what was good for him.'
> 'Anyway, he wouldn't have worn a hat like that.'
> 'Where they would have put him if he hadn't been off, he wouldn't have worn a hat at all.'
> 'Well he escaped one thing by going abroad. He missed the big scandal about your Aunt Clarissa.'
> Nelson clenched his fists. 'The jury gave Aunt Clarissa the benefit of the doubt,' he said hoarsely.
> 'Well, we all know what that means. It was accompanied, if you remember, by some very strong remarks from the bench.'
> 'I may be wrong,' said Nelson, 'but I should have thought it ill beseemed a girl whose brother Cyril was warned off the turf to haul up her slacks about other people's Aunt Clarissas.'
> A small groove was now beginning to appear in the paving-stone on which Diana stood . . . 'It is no pleasure to me,' she

said, 'to listen to your vapid gibberings. That's the worst of a man who wears his hat over his mouth—he will talk through it.' (YMS)

Buddhism: it leads to unpleasantness at Oxford when d'Arcy Cheesewright is converted to, and starts to cut chapels and go meditating beneath the nearest approach to a bo-tree (JM)

Bull and Bush Inn: Market Snodsbury, Worcs; Dahlia Travers assures Aubrey Upjohn that the Automobile Guide speaks highly of the, and advises him to transfer his unwanted presence to it (JO)

Bullett, G.: wins the Lady Jane Wix scholarship (RHJ)

Bullivant, Freddie: good at polo, and a coming man at snooker pool at the Drones; otherwise unmarked by enterprise (COJ)

Bulstrode: a skinny stripling of sixteen on whom Nature in her bounty has bestowed so many pimples that there is scarcely room on his face for the vacant grin which habitually adorns it; he represents the best talent the local board school can provide as major domo at Wyvern Hall (RJ)

Burgess, Mary: 'She's wonderful, Bertie. She is sweetly grave and beautifully earnest. She reminds me of—what is the name I want?'
'Marie Lloyd?'
'Saint Cecilia,' said young Bingo, eyeing me with a good deal of loathing (IJ)

Burgess, Wilfred: schoolboy s. of the late Matthew Burgess of Weatherley Court, Hants, and b. of Mary, has the appetite of a tapeworm and is matched in an eating contest against Master Heppenstall, the Vicar's son (IJ)

Bustard, Lt. Col. J. J., D.S.O.: of B.5 Berkeley Mansions, W., swells the chorus of neighbourly disapproval of Bertie's banjolele (TJ)

Butt, Comrade: a shrivelled Herald of the Red Dawn, reminding one of a haddock with lung trouble, is Bingo's rival for the hand of Charlotte Corday Rowbotham, q.v. (IJ)

Butterfield: butler to Sir Watkyn Bassett at Totleigh, is a confirmed listener-at-doors. Is compiling his memoirs, and loses no chance of adding suitable material (SLJ)

Byles, Sarah: Bingo Little's childhood Nannie, lives in his memory as being about eight feet tall and the same across, with hands of the consistency of cricket bats, a dominating voice and tyrannic presence. When Rosie unwisely brings the old object out of retirement to supervise their own offspring, Bingo fears that Algernon Aubrey will be giving away too much weight. In effect, Sarah's remorseless stream of anecdotes about Bingo's infancy, her admonitions and insistence on removing from his table most of the good things of life, prove an even worse menace, threatening to reduce his home status to that of a fourth-class power (NS)

Byng, old Johnnie: accompanying Major Plank on a Brazilian jungle expedition, is bitten by a puma, and still hesitates noticeably before sitting down (SLJ)

Byng, Monty: an early object lesson for Bertie:

'Jeeves,' I said, 'I am getting a check suit like that one of Mr Byng's.'
'Injudicious, sir,' he said firmly. 'It will not become you.'
Well the long and the short of it was that the confounded thing came home and I put it on, and when I caught sight of myself in the glass I nearly swooned. Jeeves was perfectly right. I looked like a cross between a music-hall comedian and a cheap bookie. Yet Monty had looked fine in absolutely the same stuff. These things are just life's mysteries (MJ)

Byng, Stephanie: far prettier, in Bertie's opinion, than she has any right to be, though on the petite side. She is a cousin (though few would think it) of the soupy Madeline Bassett, a ward of her uncle Sir Watkyn and owner of the Gaelic-speaking Aberdeen terrier Bartholomew (an animal as adept as she herself in the art of baiting the local constabulary). Stiffy is an object of worship for the village curate, the Rev. H. P. Pinker who, in the greensickness of his love, is cajoled by her to pinch the local policeman's helmet despite his apprehensions as to what the Infants Bible Class will think about it (COJ, SLJ)

C

Caesar, Caius Julius: (102?–44 B.C.) usu. in contexts of reproach on receipt of Brutus's dagger; but Bertie relaxes like, in his tent, the day he overcame the Nervii (RHJ), and Shakespearian scholars are grateful for the reminder that, on Shakespeare's authority, Caesar habitually kept all his clothes on when bathing (CT)

Caffyn, George: New York playwright (IJ)

Camberwell, S.E.: Bingo Little, that assiduous entomologist, captures a Camberwell Beauty named Mabel at a subscription dance (IJ)

Cammarleigh, Aurelia: d. of Sir Rackstraw and Lady C., is the source of Archie Mulliner's bad bout of Aurelian fever. She lives with a potty aunt who indulges in the Baconian theory (YMS)

Cammarleigh, Sir Rackstraw: retired pro-consul, of 36A Park St., W., now rates as Mayfair's biggest bore; barks at servants and club waiters and tells the same after-dinner story four nights in succession (YMS)

Cammarleigh, Lady: with good reason a pale and worn little person (YMS)

Cannes: has much to answer for, in Bertie's opinion:

> If I hadn't gone, I shouldn't have met the Bassett or bought that white mess jacket, and Angela wouldn't have met her shark, and Aunt Dahlia wouldn't have played baccarat (RHJ)

Canterbury, the Most Rev. the Archbishop of: and the incidence of frogs (MS); stings you for quite a bit (SLJ); Gussie Fink-Nottle confers with (SLJ). Information regarding the Primate is usually (as with statesmen and other celebrities) refutative. Nevertheless it is instructive to learn (SLJ) that his Grace does not keep newts (*passim*)

Carmody, Hugo: a cheerful young extrovert with few secrets from his fellow Drones or, indeed, anyone else; nephew of the miserly gourmet Lester Carmody of Rudge Hall, Worcs. Hugo was ed. at Eton and Trinity College, Cambridge. He partners Ronnie Fish in the ill-fated Hot Spot Club, and is a leading character in novels outside the Wooster-Jeeves cycle (*passim*)

Carmoyle, Lady Monica: a sister of the present Earl of Rowcester, 'the Moke'. m. Rory Carmoyle, q.v. She is instrumental in bringing the highly desirable millionairess Rosie Spottsworth to Rowcester Abbey (RJ)

Carmoyle, Sir Roderick, Bart.: in no danger of ever becoming a deep thinker, Rory Carmoyle's best achievement to date is in having married a nice girl who tolerates and even likes him. He finds happy, and almost useful, employment as a floorwalker in Harridges departmental store (RJ)

Carnaby, Lady: achieves a *succès de scandale* with her memoirs, published by Riggs & Ballinger (COJ)

Carroway, April: d. of Lady Carroway, Tudsleigh Court, Worcs, looks to Freddie Widgeon like the last word, the ultimate, bubbling cry, who could not be improved upon had he drawn up the specifications himself. She has however not only an ardent suitor in the militant Capt. Bradbury, but also a younger sister whose enterprise in gumming up the works for Bertie Wooster in VGJ is repeated with total devastation for Freddie (YMS)

Carroway, Prudence: known to the lower Fourth at St. Monica's as Teresa the Tapeworm, is the proximate cause of Bertie's arboreal adventure in the school grounds (VGJ); on being told by Freddie Widgeon that she cannot go wrong in imitating Lord Tennyson's heroines, takes Lady Godiva as her first model:

'Why aren't you at school now?' Freddie asked.
'I was bunked last term.'
'Gave you the push, did they? What for?'
'Shooting pigs. One pig, that is to say. Percival. He belonged to Miss Mapleton. Do you ever pretend to be people in books?'
'Never. And don't stray from the point at issue.'
'I'm not straying from the point at issue. I was playing William Tell.'
'The old apple-knocker, you mean?'
'I tried to get one of the girls to put the apple on her head, but she wouldn't, so I went down to the pigsty and put it on Percival's. And the silly goop shook it off and started to eat it just as I was shooting, which spoiled my aim, and I got him in the left ear. He was rather vexed about it. So was Miss Mapleton, especially as I had set the dormitory on fire the night before.'
Freddie blinked a bit. 'Any special reason, or just a passing whim?'

I was playing Florence Nightingale. The Lady with the Lamp.
I dropped the lamp.'

'Tell me,' said Freddie, 'this Miss Mapleton. What colour is
her hair?'

'Grey.'

'I thought as much.' (YMS)

CARRY ON, JEEVES: published in 1925, is dedicated to Bernard
le Strange. A collection of ten stories, four of them from **MY MAN,
JEEVES** and one more rewritten from the same. The last in the
book, **'Bertie Changes His Mind,'** is the only story in the whole
Wooster cycle which is related by Jeeves (COJ)

Cattermole, the late Elsie: who, among the older generation of
American theatregoers, does not remember this bright particular
star of the early musicals? For years her talents and personality drew
thousands of devotees to the long series of Broadway successes in
which she played leading parts. She m. the composer of the lyrics
of that outstanding success *The Blue Lady*. Much of her talent lives
on in her children Cora (Cora Starr) and Claude Potter-Pirbright
(MS *et al.*)

Chalk-Marshall, the Hon. Frederick: a shrewd and sapient
Drone, in whose presence his elder brother, the Earl of Droitwich,
sometimes feels that he is a mere babe:

'Are you trying to make me believe,' asked Lord Droitwich,
'that a girl like Violet would run after a man like me?'
'Does a mousetrap,' said Freddie, 'run after a mouse?'

Chambers, Willie: won the previous year's Choirboys 100 Yards
Race in a canter at Twing School Treat, and is now handicapped
out of it (IJ)

Charles: most young men who were not baptised Charles acquire
the name on becoming footmen. The one under review is Lord
Wickhammersley's strabismic second footman at Twing Hall:

'If you desire to ascertain Harold's form by personal in-
spection, sir,' said Jeeves, 'it would be a simple matter to arrange
a secret trial.'

'I'm bound to say I should feel easier in my mind.'

'Then I propose to bribe the lad to speak slightingly of the
second footman's squint, sir. Charles is somewhat sensitive on

the point, and should undoubtedly make the lad extend himself. (IJ)

Cheesewright, G. D'Arcy: a beefy but humourless bird, joins the Police Force via Hendon Training College and becomes village rozzer at Steeple Bumpleigh, making himself a pain in the neck to all decent citizens and to Uncle Percy Worplesdon:

> He was captain of Boats at Eton. He rowed four years for Oxford. He sneaks off each summer at the time of Henley Regatta and sweats lustily with his shipmates on behalf of the Leander Club. . . . All this galley-slave stuff has left him extraordinarily robust. . . . I remember Jeeves once speaking of someone of his acquaintance whose strength was as the strength of ten, and the description would have fitted Stilton nicely JM, JFS)

Chekhov, Anton: see **Birmingham Repertory Theatre**

Chicago, Ill.: a muffled (Kremlin) bell is rung when two old friends from the Windy City meet on some foreign shore with the reflection that 'it's a long way to Chi.' For some, it will recall that 'Old Moustache' of Napoleon's Guard who at the start of the fateful Retreat from Moscow, observed to a comrade 'I am a long way from Carcassonne'.

Chinchagook: (let us say) or Sitting Bull:

> I marked young Thos.'s demeanour closely at the time of his meeting Sebastian Moon and, unless I was much mistaken, there came into his eyes the sort of look which would come into those of an Indian chief . . . just before he started reaching for his scalping-knife (VGJ)

Chiswick, his Grace the Duke of: an uncle of Francis Bickersteth, owns half London and about five counties up north:

> 'A terrible country, Mr Wooster! A terrible country! Nearly eight shillings for a short cab drive! Iniquitous! Have you any idea how much my nephew pays for this flat?'
> 'About two hundred dollars a month, I believe.'
> 'What! Forty pounds a month?' (MJ, COL)

Christmas: those for whom *A Christmas Carol* no longer distils a heady mixture may try a draught of Bertie's seasonal stuff in 'The

Yule-Tide Spirit' (VGJ) or **'The Ordeal of Young Tuppy'** in the same book. They should not of course omit to pack the Giant Squirt and the Luminous Rabbit

Chuffnell: family name of Lord Chuffnell, q.v.

Chuffnell, the Rt. Hon. Lord: 5th Baron, was at prep school, Eton and Oxford with Bertie, yet has contrived through the years to throw a deep mantle of reserve over his Christian name. Inexorable economics compel Chuffy to spend a rusticated life at his seat, Chuffnell Hall, Chuffnell Regis, Somerset. Three or four of its bedrooms can still be occupied, and his social round is confined to the local doctor and parson, his stepmother and her son Seabury at the Dower House. But his fortunes rise in a sharp curve when he acquires the services of Jeeves (TJ)

Chuffnell, Myrtle, Lady: relict of the 4th Baron, the Dowager is a frustrated lady in her forties who is congenitally incapable of grasping why, on her husband's death, it is Chuffy, and not her own son Seabury who cops the title. She has the unpleasant habit of clasping Seabury in her arms and looking reproachfully at the fifth Baron, as if he had slipped a fast one over the widow and orphan:

> Seabury . . . was simply something his mother had picked up in the course of a previous marriage and, consequently, did not come under the head of what the *Peerage* calls Issue. And in matters of succession, if you aren't Issue you haven't a hope (TJ)

Churchill, the late Sir Winston, K.G.: might conceivably have been nonplussed, Lord Ickenham thinks, if suddenly ordered to jelly an eel. Other appearances instance his well-known views upon things up with which he would not put (YMS, *et al.*)

Clay, Bessie: loses her amateur status at the Twing School Treat (IJ)

Clementina, the Kid: on being assured by that red-haired Jezebel Bobbie Wickham that this cousin of hers is a quiet, saintly child of thirteen, Bertie might have been excused a little lip-pursing. She proves however a most sympathetic listener to his golfing troubles. Her behaviour both at dinner and the cinema is irreproachable. Only by degrees does it emerge that she is absent without leave from St. Monica's, where she had been placed under close arrest for putting sherbet in the inkwell; that Bertie is committed to smuggling her back into school by night, and that the sleepless guardian of the

St. Monica's chaingang is none other than Miss Mapleton—a twenty-minute egg and a bosom friend of Aunt Agatha, who will infallibly be furnished with all the criminal details (VGJ)

CODE OF THE WOOSTERS, THE: published 1938. In PF the author remarks that he found the finishing of it 'a ghastly sweat—I imagine because I have twice stopped writing the book for long periods' (CW)

Cohen Bros. of Covent Garden, W.C.: that fascinating shop which is the 'Mecca of all who prefer to pluck their garments ripe off the bough' rather than wait for them to grow, runs through the Wodehouse canon like an intermittent pink streak through the set of a Scotsman's kilt, (there is a story indeed in which a golfer's incandescent kilt, made by them, figures boldly—if boldly is not an understatement). The kindly brethren are at all times ready to fit a client out with a tweed suit of bold pattern with the same sense of swift service with which, had he desired it, they would provide the full costume of an Arctic explorer, a duke about to visit Buckingham Palace or a big game hunter bound for East Africa. A customer in search of a simple hat is liable, in five minutes, to find himself the temporary owner of a smoking-cap, three boxes of poker chips, a fishing-rod, some polo sticks, a concertina, a ukelele and a bowl of goldfish. The Bros. (we learn elsewhere) are Isidore, Irving and Lou. They supply the necessary raiment to convert Bertie the Sailor into Sinbad Wooster, and transmute Catsmeat Pirbright into a Borstal Rover (JM, *et al.*)

> **Collectors' Corner**

IF A COLLECTOR PINCHES SOMETHING FROM AN-OTHER COLLECTOR, IT DOESN'T COUNT AS STEALING
(SLJ)

I caught a glimpse of Uncle Tom messing about with his collection of old silver. For a moment I toyed with the idea of pausing to pip-pip, but wiser counsels prevailed. This uncle is a bird who, sighting a nephew, is apt to buttonhole him and become a bit informative on the subject of sconces and foliation, not to mention scrolls, ribbon wreaths in high relief and gadroon borders (CW)

'I remember,' said Mrs Spottsworth, 'visiting William Randolph Hearst at San Simeon, and there was a whole French abbey lying on the grass near the gates' (RJ)

'He acted from a desire to exasperate Mr Travers, sir. Collectors are never pleased when they learn that a rival collector has acquired at an insignificant price an *objet d'art* of great value' (SLJ)

'Say! What's wrong with buying you a knighthood? I wonder how much they cost nowadays. I'll have to ask Sir Roderick. I might be able to get it at Harridges' (RJ)

'If all the girls Freddie Widgeon has been in love with were placed end to end—not that one could do it, of course—they would reach from Piccadilly Circus to Hyde Park Corner. Further than that, probably, because some of them were pretty tall' (*passim*)

'Home isn't home,' he was wont to say, running a thoughtful hand through his whiskers, 'without plenty of nude Venuses.' Consequently Ickenham Hall and its gardens are reminiscent of a Turkish bath on Ladies' Night (UD)

'Yes, I have a home in Pasadena. In Carmel, too, and one in New York and another in Florida and another up in Maine.'
'Making five in all?'
'Six. I was forgetting the one in Oregon.'
'Six?' The Captain seemed thoughtful. 'Oh, well,' he said, 'it's nice to have a roof over your head, of course.' (RJ)

Coote, J. G. (Looney): outstandingly high-stepping Drone and as crazy a bimbo as ever went through life one step ahead of the Lunacy Commissioners, but rich beyond the dreams of creosote. Dreams indeed figure prominently in his fortunes (see **Racing Intelligence** for his special talents) and his luck on the turf is a standing source of gossip at the Drones (NS, *et al.*)

Cootes, Myrtle: in service at Green St., Mayfair, she improves the expression of a dead codfish on a slab with steel-rimmed spectacles, topped off with ginger hair and adenoids. Yet Myrtle is to prove the vehicle of romance whom fate selects for just retribution upon Oofy Prosser, the Drones Club creep (FO)

Corcoran, Bruce (Corky): impecunious portrait painter, discovers that there is always a way (MJ)

Cork, Nelson: a hospital nurse hears the intriguing and mysterious story of, and the Amazing Hat mix-up (see **Bruton St.**):

Percy looked warily about, and lowered his voice another notch.

'Nelson,' he said, 'you know Elizabeth Bottsworth . . . a fellow wouldn't be far out in calling her an angel in human shape.'

'Aren't all angels in human shape?'

'Are they?' said Percy, who was a bit foggy on angels (YMS)

Cornelius, Mr: doyen of the estate agency of Matters & Cornelius, of Valley Fields, S.E., no one is better qualified to compose a history of that pleasant and recurring suburb, which lightly disguises the area of Dulwich. For this bearded devotee the place has everything necessary to the good life, and in its records he can—and does—find parallels to the most exotic of travellers' tales. This gentle and far-sighted philosopher earns our further regard when he provides Freddie Widgeon with the means necessary to realise that young man's dreams (IB, *et al.*)

Cornish (Riviera) Express, the: invariably aggressive, is a frequent tapper-on-the-back of those incautious enough to pause to pick, e.g., a nosegay of wild flowers in its path; elsewhere, its sonic similarity to Aunt Agatha (*passim*)

Covent Garden Opera Co., the Royal: McGarry, talented operator behind the Drones Club bar, can accurately estimate the weight of anything at sight, from a vegetable marrow to a tenor singer in, :

'Never misses by more than half an ounce,' said an Egg. 'We call him the Human Scales.' (FO)

Craye: family name of the Earl of Worplesdon, q.v.

Craye, the Hon, Edwin: son of Lord Worplesdon, this ferret-faced child is dedicated to the Boy Scout movement and to the performance, from sheer malevolence, of his daily good deed, sparing neither age nor sex (COJ)

Craye, Lady Florence: d. of the Earl of Worplesdon, a girl with a wonderful profile but steeped to the gills in serious purpose. Author of the thoughtful novel *Spindrift*, she twice considers marriage with Bertie Wooster to the point of engaging him to herself, and he finds himself, in the course of his pre-marital education, locked in combat with a book called *Types of Ethical Theory*, with particular reference to the chapter on Idiopsychological Ethics:

This Florence, though an intellectual, is tall and willowy and handsome, with a terrific profile and luxuriant platinum blonde hair. She might, so far as looks are concerned, be the star unit of the harem of one of the better class Sultans. It is seldom that her walks abroad are unattended by the whistles of visiting Americans (COJ, JFS *et al.*)

Cream, Adela: purveyor of spine-chilling novels to the American masses, is tall, gaunt and Holmesian. Normally she wears an ink-spot on her hawk-like nose. In B. Wooster's view it is virtually impossible to write novels of suspense without getting a certain amount of ink on the beezer. Ask Agatha Christie or anyone (JO)

Cream, Homer: butter-and-eggs tycoon, makes a pilgrimage with Tom Travers to Harrogate, for the ulcers, while Jeeves journeys to Herne Bay for the shrimps. They thereby forfeit the piquant appearance of Sir Roderick Glossop in the array of a butler (JO)

Cream, Wilbert: e.s. of the Homer Creams, is a respected member of the faculty of one of the greater U.S. universities (JO)

Cream, Wilfred: y.s. of the Homer Creams, is a regular habitué of the less reputable columns of the New York tabloid press, under the label of Broadway Willie. Thrice married at time of issue, he rarely cashes a cheque without producing a gun and announcing that this is a stick-up (JO)

Cremorne, Sir Roger: writes a book called *America From Within* after a fortnight's stay in the U.S.A. (COJ)

Cripps, the late Sir Stafford, P.C.: seldom known to give an impression of a laying hen (YMS)

Crufts, Algernon: insouciant, barely sentient Drone, and (perhaps therefore) only permanent friend of the combustible Bobbie Wickham (BCE)

Cuthbert: resident cat in the Pringle ménage, beatified as indirect cause of Bertie's liberation from a fate worse than death (COJ)

D

Dalgleish, Colonel and Mrs: of Upper Bleaching, Hants, parents of the dog-girl, lavish their hospitality on the lower fauna—even on Tuppy Glossop (VGJ)

Dalgleish, Miss:

> Young Tuppy Glossop was frisking round one of those largish, corn-fed girls. He was bending towards her in a devout sort of way, and even at a considerable distance I could see that his ears were pink.
>
> 'My friend Bertie Wooster,' said Tuppy to the girl in what seemed to me an apologetic manner. You know—as if he would have preferred to hush me up (VGJ)

Damon and Pythias: symb. of sacred friendship, as of David and Jonathan, or Swan and Edgar. Elsewhere, the point is posed; Who now is able to say just what it was about Crosse which first attracted Blackwell? (RJ *et al.*)

Datchet, the Rt. Hon. the Earl of: f. of Viscount (Dogface) Rainsby, q.v., of the Drones. The Earl distinguished himself by being thrown out of the Empire Music Hall on Boat Race Night every year during his Oxford days; married happily into the chorus; now writes a gossip feature for the *Daily Post* (YMS *et al.*)

Debrett's Peerage: 'You know, Jeeves, even in these disturbed post-war days, with the social revolution turning handsprings on every side and civilisation, as you might say, in the melting-pot, it's still quite an advantage to be in big print in **Debrett's Peerage.**'

> 'Unquestionably so, m'lord. It gives a gentleman a certain standing.' (RJ)

Demosthenes Club, the: its near proximity to the Drones, which it faces in Dover St., W., earns this dreary spot a mention. To the unwary applicant for membership it might be thought a desirable thing to join a club in the heart of Mayfair, with Piccadilly at one's door, the Green Park across the way, Old Bond St. round the corner, and every attention within, including the most somniferous armchairs outside the Athenaeum itself and the conversation of such outstanding bores as Sir Raymond Bastable to induce slumber. But members do not speak of their great tragedy to the non-initiate. The truth is that Dover St. is not a judicious site for a club whose members' years and waistlines have passed the span which would permit them to run like hares for cover beneath a hail of catapulted brazil nuts. Intrepid men who have penetrated the place report that the smoking-room is full of corpses in armchairs. If it be added that the Club's leading gargoyle is old Howard Saxby the bird-watcher, and that Sir Roderick Glossop is an esteemed member, the warning may be even clearer (CT, *et al.*)

Dempsey, Jack: Kipper Herring, in Aunt Dahlia's view, looks more like, than Jack Dempsey does (JO)

Devereux, Ronnie: a Drone with a commendable talent for spotting a human tick

Deverill, Charlotte: 'One of them's deaf, and one's dotty, and they're all of them bitches,' said Corky Pirbright (MS)

Deverill, Daphne: see **Dame Daphne Winkworth, D.B.E.**

Deverill, Emmeline: This was the aunt of whom Corky had spoken as the dotty one. From start to finish of every meal she soliloquised. Shakespeare would have liked her (MS)

Deverill, the late Flora: married Haddock's Headache Hokies to the consternation of a sea of sisters, and became the m. of Esmond H., q.v. (MS)

Deverill, Harriet: 'From all I have heard of Mr Wooster,' said an aunt with a beaky nose, 'this kind of vulgar foolery will be quite congenial to him.' (MS)

Deverill, Myrtle: 'Mr Wooster is a most erratic young man,' said an aunt who would have been the better for a good facial (MS)

Deverill, the late Sir Quintin, Bart.: of King's Deverill, Hants, donated a village hall which does much to promote the steady drift to the towns (MS)

Dibble, the Rev. Cuthbert: Vicar of Boustead Parva, Glos, receives 9 minutes in the Great Sermon Handicap (IJ)

Dictyota: the strange and mysterious love life of — see **Isn't Nature Wonderful** (CW)

Dix, the Rev. W.: the incumbent at Little Clickton-in-the-Wold, Glos, receives 5 minutes in the Great Sermon Handicap (IJ)

Dobbs, P.c. Ernest: village policeman at King's Deverill, Hants, is a practising atheist, and loses no opportunity of putting awkward questions to the Vicar:

> 'He annoys Uncle Sidney,' said Corky, 'by popping out at him from side streets and making offensive cracks about Jonah

and the whale. When he isn't smirching Jonah, he's asking where Cain got his wife.'

On receiving a sharpish hint from a thunderbolt, Dobbs decided to join the Infants Bible Class in time (MS)

Dobson, P.c.: junior branch of the law at Chuffnell Regis, is nephew of P.s. Voules whose views he shares on the shackling of Britain's police force (TJ)

Drones Club, the: its postal address is Dover St., Mayfair, W.1. Expert opinion is agreed that the precise site is on the north side and that No. 16 seems to fit the evidence and implications. The windows of its smoking-room overlook the street and command the portico and front steps of the Demosthenes Club opposite (as top-hatted Demosthenians have known to their discomfiture). Years ago the Demosthenes premises were occupied by Thorpe and Briscoe, coal merchants. The Drones Club has front steps too (see **to touch Horace;** also **Petherick-Soames**). It is at the heart of the Wodehouse Metrop. and is surrounded on all sides by the town houses, streets, squares, clubs, pubs, parks, shops, churches and institutions of all kinds which wear blue plaques for the *aficionado*.

The Drones membership can be gauged, with some accuracy, at between 140 and 150. Bertie Wooster himself lets us into this secret when he comments on the universal popularity of the annual Darts Sweepstake. 'They roll up in dense crowds,' he says, 'to buy tickets at 10/-.' The winner 'stands to scoop in £56/10/-.' This would indicate 113 entrants. Allowing for absentees the total roll may be estimated at around 145. Of these, fifty-three members have been identified by name. In informal nomenclature and shorn of titles, as befitting the general atmosphere, they are:

Alistair Bingham-Reeves	Algie Martyn
Biscuit Biskerton	Archie Mulliner
Monty Bodkin	Mervyn Mulliner
Jimmy Bowles	Freddie Oaker
Tubby Bridgnorth	Horace Pendlebury-Davenport
Freddie Bullivant	Catsmeat Potter-Pirbright
Monty Byng	Oofy Prosser
Hugo Carmody	Rupert Psmith
Freddie Chalk-Marshall	Dogface Rainsby
Stilton Cheesewright	Tuppy Rogers
Berry Conway	Freddie Rooke
Looney Coote	Bill Rowcester

Nelson Cork	Oofy Simpson
Algie Crufts	Stiffy Stiffham
Ronnie Devereux	Archie Studd
Dudley Finch	Reggie Tennyson
Gussie Fink-Nottle	Freddie Threepwood
Ronnie Fish	Pongo Twistleton-Twistleton
Freddie Fitch-Fitch	Hugo Walderwick
Boko Fittleworth	Capt. J. G. Walkinshaw
Reggie Foljambe	Freddie Widgeon
Aubrey Fothergill	Ambrose Wiffin
Barmy Fotheringay-Phipps	Percy Wimbolt
Tuppy Glossop	Dick Wimple
Percy Gorringe	Bertie Wooster
Reggie Havershot	Algie Wymondham
Bingo Little	

The most chronicled (Bertie apart) are Freddie Widgeon, Bingo
Little, Psmith, Pongo Twistleton-Twistleton, Barmy Fotheringay-
Phipps, Bill Rowcester, Ronnie Fish, Hugo Carmody, Reggie
Havershot and Gussie Fink-Nottle. All these, as well as some others,
figure prominently in full-length novels. Oofy Simpson for a brief
while ranked as the Club's richest property but (though Looney
Coote and Bertie Wooster are 'stagnant with the stuff') Oofy
Prosser is the undisputed Club millionaire (his shoes by Lobb are a
point of interest for visitors). Horace Davenport was darts champion
until his resignation on marriage to Valerie Twistleton, with Bertie
as runner-up. In the Club dining-room, bread rolls are the accepted
point d'appui:

> A crusty roll, whizzing like a meteor out of the unknown,
> shot past the Crumpet and the elderly relative whom he was
> entertaining to luncheon, and shattered itself against the wall.
> Noting that his guest had risen some eighteen inches into the
> air, the Crumpet begged him not to give the thing another
> thought. 'Just someone being civil,' he explained.

The Drones is one of those clubs where they display the cold dishes on
a central table, and Catsmeat Pirbright once hit the game pie six
times with six consecutive bread rolls, from a seat at the far window.
In the smoking-room, lump sugar is the tactical missile. Members
are also pretty keen on the joke goods element. The plate lifter has
had a notable vogue. The dribble glass is a favourite ice-breaker.
The surprise salt shaker has had several successes. They still speak,
too, of Catsmeat's emotion when the bread roll he picked up squeaked

loudly and a mouse ran out of it. Strong men had to rally round with brandy. Pongo Twistleton and Barmy Phipps are the Pat and Mike of the Irish knockabout crosstalk act at the Club's annual smoker (produced in a professional manner by Catsmeat). The annual golf tournament is held usually either at Bramley-on-Sea or Marvis Bay. In the matter of I.Q. opinions are divided. Bertie Wooster is probably over-modest about his own. It is generally conceded that Bill Rowcester ranks pretty low. Some would place his intellect below that of Barmy Phipps. Others think this impossible. Looney Coote skids around one step ahead of the Lunacy Commissioners, and several others, e.g., Freddie Widgeon, have been mentally measured for a strait waistcoat by Sir Roderick Glossop. Yet when spring comes round, Barmy Phipps and the rest, like Gussie Fink-Nottle's ribbon-like seaweed, feel the stir of life along their keel and hear the voice of love, and are up and doing with the best. The record for the maiden stakes is held by Freddie Widgeon, who hears the voice of spring all the year round. The susceptible Freddie has his moments of inspiration too. The annual incursion of outsize uncles, visiting town for the Eton and Harrow Match and descending on their nephews for luncheon at the Drones (where they make for the bar like bison for a water-hole) gives Freddie the idea for the Fat Uncles Sweepstake. His own relative, Lord Blicester, starts as favourite. Apparently that super-peer, Lord Burslem, has no nephews (we are told that the Empress of Blandings is the fattest pig in Shropshire except for Lord Burslem, who lives over Bridgnorth way). It is indeed usually in company with some chance guest that we get our own rare glimpses of the interior of the egregious Club. They are always memorable occasions. We are there when Uncle Fred Ickenham (Old Sureshot) beans Beefy Bastable's topper with his first brazil nut; and when the dubious Mustard Pott organises his Clothes Stakes, and Horace Davenport emerges from the telephone alcove in the guise of a Zulu warrior.

Is there any club so hallowed (asks Richard Usborne in WAW) in English fiction? With respect to the Dickensian shades, probably not. Like Alice's Wonderland (with which they have much in common) and the Pickwick Club, and like rum to Billy Bones in *Treasure Island*, the Drones have been meat and drink, and man and wife, to men in exile the world over, and will undoubtedly be among the first earthly institutions to which our nearest neighbours in space will be introduced one day. The Club's literary roots go deep. It has strong affiliations with the Boar's Head Tavern in Eastcheap. That was a club which possessed not only a fat uncle to end all fat uncles but a parcel of sportive and spirited young sprigs of nobility for whom the Drones would lay down the red carpet of welcome, no questions asked. In a wider and nostalgic sense it is oddly evocative of the Forest of Arden:

> and a many merry men with him: and there they live like the old Robin Hood of England, and fleet the time carelessly, as they did in the golden world.

For essentially the Drones is not of this world. It is set outside time and space; and like all vintage Wodehouse, it is also set (though so gently that we need not perceive its removal) outside the world of moral law. It has been seen by some as a skilfully caricatured world before its Fall from grace. It is probably more apt to see it as the vision of a world that cannot fall; a state of guileless uninhibition whose beings, informed by a kind of divine comedy, reflect only their creator's will, speaking their own language (inimitable, yet happily intelligible to us) and who live, move and have their being for the single purpose of fleeting the time carelessly in an inspired burlesque of our own pedestrian middle-earth.

Dumbchummery

THERE ARE TREMENDOUS POSSIBILITIES IN A SNAKE. POP IT ON THE TABLE AFTER THE SOUP AND BE SOCIETY'S PET

(Scampering, sliding, hopping, climbing, flying, swimming and slithering all over the novels and stories in pleasing diversity are the Dumb Chums. Not only are they on occasion highly and colourfully characterised, but they reflect also an observation as faithful as it is amusing.)

Ambrose: late-loved spaniel of the Travers menage at Brinkley, could not be restrained from a lifelong devotion to the garbage-pail (RHJ)

Alphonse: a poodle of wide influence and not to be ignored; in Sir George Copstone's view, a mobile flea storage depot (NS)

Augustus: resident cat at Brinkley Court, suffers from a traumatic symplegia. Where other cats are satisfied with their eight hours, Augustus wants his twenty-four (JO)

Bartholomew: Stephanie Byng's redoubtable Aberdeen terrier. Beetling brows cover his eyes and he is given to muttering beneath his breath in Gaelic. Fitted out with the jaws and teeth of a crocodile he is, in a word, a bone-crusher (CW, SLJ)

Bottles: late of Bottleton, E., is of doughty and genial temperament if of uncertain breed. His mother was a popular local belle with a good deal of sex-appeal, and his paternity would set a genealogical college pursing its lips in perplexity. Makes his home with the Rev. Beefy Bingham, has cleaned up every dog in the village and is spoken of as an ornament to the village and a credit to his master's cloth (BCE)

Cyril: Valerie Twistleton's cocker, has the endearing habit of snapping the nose off such visitors as care to avail themselves of the privilege (NS)

Clarkson: Elizabeth Bottsworth's hostess's Peke (YMS)

Cuthbert: (already noticed) heroine cat of the Pringle ménage, rescues Bertie from a shotgun wedding (COJ)

Jabberwocky: (fl. c. 1880); the pug who played a leading if silent part in laying the foundations of Sir Thomas Lipton's fortunes when walking in Grosvenor Square with Pongo Twistleton's great-aunt Brenda (UFS)

Lysander: the snores of Aurelia Cammarleigh's bulldog are reminiscent of a lumber camp when the wood-sawing is at its briskest

McIntosh: Agatha Spenser Gregson's Aberdeen, an enthusiastic being of weak intellect, is rashly boarded out with Bertie (VGJ)

Mike: Lord Rowcester's amiable Irish terrier responds to treatment with American ointment by Jill Wyvern (RJ)

Mittens: a sheepdog resident at Pongo's ancestral home whose memory helps to retrieve the honour of the Twistletons (UD)

Nigger: doubtfully considered by experts to be a Gorgonzola cheese-hound. Writes his autobiography in *The Mixer* (MT)

Percy: a woolly, white effort with a penchant for evicting young men from behind Madeline Bassett's sofa (MS)

Ping-Poo: one of Mrs Bingo Little's coloratura sextet of Pekes (EBC)

Pirbright: the Pekinese, naturally incensed when a wolfhound comments on the situation in China, rolls up his sleeves preparatory to mixing it when he is suddenly airborne (NS)

Pomona: Mrs Spottsworth's Pekinese, registers joy by a series of piercing shrieks as though being tortured. In moments of unrestrained ecstasy she screams partly like a lost soul, partly like a scalded cat (RJ)

Poppet: a low-slung chassis type Dachshund, wears his ears inside out (JO)

Rollo: dubious bull-terrier won by Lord Pershore in a raffle (COJ)

Robert: Aunt Agatha's spaniel; a notable exponent of retrieving and wolfing any such overlooked trifles as cucumber sandwiches (VGJ)

Sam Goldwyn: parentage indeterminate, is acquired by Corky Pirbright at the Battersea Dogs Home. Shows his affectionate nature by knocking Bertie base over apex, but wins his undying admiration by biting Uncle Charlie Silversmith. In appearance is the original Shaggy Dog, has a tongue like an anteater, and niffs to high heaven (MS)

Sidney: the snake, is put to bed with Sir Claude Lynn, Bart., thus making two of them

Susan: one of Lady Alcester's perturbation of Pekes (BCE)

Tibby: a mobile target for the bow and arrows of Sippy's boyhood and a remote agent of Bertie's rescue from a fate worse than death (COJ)

Toto: greatly resembles a rat and is taken for one by Nigger (MT)

Wilhelm: an Alsatian of (apparently) 5% dog and 95% wolf descent, one of the principal menaces at Matcham Scratchings, where cats form his main diet. Is put to ignominious flight by a Pekinese puppy (YMS)

Wing-Fu: a treble in the Bingo Littles' Peke choir, goes A.W.O.L. (EBC)

The whole situation recalled something that had happened to me once up at Oxford, when the heart was young. It was during Eights Week, and I was sauntering on the river bank with a girl when there was a sound of barking and a large, hefty dog came galloping up, obviously intent on mayhem. And I was just commending my soul to God and feeling that this was where the old flannel trousers got about thirty bob's worth of value bitten out of them, when the girl, waiting till she saw the whites of its eyes, suddenly opened a coloured

Japanese umbrella in the animal's face. Upon which, it did three back somersaults and retired into private life (CW)

The Vicar happened to be speaking of Pharaoh and all those Plagues he got when he wouldn't let the Children of Israel go. And it occurred to Corky that if P.c. Dobbs were visited by a Plague of Frogs, it might quite possibly change his heart and make him let Sam Goldwyn go. She felt that the Plague of Lice might be even more effective, but she is a practical, clear-thinking girl and realised that lice are hard to come by (MS)

'The shock was of the severest,' said Sir Roderick. 'Knowing the Dower House to be unoccupied, I repaired thither.' He shuddered. 'Mr Wooster, that house is—I speak in all seriousness—an Inferno. Shall I tell you of my experiences beneath that roof?'

'Do,' I said cordially. 'We have the night before us.'

He handkerchiefed the b. once more.

'It was a nightmare. I had scarcely entered the place when a voice addressed me from a dark corner of the kitchen. "I see you, you old muddler," was the phrase it employed.'

'Dashed familiar.'

'I need scarcely tell you what consternation it occasioned me. I bit my tongue severely. Then, divining that the speaker was merely a parrot, I hastened from the room. I had scarcely reached the stairs when I observed a hideous form. A little, short, broad, bow-legged individual with long arms and a dark, wizened face. He was wearing clothes of some description and he walked rapidly, lurching from side to side and gibbering. . . . The room in which I next found myself seemed to be completely filled with small dogs. They pounced upon me, snuffling and biting at me. I escaped and entered another room. Here at last, I was saying to myself, even in this sinister and ill-omened house there must be peace. Mr Wooster, I had scarcely framed the thought when something ran up my right trouser leg. I sprang to one side and in so doing upset what appeared to be a box or cage of some kind. I found myself in a sea of mice. I detest the creatures. I endeavoured to brush them off. They clung the more. I fled from the room, and I had scarcely reached the stairs when this lunatic appeared and pursued me.' (TJ)

Mrs Bingo's Pekes were all in bed when Bingo went and sprang the little stranger on them. Too often, when you introduce a ringer into a gaggle of Pekes, there ensues a scrap like New Year's Eve in Madrid. But to-night, after a certain amount of tentative sniffing, the home team issued their O.K., and he left all them curled up in their basket like so many members of the Athenaeum. (EBC)

Lord Brancaster at that time (said Jeeves) owned a parrot to which he was greatly devoted. One day the bird chanced to be lethargic, and his lordship, with the kindly intention of restoring it to its customary animation, offered it a portion of seed-cake steeped in the '84 Port. The bird accepted the morsel gratefully and consumed it with every indication of satisfaction. Almost immediately afterwards, however, its manner became markedly feverish. Having bitten his lordship in the thumb and sung part of a sea-shanty, it fell to the bottom of the cage and remained there for a considerable period of time with its legs in the air, unable to move (RHJ)

'I don't mind telling you that there are a couple of notches on my gun that aren't for buffalo, or lions, or elands, or rhinos.'
'Really? What are they for?'
'Cheaters.'
'Ah, yes, those leopard things that go as fast as racehorses.'
Jeeves had a correction to make.
'Somewhat faster, m'lord. A half-mile in 45 seconds.'
'Chea-*ters* was what I said.' (RJ)

In the drive I met Jeeves, at the wheel of Stiffy's car. Beside him, looking like a Scotch elder rebuking sin, was the dog Bartholomew.
'Good evening, sir,' he said. 'I have been taking this little fellow to the veterinary surgeon. Miss Byng was uneasy because he bit Mr Fink-Nottle. She was afraid he might have caught something.' (SLJ)

I had looked in at his place while on a motor trip, and he had put me right off my feed by bringing a couple of green things with legs to the luncheon table, crooning over them like a young mother and eventually losing one of them in the salad (RHJ)

'There are all sorts of ways of nobbling favourites,' said Bingo in a sort of deathbed voice. 'In *Pipped On the Post* Lord Jasper as near as a toucher outed Bonny Betsy by bribing the head lad to slip a cobra into her stable the night before the Derby.'
'What are the chances of a cobra biting Harold, Jeeves?'
'Slight, I should imagine, sir. And in such an event, knowing the boy as intimately as I do, my anxiety would be entirely for the snake.' (IJ)

Pirbright wasn't well, she said, and the vet talked me into trying some sort of tonic port which he said was highly recommended. We gave Pirbright a saucerful and he seemed to enjoy it. Then he suddenly uttered a piercing bark and ran up the side of a wall. When he returned his manner was lethargic. I thought a walk would do him good, but as we came on to the the bridge, he staggered and fell into the lake. He must have had some form of vertigo (MS)

I don't know if you have ever leaped between the sheets, all ready for a spot of sleep, and received an unforeseen lizard up the left pyjama leg? It is an experience which puts its stamp on a man (TJ)

Dunstable, 4th Duke of: g.g.f. of Horace Pendlebury-Davenport, while lunching at his club in St. James's rubs the nose of a committee member in an unsatisfactory omelette. The egg motif would appear to be endemic in the family. Blandings devotees will recollect that this nobleman's grandson, the present Duke, converts an unpopular secretary into an omelette on the Castle terrace.

Dunstable, 5th Duke of: twice cuts down the barbed wire fence separating his garden on the Cote d'Azur from the local golf links.

Dunstable, his Grace the Duke of: Alaric Pendlebury-Davenport, 6th Duke, s. his f. the 5th Duke. His Grace is unm.; heir-pres., Horace Pendlebury-Davenport, his nephew, q.v., Bloxham Mansions, Park Lane, W. His Grace res. principally on his Wiltshire estates, but inheriting his forbears' mercurial temperament, is prone to making unpremeditated descents, for indefinite periods, upon the country homes of his acquaintances. A confirmed believer, like his noble ancestors, in the efficacy of direct action, the Duke can say it indifferently with either eggs or pokers. Is claimed by some to be now as fat as the Earl of Blicester. In his youth his Grace conceived a tender regard for the then Lady Constance Threepwood, y.d. of the 8th Earl of Emsworth and sister of the present peer. Hobbies; pokerwork, omelette making, training racing pigs. His chief allergies include nephews, Scottish traditional songs, male secretaries. Few coots could have less hair than, and any walrus would be proud of the moustache through which he strains his soup:

> The cosy glow which had been enveloping the Duke became shot through with a sudden chill.
> 'My cheque? What do you mean, my cheque?'
> 'For two hundred and fifty pounds.'
> The Duke shot back in his chair, and his moustache, foaming upwards as if a gale had struck it, broke like a wave on the stern and rockbound coast of the Dunstable nose.

Durante, Schnozzle: 'You are a splendid, chivalrous soul,' said the Bassett. 'You remind me of Cyrano.'

'The chap with the nose?'

'Yes.'

I felt the old beak furtively. It was a bit on the prominent side, perhaps, but, dash it, not in the Cyrano class. It began to look as if the next thing this girl would do would be to compare me to Schnozzle Durante (RHJ)

E

East Wibley: Steeple Bumpleigh's nearest market town, Hants, and scene of the fancy dress dance where Lord Worplesdon does a secret deal with King Edward the Confessor and Bertie is scheduled to appear as Sinbad the Sailor (JM)

EGGS, BEANS AND CRUMPETS: a collection of nine short stories of which one, **Anselm Gets His Chance,** is one of the author's favourites. Published 1940 (EBC)

Eisenhower, General Dwight: Jeeves has no doubts that even Ike in certain circumstances might resort to a tactical retreat to a prepared position (RJ)

Ela of Salisbury, the Countess: see Rowcester Abbey (RJ)

Emperor Marcus Aurelius: quoted as holding to the Christian ethic that nobody is called on to bear things beyond his powers; e.g., Jeeves and the future yet unseen (RJ) (*passim*)

a sort of primitive Bob Hope, given to throwing off wisecracks (RJ)

Empress Catherine of Russia, H.I.M. the: it is generally considered that her Imperial Majesty was not everybody's girl. (Historians are agreed, however, that she was quite a lot of people's—Ed.) (*passim*)

Emsworth, the Rt. Hon. the Earl of: f. of the well-known Drone Freddie Threepwood, is Clarence, 9th of his line, of Blandings

Castle, Shropshire. Is cited elsewhere as sharing, with the majority of the peerage, the view that younger sons are a drug on the market and a general headache to everyone around them. Clarence makes a single but very illuminating entry in the Wooster-Jeeves canon. Florence Craye, detailing the ribald reminiscences she had found in Willoughby Wooster's family history, observes:

> 'There is a dreadful one about Lord Emsworth.'
> 'Lord Emsworth? Not the one we know? Not the one at Blandings?' A most respectable old Johnnie. Doesn't do a thing nowadays but dig in the garden with a spud.
> 'The very same. That is what makes the book so unspeakable. It is full of stories about people one knows who are the essence of propriety to-day, but who seem to have behaved, when they were in London in the 'eighties, in a manner that would not have been tolerated in the fo'c'sle of a whaler (COJ)

(Initiated readers may well take a conservative view of Uncle Willoughby's powers of memory. Nameless orgies are difficult to associate with the amiable but vacuous Clarence. It is difficult to imagine that his brother Galahad, when composing his own reminiscences for publication, would have omitted the opportunity to present Clarence as a gay boulevardier. Yet Gally specifically records that at the height of his powers Clarence's sole West End exploit was the ability to mix a wonderful salad)

enter the foul fiend: 'Oh, and by the way,' said Mrs Bingo, opening her bag and producing currency. 'when you go to Boddington and Biggs will you pay their bill? It will save me writing out a cheque.' She slipped him a couple of fivers, embraced him fondly and drove off, leaving him waving on the front steps. This waving had an important bearing on what followed. You cannot wave a hand with a couple of fivers in it without them crackling. And a couple of fivers cannot crackle in the hand of a man who has received direct information from an authoritative source that a 7–1 shot is going to win the two o'clock race at Hurst Park without starting in his mind a certain train of thought (EBC)

Erbut: a plug-ugly with the cold grey eye of a parrot, is presented to Bingo (EBC)

Eton and Harrow Match, the: always a big day at the Drones. Fathers and uncles roll up in droves to lunch with sons and nephews, making first for the bar like bison for a water-hole (FO)

Eulalie Soeurs: fashion designers, Bond St., W. The mysterious sisters have a spectacularly sedative effect upon Roderick Spode, anthropoid leader of Britain's Black Shorts. The mention of their name provokes a reaction more instantaneous than that of a drugged dart upon a charging rhinoceros, transmuting him instantly from a ravening cave-bear to a filleted yes-man. Equally pleasing (if not more so) is the counter-reaction by which Bertie, all fear instantly forgotten, slips automatically into the tyrant's place, assuming to the manner born the voice and jargon of authority:

'I shall be very sharp on that sort of thing in the future, Spode.'
'Yes, yes, I understand.'
'I have not been at all satisfied with your behaviour since I came to this house. The way you were looking at me at dinner. You may think people don't notice these things, but they do.'
'Of course, of course.'
'And calling me a miserable worm.'
'I'm sorry I called you a miserable worm, Wooster. I spoke without thinking.'
'Always think, Spode. Well, that is all. You may withdraw.'
(CW)

Everett, Sir Everard: His Britannic Majesty's Ambassador at Washington leaves London to take up his post, thereby causing a far-reaching modification of plans at the Junior Ganymede Club, Curzon St., W. (JFS)

F

Fath, Jacques: a sports costume by, clings lovingly to Rosalinda Spottsworth's undulating figure (RJ)

Ferraro: Archie Mulliner thinks it unlikely that the celebrated head waiter at the Berkeley would take a fellow by the seat of the trousers and play quoits with him along Piccadilly (YMS)

Fifty-Seventh Street: New York City; Bertie's bachelor H.Q. and the prepared position to which he retreats on hearing the clash of Aunt Agatha's tomahawk (COJ)

Filmer, the Rt. Hon. A. B., P.C.: A Cabinet Minister who learns that it is unwise to report the misbehaviour of schoolboys to their parents. Thos. Spenser Gregson bases his retaliatory measures on the tactics of that other scourge, Capt. Flint, in *Treasure Island*, and the parliamentary informer shortly finds himself occupying (for the first time in years) an unsafe seat (VGJ)

Finch, Dudley: graces a flat in Jermyn St., W., and occasionally adorns the Drones:

> like a male Lady of Shalott, is so sartorially right that you feel that, if this is the sort of chap who lunches at Claridges, old man Claridge is in luck

Fink-Nottle, Augustus: made his debut brilliantly in 1934 and has been delighting us ever since. His must be (one thinks) a country membership of the Drones, since he 'lives year in, year out, in a remote Lincolnshire village, covered with moss', studying the habits of newts. Enslaved by the charms of Corky Pirbright, following his super-heated affair with Madeline Bassett, he ventures occasionally to town and undergoes the rigours and perils of country house parties at Brinkley, King's Deverill and Totleigh. But though Bertie promises to be present in a ringside pew at his wedding, singing 'Now the labourer's task is o'er' with the best, no business results, until the practical Emerald Stoker whisks Gussie off to well-fed, marital security. Emerald, one feels, will take newts in her stride. The character was early marked for greatness. Gussie's school prize presentation sequence in RHJ is of course a classic. He was to attain the laurel crown, publicly bestowed, when the late Dr Cyril Bailey, Public Orator of Oxford University, referred to him at the Encaenia at which Dr. P. G. Wodehouse (*vir lepidissimus, facetissimus, venustissimus, iocusissimus, ridibundissimus*) received his Doctorate *in honoris causa*. In sonorous, Vergilian measure, Gussie was among the two or three characters singled out (together with his 'little newts') for special mention:

> . . . *Augustus item qui novit amores*
> *ranucularum, aliusque alio sub sidere natus* (RHJ, MS, SLJ *et al.*)

Fish, Miss: a sumptuous blonde of Bwana Biggar's acquaintance, dances the can-can in her step-ins (RJ)

Fish, Ronald Overbury: a Drone whose adventures belong to the Blandings saga, is o.s. of the late Major-General Miles Fish, Brigade of Guards, and of Lady Julia Fish (née Threepwood). He m. Sue Cotterleigh

Fittleworth, George Webster (Boko): a valued member of Bertie's inner entourage, presents to the beholder a face like an intellectual parrot. Like so many of the younger literati, dresses like a tramp cyclist left out overnight in the rain in an ashcan. It is indeed on record that he, alone among the world's teeming millions, at first appearance 'really got Jeeves rattled':

> He winced visibly and tottered off to the kitchen, no doubt to pull himself together with cooking sherry (JM)

Flint, Capt. Jas.: master of the Walrus in R. L. Stevenson's *Treasure Island*, a formative influence on young Thos., that promising candidate for Devil's Island (VGJ)

Foljambe, Reggie: the serpent in the Drones' Eden, tries to sneak Jeeves from Bertie's service by offering to double his salary (COJ)

Foreign Legion, the: perhaps its most frequent aspirant is Freddie Widgeon. After, e.g. his abortive affair with Drusilla Wix he announces at the Drones, with a hideous laugh, that he is going to join that Cohort of the Damned in which broken men may toil and die and, dying, forget (YMS)

Foster, Sally: the end of the (Piccadilly Circus-Hyde Park Corner) road for Freddie Widgeon, and the cancellation of his plans for death in the Cohort of the Damned. Sally, a small, trim girl with copper hair and eyes of cornflower blue, eventually decides to overlook the mile of recumbent damsels and to accompany Freddie to a new life on his Kenya coffee plantation (IB)

Fothergill, Aubrey: tells Bertie at the Club, with absolute tears in his eyes, poor chap, that he has had to give up a pair of favourite brown shoes because his man Meekyn disapproved of them (COJ)

Fothergill, Cornelia: novelist who specialises in rich and stearine goo for the feminine book market. Where Rosie M. Banks merely touches the heart-strings, Cornelia grabs them in both hands and ties them in knots (FO)

Fothergill, Edward and Everard:

> Three souls were present when I made my entry, each plainly as outstanding a piece of cheese as Hampshire could

provide. One was a small, thin citizen with a beard of the type
that causes so much distress, and seated near him was another
bloke of much the same construction but an earlier model,
whom I took to be the father. He, too, was bearded to the
gills (FO)

Fotheringay-Phipps: (pron. 'Fungy'); family name of Lord
Binghampton, q.v.

Fotheringay-Phipps, Cyril (Barmy): a nephew of Lord Binghampton, q.v., is tall and willowy, his disposition intensely amiable,
his hair the colour of creamery butter and his face of the open,
engaging type which arouses the maternal instinct in women but
other instincts in male employers. Even at the Drones, Barmy's I.Q.
is held to be rather lower than that of a backward clam. He shares
the Maiden Eggesford misadventure with Pongo Twistleton, and has
his name in lights in the novel **BARMY IN WONDERLAND**
(YMS, *et al.*)

Fotheringay-Phipps, George: joins the police via the Hendon
Training College, and makes an auspicious start by pinching his
cousin Cyril in Leicester Square on Boat Race Night (JM)

French, Ellen Tallulah:

He stared, at a loss, at a tall, good-looking girl who had just
entered. . . . But Monica saw more clearly into the matter.
Observing the cap and apron, she deduced that this must be
that almost legendary figure, the housemaid (RJ)

French, R.B.D.: every devotee will find pleasurable stimulus as
well as fun in his **P. G. WODEHOUSE** published in 1966. Partly
complementary to Usborne, he cuts much new ground, and his
studies of the school stories, the 'romantic' novels and of Ukridge
are signally successful. Like this notice, alas, the book is far too
short (PGW)

fried to the tonsils: see **full to the back teeth**

Frobisher, Major Augustus (Tubby): doyen of the Anglo-Malay
Club at Kuala Lumpur and a constant, if invisible, mentor of Bwana
Biggar, steeling him to stiffness about the upper lip and bidding him
remember a Sahib's moral responsibilities. This soul of rectitude, the
Bwana is to learn, has let down the British Raj by marrying the
widow of Sigsbee Rockmeteller. Tubby is a Charleston addict, of
the barrack-square order, and when the dance is over, his partner
knows she has been in a fight, all right (RJ)

full to the back teeth: see **lathered**

G

gadroon: borders (a form of decoration prized highly by e.g. Tom Travers—see **Collectors' Corner**); one of a set of convex curves or arcs joined at their extremities (says the S.E.D.) to form a decorative pattern used in ornamenting plate. Inverted fluting, usually referring to edging, of silverware (CW)

Gadsby, Ephraim: would live at The Nasturtiums, Jubilee Rd., Streatham Common, S.W., had he not suddenly occurred to B. Wooster as a life-saver at a West End night club when the joint is pinched. Ephraim duly pays his debt to society in the dock the following morning (JFS)

Gandle, Clifford, M.P.: quondam President of the Union at Oxford, shares Mr Potter's alleged rest-cure at Skeldings with even bitterer regrets. To be plunged into a moat while proposing marriage to a red-haired Jezebel, to be prodded with a punt-pole, to catch a cold and swallow a newt are experiences which do not conduce to sunniness (BCE)

Garbo, Greta: for whose sweet sake Cupid hath enpierced with his shaft the fourteen-years-old heart of Thos. Gregson (VGJ)

> **Gazetteer of Village England**
> **(With Occasional Trips Overseas)**

AND ONCE YOU'RE ON THE BRANCH LINE, IT'S QUICKER TO WALK

Ashendon Oakshott, Hants (UD)
Badgwick, Glos (IJ)
Beckley-in-the-Moor, Yorks (COJ)
Bingley-on-Sea (VGJ)
Bishop's Ickenham, Hants (for Ickenham Hall) (UD)
Bottsford Mortimer, Somerset; the Vicar of Maiden Eggesford proposes lunch among the Abbey ruins at, (YMS)
Boustead Magna, Glos (IJ)
Boustead Parva, Glos (IJ)
Bramley-on-Sea, Dorset (NS, FO)
Bridley-in-the-Wold (MT)

Bridmouth-on-Sea, Dorset (YMS)
Brinkley-cum-Snodsfield-in-the-Marsh, Worcs; nr. Market Snodsbury;
    junction for Brinkley Court (CW, IJ, VGJ, JFS, FO, SLJ)
Carterville, Ky (or was *Carterville*, Mass, Pop Stoker's birthplace?)
    (TJ)
Chilicothe, Ohio; Rosie Spottsworth's home town (RJ)
Chipley-in-the-Glen, Dorset (IJ)
Chuffnell Regis, Somerset (TJ)
Cooden Beach, Long Island, N.Y. (NS)
Ditchingham, Southmoltonshire (RJ)
Ditteredge, Hants; Sir Roderick Glossop's rural lair (IJ)
Dovetail Hammer, Berks (CT)
East Bampton, (NS)
East Wibley, Hants (JM)
Eggmarsh St. John, Hants (UD)
Fale-by-the-Water, Glos (IJ)
Gandle-by-the-Hill, Glos (IJ)
Greenwich Village, N.Y.; Rosie takes a course in starkness at, (RJ)
Hockley-cum-Meston, Hants; Tuppy Glossop in bloodbath at, (VGJ)
King's Deverill, Hants (MS)
Kilimanjaro, Mt., E. Africa (RJ)
Kingham, Worcs; Bertie springs to the saddle (RHJ)
Knopp, (FO)
Kuala Lumpur, *F.M.S.* (RJ)
Lakenham, Norfolk (see **Racing**) (VGJ)
Little Chilbury, (RHJ)
Little Clickton-in-the-Wold, Glos (IJ)
Lower Bingley, Glos (IJ)
Lower Rumpling, Norfolk (LEO)
Lower Shagley, Dorset (UD)
Lower Smattering-on-the-Wissel, Worcs (FO)
Lower Snodsbury, Southmoltonshire (RJ)
Maiden Eggesford, Somerset; two Drones struck by lightning at (YMS)
Market Deeping, Sussex (EBC)
Market Snodsbury, Worcs (RHJ, CW, FO, SLJ, JO)
Marsham-in-the-Vale, Hants (FO)
Marvis Bay, Dorset (NS, LEO)
Much Middlefold, Shropshire (VGJ)
Rising Mattock, Hants (EBC)
Roville-sur-Mer, A.M. (IJ)
Sheepshead Bay, New England (RJ)
Skeldings, Herts (IJ, FO)
Southmolton, Southmoltonshire (RJ)

Totleigh-in-the-Wold, Glos (CW, JFS)
Tudsleigh, Worcs (YMS)
Twing, Glos (IJ)
Upper Bingley, Glos (IJ)
Upper Bleaching, Hants (JFS)
Upton Snodsbury, Worcs (YMS)
Waterbury, Connecticut (YMS)
Wibbleton-in-the-Vale, Worcs (YMS)
Wooster, Ohio; see **Wooster, B. W.**

Gervase-Gervase, Sir Stanley, Bart.: a leading light of London's *Pink Un* and Pelican days, figures colourfully in Uncle Willoughby Wooster's *Recollections of a Long Life*, to the shocked horror of Florence Craye:

> 'There is a story about Sir Stanley Gervase-Gervase at Rosherville Gardens which is ghastly in its perfection of detail. It seems that Sir Stanley—but I can't tell you!'
> 'Have a dash!' (COJ)

ghosts: the earnest seeker should tour the **Stately Homes** section for details of their astral residents. Mrs Spottsworth pins her faith to Rowcester Abbey, q.v. Several noble lords, e.g. the Earls of Wivelscombe (who has the Sight) and Yaxley may also be consulted (*passim*)

> 'But I must have ghosts,' said Mrs Spottsworth. 'Don't tell me there aren't *any*?'
> 'There's what we call the haunted lavatory on the ground-floor,' said Rory. 'Every now and then, when there's nobody near it, the toilet will suddenly flush, and when a death is expected in the family it just keeps going and going. But we don't know if it's a spectre or just a defect in the plumbing.'
> 'Probably a poltergeist,' said Mrs Spottsworth, seeming a little disappointed (RJ)

(For the real life origin of the haunted lavatory, see the joyous account of the weekend spent by Guy Bolton at Knole in BG. The bedroom adjoining the ghost's quarters had been allotted to Adele Astaire, who was rendered sleepless by the monotonous sound of water finding its own level.—*Ed.*)

Gish, Lillian: for love of whom, Bonzo Travers's prime of youth is but a frost of cares, his feast of joy a dish of pain (VGJ)

Glossop, Hildebrand: nephew of Sir Roderick G. and a stalwart of the Drones, is 'Tuppy' to them and to most of us. He is the perpetrator of the compulsive bath act in the club swimming pool (VGJ) which Bertie has not forgotten or forgiven:

> To execute a fitting vengeance had been the ruling passion of my life.
> 'I'm rather pinning my faith on the Luminous Rabbit, Jeeves. You wind it up and put it in someone's bedroom in the night watches, and it shines in the dark and jumps about, making odd squeaking noises the while.'

While genuinely fond of Angela Travers, Bertie's cousin, Tuppy wavers temporarily in favour of the light-heavyweight coloratura singer Cora Bellinger (TJ). He 'somewhat resembles a bulldog', and after the second breaking off of his engagement to Angela, consequent on the shark episode, he looks like a bulldog who has just been refused a slice of cake (RHJ):

> 'I suppose,' he said, 'Aunt Dahlia cursed me properly?'
> 'Oh, no. Beyond referring to you as "this blasted Glossop" she was singularly temperate for a woman who at one time hunted regularly with the Quorn.'
> If anything he was now looking more moth-eaten. If you can visualise a bulldog which has just been kicked in the ribs and had its dinner sneaked by the cat, you will have Hildebrand Glossop as he stood before me now.
> 'Stap my vitals, Tuppy, old corpse,' I said, concerned, 'you're looking pretty blue round the rims.'
> Jeeves slid from the presence in that tactful, eel-like way of his, and I motioned the remains to take a seat.

(See **Angela Travers: Old Austinians**) (IJ, VGJ, RHJ)

Glossop, Honoria Jane Louise: o.d. of Sir Roderick and Lady Glossop, is a budding Aunt Agatha of a girl with amplified sound effects. She has an ingrained habit of seeking out young males in need of moulding, and has periodically taken in hand the apprentice minds of Freddie Threepwood, Bertie Wooster, Bingo Little and the absent-minded 'Biffy' Biffen. They are unanimous in their opinion that Honoria is an Act of God. One of those dashed, large, strenuous, dynamic girls you see so much of these days, Bertie tells us:

She had been at Girton, where in addition to enlarging her brain to the most frightful extent she had gone in for every kind of sport and developed the physique of a middleweight wrestler. I'm not sure she didn't box for the 'Varsity while she was up (IJ).

One of those robust girls with the muscles of a welterweight and a laugh like a squadron of cavalry charging over a tin bridge. The sort of girl who reduces you to pulp with sixteen sets of tennis and a few rounds of golf, and then comes down to dinner as fresh as a daisy, expecting you to take an intelligent interest in Freud (COJ)

Considering how early (IJ) the warning light is on for Bertie, it is remarkable that the Honorian candle continues to dazzle him through the years; mark the doom-laden words:

'Bertie,' she said suddenly, as if she had just remembered it, 'What is the name of that man of yours—your valet?'
'Eh? Oh, Jeeves.'
'I think he is a bad influence for you.' said Honoria. 'When we are married you must get rid of Jeeves.'
It was at this moment that I jerked the spoon and lofted six fried potatoes on to the sideboard, with Spenser gambolling after them like a dignified retriever (IJ)

Glossop, Lady: née Blatherwick, is a sister of Mrs Pringle, q.v., and m. the well-known alienist, Sir Roderick Glossop. Her demise is not specifically recorded, but may be assumed to have occurred before TJ, in which Sir Roderick becomes affianced to Myrtle, Lady Chuffnell (COJ)

Glossop, Oswald: o.s. of Sir Roderick and Lady Glossop and pretty snooty about it, too. Is periodically tutored by Bingo Little after things come unstuck at Haydock Park and elsewhere:

'I haven't met the Glossop kid,' I said.
'Don't,' advised Bingo briefly (IJ)

Glossop, Sir Roderick: 6b Harley Street, W., and Ditteredge Hall, Hants; as familiar a London landmark as St. Paul's Cathedral (with whose top storey indeed he has much in common), the celebrated specialist has become so much a creature of flesh and blood that, were we to encounter him in Harley Street we should accept him automatically as part of the landscape. The dome-like bald cranium, the eyebrows which so urgently need bobbing or shingling, the piercing, speculative eyes so manifestly intent on diagnosing, in a few seconds, precisely how many weeks hence your nearest and dearest will be ringing him up for an urgent opinion—these are the concomitants of a three-dimensional character of weight and substance. He is 'always called a nerve specialist, because it sounds better, but everybody knows that he's a sort of janitor to the looney-bin'. . . . :

> When your uncle the Duke begins to feel the strain a bit and you find him in the blue drawing-room sticking straws in his hair, old Glossop is the first person you send for. He toddles round, gives the patient the once-over, talks about over-excited nervous systems, and recommends complete rest and seclusion. . . . I suppose that constantly having to sit on people's heads . . . does tend to make a chappie take what you might call a warped view of humanity (COJ)

The warped view explains why, for the first thirty-five years of our acquaintance, Sir Roderick was ever a constant menace to the liberty of the young master. John Aldridge sees him as a father-surrogate figure. It is sufficient to match him, one thinks, to the ever-incursive element of comic destruction represented by Master Ford in *The Merry Wives.* When Sir Roderick discovers a skeletal salmon, one black cat, one tabby and one small, lemon-coloured effort in Bertie's bedroom, he grabs the nearest umbrella, waves it overhead and shouts 'Stand back, sir! I am armed!' and it is then that we hear the muted voice of Bertie's good angel echoing Mrs Ford's friend Mrs Page, in that same play: 'Defend your reputation, or bid farewell to your good life forever!'

But a few years ago (in JO) a promising change occurred in the climate. There had indeed been a rift in the storm clouds as far back as TJ, when Sir Roderick, mice-infested and shaken after his experiences in the Chuffnell dower house, related to a black-faced Bertie the horrors of his experiences there:

> 'Mr Wooster, we have had our differences in the past. The fault may have been mine. I cannot say. . . . We must see more of one another. Let us lunch together one of these days.'

And by JO (1960) when Sir Roderick, woofing after the supposed nutcase Cream, is disguised at Brinkley as Swordfish the butler, an air of sunset benison has descended upon the hunter and the hunted. Bertie's artless prattle about patients who are 'foggy between the ears' may still jar slightly upon Sir Roderick's professional instincts, and cause him to remind Bertie:

> 'We must not judge hastily, Mr Wooster. . . . At one time I reached a hasty judgment regarding your sanity. Those twenty-three cats in your bedroom. . . .'

but with luck, and Jeeves's vigilance, and Bertie's continued prudence in avoiding the subject of hot water bottles, the glass should, we feel, remain set fair. (See **Now We Know: Hungerford: Master in Lunacy: Dumbchummery**) (IJ. COJ, TJ, JO *et al.*)

Gobi Desert, the: Col. Wyvern's child cook, a pigtailed incompetent under the impression that she is catering for a covey of buzzards in (RJ); the Rev. Harold Pinker still well up among those who could not walk over it without knocking something over (CW)

Godiva, the Lady:

> As April Carroway appeared, Freddie Widgeon braced himself to break the bad news.
>
> 'I say,' he said, 'a rather rummy thing has occurred. I seem to have lost your sister Prudence.'
>
> 'So I gathered. Well, I've found her.'
>
> At this moment a disembodied voice suddenly came from inside one of the bushes, causing Freddie to shoot a full couple of inches out of his seat. He tells me he remembered a similar experience having happened to Moses in the Wilderness, and he wondered if the prophet had taken it as big as he had done.
>
> 'That was Prudence,' said April coldly. 'She is obliged to remain in those bushes, because she has nothing on.'
>
> 'Nothing on? No particular engagements, you mean?'
>
> 'I mean no clothes. The horse kicked hers into the river.'
>
> 'A horse kicked the clothes off her?'
>
> 'It didn't kick them off me,' said the voice. 'They were lying on the bank in a neat bundle. You see, I was playing Lady Godiva, as you advised me to.'
>
> Freddie clutched at his brow. He had studied Woman, and knew that when Woman gets into a tight place her first act is to shovel the blame off on to the nearest male.
>
> 'When did I ever advise you to play Lady Godiva?'
>
> 'You told me I couldn't go wrong in imitating any of Tennyson's heroines' (YMS)

Gooch, the Rev. Sidney: Vicar of Rising Mattock, Hants (MS)

Goode, Jimmy: a mere starter in the Choirboys Handicap (IJ)

Gorringe, Lionel: an anguished soul with side-whiskers who pens *avant garde* verse with titles like 'Caliban At Sunset'. He also dramatises Florence Craye's novel *Spindrift*. However, there is a brighter side; see **Rex West**, (JFS)

Gospodinoff: Hero of the People's Glorious Bulgarian Soviet Socialist Republic, plays the Glorious etc. Bulgarian bagpipes continuously for twenty-four hours (TJ)

Greaseley, Clarence (Poisonpot): not a fair criterion by whom to judge Mayfair (YMS)

Great Neck, N.Y.: Freddie Threepwood's screen idol, Pauline Petite, takes a house at (BCE)

Greenlees, Mrs: ably conducts Steeple Bumpleigh's one and invaluable shop, supplying the peasants with string, pink sweets, sides of bacon, tinned goods, Old Moore's Almanac and the other concomitants of rural civilised life (JM)

Gregson, Spenser: a strange note as of muted sadness seems to inform the few references to this 'battered little chappie on the Stock Exchange' who earns fame by taking Aunt Agatha to the altar. Can we see a reflection of his facial features in his son Thos., who so diverges from Agatha's aquiline angularity? Bertie is our only informant, and Spenser remains offstage, cleaning up plentifully in Sumatra rubber and supplying the means to buy Woollam Chersey. Some time before 1947 he goes to dwell with the morning stars, leaving Agatha free to wed her first fiancé, the now widowed Percy Craye (*passim*)

Gregson, Thomas Spenser: the nose is snub, the eyes are green, the aspect that of one studying to be a gangster. A chunky kid, Bertie informs us, whom a too-indulgent public has allowed to infest the country for fourteen years. Aunt Dahlia (a recognised authority on form) bears this out; 'When it comes to devilry, Thomas is a classic yearling'. Thos. has, indeed, inherited his father's commercial drive as well as his mother's ruthlessness, and the combination is formidable. As to the former, he corners fifty autographs of the screen star Corky Pirbright, selling them for a shilling each at his prep school. For the latter, see his excellently conceived vengeance on a Parliamentary informer in VGJ. He is 'a boy of volcanic passions who, if he had but threepence in the world, would spend it on a stamp, writing to Dorothy Lamour for her autograph'. It is on record that he has twice, to date, absconded from school, once to attend the Cup Final, once to organise a treasure expedition to the Caribbees. Possibly his forcible kidnapping in the middle of term (MS) gave him even greater satisfaction (RHJ, VGJ, MS)

Grindle, Pomona: is lushly lunched by Dahlia Travers who hopes to serialise her new novel (CW)

Grosvenor Square, W.: of many references to the Square during the days when the British flag still flew over it, we are liefest to the bizarre events by which Sir Thomas Lipton got his first chance in life through the happy accident of Pongo Twistleton's great-aunt Brenda taking her pug-dog Jabberwocky for an airing (*passim*)

Gudgeon, Hilda: A strapping ex-Roedean hockey-knocker with whom Madeline Bassett takes refuge at Wimbledon. Hilda has taken such a toss in love's lists that even the changing of the l.b.w. rule cannot stir her apathy. She recovers sufficiently, though, to prise Bertie at pistol point from his refuge behind the sofa (MS)

H

Haddock, Esmond, J.P.: this offspring of the union between the late Flora Deverill and Haddock's Headache Hokies, although nominal owner of Deverill Hall and Squire of King's Deverill, Hants, has been for so long the plaything of the resident arpeggio of aunts that he has sunk to the status of a fourth-rate power. An outsize Greek god as to the outer crust, he is in fact little more than an overgrown Fauntleroy. But the stiffening of the fibres, consequent on the grim ultimatum issued by his adored Corky Pirbright, plus the moral rearmament of discovering that he has a concert platform public and (it has to be admitted) the working of a fate whose other name is Jeeves, combine to bring solid and lasting results. There is, in the final upshot, that about the seigneur of King's Deverill, as he sits dispensing rough justice, something that can fairly be likened to Judge Jeffreys about to do his stuff:

> 'I really cannot have any discussion or argument about it. Silence, Aunt Daphne. Less of it, Aunt Emmeline. Desist, Aunt Harriet. Aunt Myrtle, put a sock in it. In Turkey, all this insubordinate stuff, these attempts to dictate to the master of the house and the head of the family, would have led long before this to your being strangled with bowstrings and bunged into the Bosphorus. Aunt Daphne, you have been warned. One more yip out of you, Aunt Myrtle, and I stop your pocket money.' (MS)

Hamlet, Prince of Denmark: one of the three Shakespearian plays (the others are *Julius Caesar* and *Macbeth*) most drawn upon for imagery and quotation; for Shakespeare's comments on the plot of, see **THANK YOU, JEEVES** (*passim*)

Harlequins Rugby Football Club: 'Stinker' Pinker, after playing for Oxford for four years and England for six, still turns out for the, reports Bertie to whom, as an Etonian, the game is 'a sealed book':

> But even I could see that he was good. The lissomness with which he moved hither and thither was most impressive, as was his homicidal ardour when doing what I believe is called tackling. Like the Canadian Mounted Police he always got his man, and when he did so the air was vibrant with the excited cries of morticians in the audience making bids for the body (SLJ)

Harley Street, W.: where almost every door has burst out into a sort of eczema of brass plates. Here Sir Abercrombie Fitch-Fitch and his four merry messmates are equipped to cope with most human ills, and E. Jimpson Murgatroyd is qualified to chase pink spots from the chests of overwrought young millionaires. Approaching (with caution) No. 6b the visitor may note the coroneted limousines lining the pavement outside, varied perhaps by one plain van delivering a fresh supply of strait-jackets (*passim*)

Harold: page boy at Twing Hall, Glos, though virtually spherical, is thought by Jeeves, on good grounds, to be a certainty for the Choirboys 100 yards handicap (IJ)

Harrogate: Bertie, contrary to his forebodings, finds the Yorkshire spa not unpleasant:

> What I had overlooked was that I should be in the middle of a

bevy of blokes who were taking the cure and I shouldn't be taking it myself. You've no notion what a dashed cosy, satisfying feeling that gives a fellow. There was old Uncle George, for instance. The medicine-man, having given him the once-over, had ordered him to abstain from all alcoholic liquids, and in addition to tool down to the Royal Pump Room each morning at eight-thirty and imbibe twelve ounces of warm crescent saline and magnesia. It doesn't sound much, put that way, but I gather it's practically equivalent to getting outside a couple of little old last year's eggs beaten up in sea-water. And the thought of Uncle George, who had oppressed me sorely in my childhood, sucking down that stuff and having to hop out of bed at eight-fifteen to do so was extremely grateful and comforting of a morning. At four in the afternoon he would toddle down the hill and repeat the process, and at night we would dine together and I would loll back in my chair, sipping my wine, and listen to him telling me what the stuff had tasted like. In many ways the ideal existence (COJ)

haymaker, a: may be likened to a humdinger with, perhaps, some aspects of a rannygazoo. B. W. Wooster supplies an example in recalling the guest list for the house party at Brinkley, as announced over the telephone by Aunt Dahlia:

> I was still tottering under this blow when the old relative landed another, and it was a haymaker.
> 'Then there's Aubrey Upjohn and his stepdaughter,' she said. 'That's the lot. What's the matter with you? Got asthma?' (JO)

Hayward, the Rev. G.: the incumbent at Lower Bingley, Glos, receives 12 minutes in the Great Sermon Handicap (IJ)

Heber the Kemite: patron of absentee husbands (see also **Jael**) (*passim*)

Hemmingway, Aline: alleged sister of the supposed Curate of the *soi-disant* village of Chipley-in-the-Glen, Dorset, is selected by Aunt Agatha as an ideal bride for Bertie. The light-fingered young lady elects instead to steal Aunt Agatha's pearl necklace, presenting Bertie with an opportunity to which he does full justice:

> I don't want to rub it in,' I said coldly, 'but good heavens, do you realise that if you had brought the thing off I should probably have had children who would have sneaked my

watch while I was dandling them on my knee? I'm not a complaining sort of chap, but I must say that another time I do think you ought to be more careful. . . .' I gave her one look, turned on my heel and left the room (IJ)

Hemmingway, the Rev. Sidney: potential brother-in-law for Bertie, has a face like a benevolent sheep, and is more widely known as Soapy Sid (IJ)

Hendon Police Training College, N.W.: since its inception the Force seems to have become congested with Bertie's buddies. See e.g., **Cyril Widgeon,** and **George Fotheringay-Phipps** (JM, *et al.*)

Heppenstall, the Rev Francis: Vicar of Twing, Glos, a hot favourite for the Great Sermon Handicap:

> Never used to preach under half-an-hour, and there was one sermon of his on brotherly love which lasted forty-five minutes if it lasted a second (IJ)

Heralds of the Red Dawn, the: the thing started in the Park at the Marble Arch end, where weird birds of every description collect on Sunday afternoons and stand on soap boxes and make speeches. Here the Heralds of the Red Dawn are slipping it into the idle rich when Bertie is joined by Lord Bittlesham:

> 'Look at them! Drink them in!' the bearded egg was yelling. 'There you see two typical members of the class which has down-trodden the poor for centuries. Idlers! Non-producers! Look at the tall thin one with the face like a motor-mascot. Has he ever done an honest day's work in his life? No! A trifler and a bloodsucker! And I bet he still owes his tailor for those trousers!'
>
> He seemed to me to be verging on the personal, and I didn't think a lot of it. Old Bittlesham, though, was pleased and amused.
>
> 'Great gift of expression these fellows have,' he chuckled.
>
> 'Very trenchant.'
>
> 'And the fat one!' proceeded the chappie. 'Don't miss him. Do you know who that is? That's Lord Bittlesham! One of the worst! What has he ever done except eat four square meals a day? His god is his belly. If you opened that man now you would find enough lunch to support ten working-class families for a week!'

'You know, that's rather well put,' I said, but the old boy didn't seem to see it. He had turned a brightish magenta and was bubbling like a kettle on the boil.

'Come away, Mr Wooster,' he said. 'I am the last man to oppose the right of free speech, but I refuse to listen to this vulgar abuse any longer!' (IJ)

Herring, Reginald (Kipper): having gone in for boxing since infancy, would be an unsafe entrant in a beauty contest, even if the only other competitors were Boris Karloff, King Kong and Oofy Prosser of the Drones. A lifelong buddy of B. Wooster, no minutest detail of life at Aubrey Upjohn's school has ever escaped his memory and, as a book reviewer, he finds himself ideally placed to square the game (JO)

Higgins, Marlene: a shapely damsel from Brixton, awarded first prize by Jeeves at the Bathing Belle contest which he judges while on holiday at Folkestone (JO)

His Majesty's Royal Mail: Bertie plans a raid on, involving a risk of about forty years in the coop (MS)

Hockley-cum-Meston: Hants village renowned for its annual Christmas ball-game (officially termed a Rugby football match) against Upper Bleaching:

> There's nothing much to do in the long winter evenings but listen to the radio and brood on what a tick your neighbour is. . . . How this particular feud had started I don't know, but the season of peace and goodwill found it in full blast. The only topic of conversation was Thursday's game, and the citizenry seemed to be looking forward to it in a way that can only be described as ghoulish (VGJ)

Hodgkin's Disease: 'Tom's been feeling rather low of late because of what he calls iniquitous taxation,' said the old relative. 'I thought having to fraternise with Bassett would take his mind off it—show him that there are worse things in the world than income tax. Our doctor here gave me the idea. He was telling me about a thing called Hodgkin's Disease that you cure by giving the patient arsenic' (SLJ)

Holmes, Martin, F.S.A.: Shakespearian scholar, has drawn attention to the piquant parallels of character and situation between the households of Lord Emsworth at Blandings and Olivia in *Twelfth Night*. There are also pertinent references in his stimulating book *Shakespeare's Public* (1960). Of Bassanio, e.g., he says:

Because Shakespeare is Literature, and a National Institution, we are tempted to take all his characters somewhat too seriously, and to consider Bassanio a scheming hypocrite because he wants to dress in a style he cannot afford, so as to make a good impression on an heiress. He has been called a cad and a fortune-hunter for expressing sentiments, and for formulating designs, which we should admit without question had his creator been not Shakespeare but Dr P. G. Wodehouse. The young man with a big heart, big ideas and a still bigger overdraft, 'touching' a friend for a loan so that he may equip himself for a house-party where there is a girl who combines all lovable qualities with a satisfactory fortune, was as good entertainment then as he is now.

Elsewhere he cites 'the various chronicles of Blandings Castle, in which Dr Wodehouse has achieved the rare feat of creating a modern-dress Malvolio in the person of the Efficient Baxter.' (Maria, Olivia's young kinswoman, who hatches the fun and games against the pompous Malvolio, is, of course, a Bobbie Wickham archetype —Ed.)

Holmes, Sherlock: *passim* in the usual context, but instanced by Jeeves as the vehicle for Sir Arthur Conan Doyle's maxim that the instinct of everyone, upon an alarm of fire, is to save the object dearest to them (RHJ)

hoosegow: calaboose, calahoose, or the big house; Anglice—jug, stir, glasshouse, cooler, hulks, pound, coop, brig, quod, bastille, bridewell, paddock, pen, nick, chokey, hold, clink, black-hole, jankers, in irons or, if you prefer it, *in vinculis (passim)*

Hope, Bob: see **Emperor Marcus Aurelius,**

Hopwood, the late Roderick: apart from a brief word of devotion from his daughter Nobby, the records are sparing, and rest on the evidence of Lord Worplesdon at a time when he was suffering from magnums:

'When confiding her to my care, I remember, her poor old father, as fine a fellow as ever stepped, though too fond of pink gin, clasped my hand and said "Watch her like a hawk, Percy, old boy, or she'll go marrying some bally blot on the landscape." And what happens? First thing you know, up pops probably the worst blot any landscape was ever afflicted with.'

74

'But her father wasn't thinking of a chap like Boko.'

'There are limits to every man's imagination.' (JM)

Hopwood, Zenobia: like Corky, Stiffy and Bobbie, Nobby Hopwood was born under a dancing star:

> 'Miss Hopwood called while you were still asleep, sir. She was desirous of rousing you with a wet sponge, but I dissuaded her. I considered it best that your repose should not be disturbed.' I applauded this watchdog spirit, but tut-tutted a bit at having missed the young pipsqueak, with whom my relations had always been of the matiest. This Hopwood was old Worplesdon's ward, as I believe it is called. She is a blue-eyed little half-portion with an animated dial.

That the dial is not so animated at the moment is because Authority takes a dim view of wards who want to wed young men who earn a scanty living with their pens (JM)

Hough, the Rev. Orlo: Vicar of Boustead Magna, starts at odds of 6–1 in the Great Sermon Handicap (IJ)

Hungerford: family name of the Duke of Ramfurline, q.v.

Hungerford, Lord Alastair: y.s. of the Duke of Ramfurline, visits Sir Roderick Glossop on a delicate mission:

> 'His grace, he informed me, had exhibited a renewal of the symptoms which have been causing the family so much concern.'
>
> 'So the Duke is off his rocker, what?'
>
> 'The expression is not precisely the one I should have employed myself with reference to the head of perhaps the noblest family in England, but there is no doubt that cerebral excitement does, as you suggest, exist in no small degree.' (IJ)

I

Ibsen, Henrik: *passim* and usually pessim.

ICE IN THE BEDROOM: published 1961. A return to Valley Fields, S.E., it marks the end of Freddie Widgeon's long and painful apprenticeship to marriage. In it we meet again Soapy and (Fainting) Dolly Molloy, and incidentally learn, at last, the address of Barribaults—it is in Clarges St., W. (IB)

Ickenham, 2nd Earl of: g.g.f. of Pongo Twistleton, an art lover in the broader sense, filled his house and grounds with statuary:

> 'Home isn't home,' he was wont to say, running a thoughtful hand through his whiskers, 'without plenty of nude Venuses.' Consequently Ickenham Hall and its gardens are reminiscent of a Turkish bath on Ladies Night (UD)

Ickenham, 3rd Earl of: Pongo's grandfather gave his offspring sound advice:

> 'Never put anything on paper, my boy, and never trust a man with a small black moustache.' (CT)

Ickenham, the Rt. Hon the Earl of: the chronicles of Frederick Altamont Cornwallis Twistleton-Twistleton, 5th Earl, are a saga in their own right. His incursions into the Wooster-Jeeves cycle, though many and unavoidable, will be kept under control (a feat usually regarded by his acquaintance as impossible). An outstanding survivor (like his friend Gally Threepwood) of the Romans and Pink 'Uns of a less inhibited London, he succeeded his b. the 4th E. after a varied career in the U.S. He m. Jane Bastable after she had six times broken off the engagement. The initiator and advocate of the Ickenham Wooing System (grab—waggle—murmur 'My mate!') the Earl's advice to all young men is to marry a girl whom they can tickle. Is dedicated to the correction of what he considers the Hamlet-like gloom of his nephew and heir, Reginald (Pongo) Twistleton, q.v. Res: Ickenham Hall, Bishop's Ickenham, Hants (YMS, UFS, UD, CT)

ideal diet: Jeeves propounds the,

> 'Medical research has established, sir, that the ideal diet is one in which the animal and vegetable foods are balanced. A strict vegetarian diet is not recommended by the majority of doctors, as it lacks sufficient protein and in particular does not contain the protein which is built up of the amino-acids required by the body. Competent observers have traced some cases of mental disorder to this shortage.' (SLJ)

Illuminated Items

THE SPECTACLE OF AN UNCLE GOING DOWN FOR THE THIRD TIME IN A SEA OF DANCE CHAMPAGNE CAN NEVER BE A PLEASANT ONE (JM)

I am told by those who know that there are six varieties of hangover—the Broken Compass, the Sewing Machine, the Comet, the Atomic, the Cement Mixer and the Gremlin Boogie—and his manner suggested that he had got them all (RHJ)

'Have you ever been in Trafalgar Square at five in the morning? Very picturesque, that fountain in the first early light of the dawn. It was as we stood on its brink with the sun just beginning to gild the house tops that I got an idea which I can now see, though it seemed a good one at the time, was a mistake. It struck me as a possibility that there might be newts in the fountain, and knowing how keen Gussie is on newts I advised him to wade in and hunt around.'

'With all his clothes on?'

'Yes, he had his clothes on. I remember noticing.'

'But you can't go wading in the Trafalgar Square fountain with all your clothes on.'

'Yes, you can. Gussie did, but I seem to recall that he took a bit of persuading. I said if he didn't wade I would bean him with my magnum. So he waded.'

'You still had the magnum?'

'This was another which we had picked up in Limehouse.'

'I wonder he wasn't pinched.'

'He was. A cop came along and gaffed him, and this morning he was given fourteen days without the option at Bosher Street' (MS)

'If you ask me, Aunt Dahlia,' I said, 'I think Angela is well out of it. This Tuppy Glossop is a tough baby. I was trying to tell you just now what he did to me one night at the Drones. First having got me in sporting mood with a bottle of the ripest, he betted I wouldn't swing myself across the swimming bath by the ropes and rings. I knew I could do it on my head, so I took him on, exulting in the fun, so to speak. And when I'd done half the trip and was going as strong as dammit, I found he had looped the last rope back against the rail, leaving me no alternative but to drop into the depths and swim ashore in correct evening costume.'

'He did?'

'He certainly did. It was months ago and I haven't got really dry yet. You wouldn't want your daughter to marry a man capable of a thing like that?'

'On the contrary, you restore my faith in the young hound. I see that there must be lots of good in him after all' (VGJ)

The barman said that in a situation of that sort he usually prescribed a lightning whizzer, an invention of his own. He said this was what rabbits trained on when they were matched against grizzly bears, and there was only one instance on record of the bear having lasted three rounds (MT)

'You ate something that disagreed with you last night, didn't you?' I asked him, by way of giving him a chance to slide out of it if he wanted to.

'No,' he replied firmly. 'I drank too much. Much too much. Lots and lots too much. And, what's more, I'm going to do it again. I'm going to do it every night. If ever you see me sober,' he said with a sort of holy exaltation, 'tap me on the shoulder and say "Tut, tut!", and I'll apologise and remedy the defect. All my bally life I've been cooped up in the family home at Much Middlefold, in Shropshire, and till you've been cooped up in Much Middlefold you don't know what cooping is. I've got about a month of New York and I mean to store up a few happy memories for the long winter evenings. This is my only chance to collect a past, and I'm going to do it.'

The only time I met him late at night after that was once when I passed the door of a fairly low-down sort of restaurant and had to step aside to dodge him as he sailed through the air *en route* for the opposite pavement, with a muscular looking sort of fellow peering out after him with a kind of gloomy satisfaction (COJ)

I had never listened in on a real, genuine, female row before, and I'm bound to say it was pretty impressive. The combatants had reached the stage now where they had begun to dig into the past and rake up old scores. Mrs Bingo was saying that the Pyke would never have got into the hockey team at St. Adela's if she hadn't flattered and fawned upon the captain in a way that it made Mrs Bingo, even after all these years, sick to think of. The Pyke replied that she had refrained from mentioning it until now, having always felt it better to let bygones be bygones, but that if Mrs Bingo supposed her to be unaware that Mrs Bingo had won the Scripture prize by taking a list of the Kings of Judah into the examination room, tucked into her middy-blouse, Mrs Bingo was vastly mistaken. Furthermore, the Pyke proceeded, Mrs Bingo was also labouring under an error if she imagined the Pyke proposed to remain a night longer under her roof. Rather than endure it, the Pyke was quite willing to walk to London.

To this, Mrs Bingo's reply was long and eloquent and touched on the fact that in her last term at St. Adela's a girl named Simpson had told her (Mrs Bingo) that a girl named Waddesley had told her (the

Simpson) that the Pyke, while pretending to be a friend of hers (the Bingo's) had told her (the Waddesley) that she (the Bingo) couldn't eat strawberries and cream without coming out in spots and, in addition, had spoken in the most catty manner about the shape of her nose.

It was when the Pyke had begun to say that she had never had such a hearty laugh in her life as when she read the scene in Mrs Bingo's last novel where the heroine's little boy dies of croup that we felt it best to call the meeting to order before bloodshed set in (VGJ)

'Are you going for a stroll?' said Aunt Dahlia with a sudden show of interest. 'Then I wonder if you'd mind doing something for me?'

'Give it a name,' I said.

'It won't take you long. You know that path that runs past the greenhouses into the kitchen garden. If you go along it you come to a pond.'

'That's right.'

'Well, will you get a good piece of stout rope or cord and go down that path till you come to the pond—'

'To the pond. Right.'

'—and look about you till you find a nice, heavy stone. Or a fairly large brick would do.'

'I see,' I said, though I didn't, being still fogged. 'And then?'

'Then,' said the relative, 'I want you, like a good boy, to fasten the rope to the brick and tie it around your damned neck and jump into the pond and drown yourself. In a few days I will send and have you fished up and buried because I shall need to dance on your grave' (RHJ)

Jeeves returned with the tissue-restorer. I loosed it down the hatch, and after the passing discomfort, unavoidable when you drink Jeeves's patent morning revivers, of having the top of the skull fly up to the ceiling and the eyes shoot out of their sockets and rebound from the opposite wall like racquet balls, felt better (CW)

And so it proved. Oofy Prosser was lying with his head in the fender and his mouth open. He had on an opera hat and what would have been faultless evening dress if he had had a tie on instead of a blue ribbon of the sort which the delicately nurtured use to bind up their hair. In one hand he was clutching a pink balloon, and across his shirt-front was written in lipstick the word 'WHOOPS!' (TJ)

Indians, Red: never in livelier spirits than when being cooked on both sides at the stake (SLJ)

Infant Samuel at Prayer, the: heads the list of disposable trifles, yet the supply surprisingly continues:

> Aunt Dahlia rose and moved restlessly to the mantelpiece. I could see that she was looking for something to break as a relief to her surging emotions—what Jeeves would have called a palliative—and courteously drew her attention to a terra-cotta figure of the Infant Samuel At Prayer. She thanked me briefly and hurled it against the opposite wall (CW)

Infants Bible Class: on receiving a strong hint from a passing thunderbolt, the atheistic P.c. Dobbs, perceiving the error of his ways, anxiously asks the Vicar whether he may join the choir at once, or whether he must serve a probation in the, (MS)

INIMITABLE JEEVES, THE: published in 1923, is a loosely-knit novel of episodic type. Its eighteen chapters make ten short stories in **THE JEEVES OMNIBUS;** but in those eighteen chapters, Jeeves and Bertie Wooster definitely arrived on the world stage (IJ)

Irish interlude: 'Irishmen don't talk like that,' said Gussie. 'Have you read J. M. Synge's *Riders to the Sea*? If you can show me a single character in it who says "Faith and begob" I'll give you a shilling. Irishmen are poets. They talk about their souls and mist and so on. They say things like "An evening like this, it makes me wish I was back in the County Clare, watching the cows in the tall grass" '. (MS)

Israelite Mothers S.S.A., the: 'Permit me,' said Freddie, suave to the eyebrows. And, bounding forward, he barged right into a cat.

> 'Oh, sorry,' he said, backing and bringing down his heel on another cat.

> 'I say, most frightfully sorry,' he said. And tottering to a chair, he sank heavily on to a third cat. Well, he was up and about again in a jiffy, of course, but it was too late. Lady Prenderby's eyes had rested on him only for a brief instant, but it had been enough. His standing with her, he perceived, was now approximately what King Herod's would have been at an Israelite Mothers' Social Saturday Afternoon (YMS)

Issue: the importance of being; most of us have to be content to be issue; only if you are Issue have you a hope of being seen in *Debrett*. See, e.g., **Myrtle, Lady Chuffnell** (TJ)

Ivan the Terrible: it is conjectured that when a mediaeval Russian potentate was nicknamed 'the Terrible', things were pretty bad

J

Jael the wife of Heber: the Kemite, is recalled by Bertie the Scripture Prize winner as an example of mayhem by the gentler sex ('dug spikes into the guest's coconut while he slept and then went swanking about like a Girl Guide'). Normal citations speak of a certain gleam in the eye of, just before she gets down to the rough work. Elsewhere is a derogatory reference to the spikes used by, as compared with the red-hot variety experienced by those who have dined unwisely at the Drones Club (RHJ, CW, *et al.*)

Jane: neurotic domestic at Brinkley Court, skips like the high hills on encountering Bertie at a sharp corner (RHJ)

Jeeves: it is presumable that he was baptised and possesses at least one Christian name. No one has had the temerity to inquire, and he shares the distinguished anonymity of a few forceful Wodehouse characters such as Donaldson. Minor forces of nature (earthquakes, and even hurricanes) receive names: a superman needs none. His surname (as Belloc observed a generation ago) is already part of the English language. His background, too, is frugally recorded. Of his parents we know next to nothing. His mother thought him intelligent as a child ('But then, you can't go by that,' Bertie observes. 'My mother thought me intelligent.') and a sketchy picture emerges from relatives (listed below) of a contented, average family background. Besides these there are one or two unnamed; the aunt who carried her passion for riding in hansom cabs to the point of rifling the children's money-boxes, until dissuaded by the Vicar; the aunt who got inflated ideas when her photograph was published as a sponsor for Walkinshaw's Supreme Ointment; the aunt who was a devotee of Rosie M. Banks's novels; the expert jeweller cousin who passed on his knowledge to Jeeves.

In infancy he was dandled on the knee of Uncle Charlie Silversmith, he tells Bertie, who comments that he must have been a child of blood and iron, and that he was privately educated. Posterity will want to know who his mentors were. Is there a nautical strain in his ancestry? The evidence is tenuous but need not be disregarded. One has felt it significant that Bertie, hearing him singing sea shanties in the kitchen, should tell us:

He has always had the urge of the salt sea in his blood. I have noticed him on liners, when we were going to America, striding the deck with a nautical roll and giving the distinct impression of being just about to heave the main-brace or splice the binnacle.

Jeeves himself admits that he 'dabbled in the First World War to some extent' and it is my own guess that this was in the Senior Service. The war apart, and discounting the months spent with the jeweller cousin, he seems never to have deviated from his chosen calling, that of domestic service. As a lad, his first employment was in a school for young ladies; an education in itself for an intellect intent on steeping itself in the psychology of the individual. It is a salutary comment on the ingrowing stupidity of his own sex that no fewer than five employers at least should (like 'Lo' the poor Indian) have doltishly cast away this treasure among manservants before he joins Bertie, who himself is to play with fire by periodically returning him to circulation for puerile reasons. Lord Worplesdon lost him through insisting on wearing a flannel shirt and shooting jacket with evening trousers. He was in service with Digby Thistleton, later Lord Bridgworth; with Lord Brancaster the psittaphile; with Lord Frederick Ranelagh, and with the financier Montague Todd, 'now in the second year of his sentence'—a fate, one feels, which would have been easily avoidable had he retained Jeeves. After joining the young master he is to have other employers; Lord Chuffnell, Lord Rowcester (as butler), Gussie Fink-Nottle (for a few days), Sir Watkyn Bassett (a matter of inducement) for a week, old Pop Stoker for even less time and (strictly on loan) Aunt Agatha.

Why (it has been asked) did this gem among valets come to be unemployed at all, and on the books of an agency, at the moment when Bertie was constrained to give Meadowes the elbow? For me, the answer is simple. The whole sequence has an air of Jeevesian inevitability. I believe Jeeves had had an eye on the young master for some time, and had long concluded that he represented stubborn, virgin soil most suitable for tillage beneath his, Jeeves's, talented and devoted hands. I believe Jeeves had been keeping an eye on a possible berth at Crichton Mansions ever since some past day when he had lighted on Meadowes's contribution to the Ganymede Club Book under 'Wooster, B. W.' one rainy afternoon in Curzon Street; that the domestic agency was merely a matter of a telephone call; that the master-mind saw to it that the hour produced the man.

In appearance Jeeves is 'a tallish man, with one of those dark, shrewd faces.' His eye gleams with the light of pure intelligence. His head bulges markedly at the back. ('That's where the brain is,' Bertie tells us helpfully, 'packed behind the ears.') He wears a size eight bowler hat; but despite popular impression, he is not addicted to sardines, nor over-fond of fish. He is, however, a keen fisherman, whether dry line in Hampshire or shrimping at Bognor. A keen racegoer, who forfeits a visit to Cannes rather than miss Ascot, he is a successful punter with an immense knowledge of form. When attending a subscription dance he 'swings a dashed efficient shoe.' An occasional smoker, he carries a case of cigarettes ('Virginian this side, sir, Turkish on that') and he does not drink. ('Alcohol has a sedative rather than a stimulating effect on me'). Dogs regard him with respectful devotion:

> The most febrile dog recoils before the majesty of Jeeves. He ... views the animal kingdom with a benevolent eye and is the first to pat its head and offer it a slice of what is going, but he does not permit it to lick his face.

His intelligence network is second to none. Barely arrived in New York, he is advised to patronise Reigelheimers on Forty-Second Street:

> 'Pardon me, sir,' he comments, 'people are no longer going to Reigelheimers. The place at the moment is Frolics on the Roof.'

Has Jeeves (as Bertie avers) a sixth sense denied to ordinary men? Water (they taught us at school) does not actually possess a skin on its surface, but behaves as though it did; Jeeves, one imagines, is endowed with an intensified perceptivity which, allied to an intellect of outstanding order, produces a civilised being of almost limitless potentiality. Returning for a moment to the perceptivity:

> He seems to know when I am awake by a sort of telepathy. He always floats in with the cup exactly two minutes after I come to life.
>
> I hadn't heard the door open, but the man was on the spot. My private belief is that Jeeves doesn't have to open doors. He's like one of those birds in India who bung their astral bodies about. . . . He just seems to float from Spot A to Spot B like some form of gas.

Some will associate the gift with that of the mystery cat Macavity, who not only isn't there but even breaks the law of gravity. He is the Stoic Philosopher of our day. He is not unemotional, but his emotions are innately controlled. Twice only, in all the years, he has been seen to blench. On being confronted with Boko Fittlesworth's Bohemian attire he retires to the kitchen to pull himself together; and when Bingo Little appears in a beard he clutches at the table for support. But when Lady Malvern tries to freeze him with a look, he is look-proof; and when, for Bertie, hell's foundations are quivering, Jeeves is ready to observe that phenomenon with an indulgent and philosophic interest. His reading is wide, catholic and critical. The early classics, the Bible, a fine assortment of poets from Vergil, Shakespeare and Milton down to Kipling; Dostoevsky and the other Russians; Spinoza, Nietzsche. . . . He may, like Lord Ickenham, have dabbled in Pierre Louÿs, or like Beach the butler have read Dunsany. None has swayed his own judgment, and though they enrich his speech with a flow of apt quotation, they are not allowed to cloud his own perpetual spring of Augustan English, the English of Gibbon and of *The Times* first leader.

What of his other emotions? He is as incapable of betraying annoyance, despite frequent provocation, as alarm, envy, ambition, jealousy or any other human weakness. He never hates. He is the prime mover in his own limited world—'limited' only in the sense that he has fashioned it to his own chosen limits—and prime movers are not prone to the emotions. But he is capable of showing an indulgent affection. In the affair, e.g., of the check suit:

> 'All right,' I said, 'give the bally thing away to somebody.'
> He looked down at me like a father gazing tenderly at the wayward child.
> 'Thank you, sir. I gave it to the under-gardener last night. A little more tea, sir?'

That (in terms of publication) was forty-two years ago. In the last Wooster-Jeeves novel, Bertie tells him that in his absence

> 'I felt like a child of tender years deprived of its Nannie. If you don't mind me calling you a Nannie.'
> 'Not at all, sir.'
> Though, as a matter of fact, I was giving myself a slight edge, putting it that way. My Aunt Agatha generally refers to Jeeves as my keeper.

The passage is of high significance. In six lines it illustrates, with a lightning clarity, both the mutual awareness of the Nannie situation and at the same time Bertie's native (and sharp) intelligence in that awareness—tempered as always by his humility and over-honesty in the quite unnecessary reference to Aunt Agatha's acerbity. Bertie's perceptions, when not occluded by obstinacy or bedevilled by the desire to be clever, are always direct, limpid and simple. Here he is consciously avowing a relationship which he had subconsciously recognised at the start, and which Jeeves had envisaged on that rainy afternoon in Curzon Street.

Of Jeeves's love-life, if any, we know practically nothing. Prime movers can choose to conduct their affairs beneath a veil of discretion. He has red blood however. There is an 'understanding' between him and Jane Watson, who becomes Lady Bittlesham, by which time Jeeves has an eye upon Bingo's Camberwell girl friend. This in turn apparently peters out. He confesses that he has greatly appreciated the official invitation to judge a seaside Bathing Belle contest. One may perhaps allow oneself to hazard a guess that Jeeves, like the young master, is a not unwilling bachelor whose emotional needs are well repaid in supervising the life and well-being of Bertie and of the occasional friend in need. Employers are like horses, he tells us. They need managing. Few if any employers in fiction have had their affairs managed so smoothly, and none more ingeniously. In each extrication, Jeeves is both the potter and the wheel. He is the vehicle for the consummately skilful plots which Wodehouse has planned, working on them sometimes for months in advance, before a word is put to paper.

> 'It beats me why a man of his genius is satisfied to hang around pressing my clothes and whatnot,' says Bertie. 'If I had half Jeeves's brain, I should have a stab at being Prime Minister or something.'

And the 'something' could conjecturally be anything. It is virtually certain that had Jeeves been valet at No. 10 Downing Street before the First World War, neither the first nor the second war would have happened. A pregnant remark is made by one well-known Wodehouse character to the effect that, had Drake been playing golf instead of bowls that historic day on Plymouth Hoe, he would have ignored the Armada altogether. With respect we may submit that, had the Almighty in His wisdom decided to endow Adam with a gentleman's personal gentleman, there would have been no Fall. If Adam (which we doubt) had got as far as to raise the forbidden fruit halfway to his mouth, the action would have been halted by a soft voice, sliding across Eden like the note of a far-off sheep: 'Injudicious, sir, if I may be allowed to say so.' Should that have failed, a well directed blow on the occiput would have followed from a broken-off branch of the Tree of the Knowledge of Good and Evil. Upon receipt of this sharpish hint from a passing thunderbolt, Adam would infallibly have applied for immediate readmission to the Infants Bible Class.

JEEVES AND THE FEUDAL SPIRIT: Published 1954; later in the U.S. as **BERTIE WOOSTER SEES IT THROUGH** (JFS)

Jeeves, Annie: 'It is a recognised fact, sir, that there is nothing that so satisfactorily unites individuals who have been so unfortunate as to quarrel among themselves as a strong mutual dislike for some definite person. In my own family, if I may give a homely illustration, it was a generally accepted axiom that in times of domestic disagreement it was necessary only to invite my Aunt Annie for a visit to heal all breaches between the other members of the household.' (RHJ)

Jeeves, Cyril: an uncle of the outstanding thinker, had a sense of humour bordering on the *farouche* (see **Nicholls and Jackson**) (RHJ)

Jeeves, P. C. Egbert: is custodian of the King's peace at Beckley-in-the-Moor, Yorks, where (for a slight consideration) he augments Jeeves's masterly plan to rehabilitate an errant nephew (COJ)

Jeeves, the late Emily: on Lord Rowcester's observing that he is not interested in the late Aunt Emily, Jeeves remarks that in the course of her long life few people were (RJ)

Jeeves, George: 'Gentlemen who have been discarded by one young lady are often apt to attach themselves without delay to another, sir. It is known as a gesture.'
'I see what you mean. Defiant stuff.'
'Precisely, sir. My cousin George—'
'Never mind about your cousin George, Jeeves.'
'Very good, sir.'
'Keep him for the long winter evenings, what?' (RHJ)

JEEVES IN THE OFFING: published in serial form in Britain, 1949; in the U.S. the same year as **HOW RIGHT YOU ARE, JEEVES;** appeared in book form in Britain in 1960 with an outstanding jacket. As collectors know, the first British edition, through a publishing error, carried the half-title **A FEW QUICK ONES** (JO)

Jeeves, Mabel: a decorative niece of the master psychologist, accepts the hand and fortune of **Charles Biffen,** q.v., mislays him in the New York custom shed and is reunited to him in the Palace of Beauty at the British Empire Exhibition, Wembley (COJ)

JEEVES OMNIBUS: published in 1931, collects in edited and tidied-up form the thirty-one Wooster-Jeeves stories issued up to that date. In the introduction, the author observes:

> This trackless desert of print . . . winding on and on into the purple distance, represents my first Omnibus Book: and I must confess that . . . I cannot overcome a slight feeling of chestiness, just the faint beginning of that offensive conceit against which we authors have to guard so carefully. I mean, it isn't everyone . . . I mean to say, an Omnibus Book . . . Well, dash it, you can't say it doesn't represent an epoch in a fellow's career and put him just a bit above the common herd. . . . The bulk of this volume makes it almost the ideal paperweight. Placed upon the waistline and jerked up and down each morning, it will reduce *embonpoint* and strengthen the abdominal muscles. And those still at their public school will find that between, say, Caesar's Commentaries in limp cloth and this Jeeves book there is no comparison as a missile in an inter-study brawl (JOM)

Jennings, Myra: of Waterbury, Conn., is the recipient of a knightly action by Beau Widgeon (YMS)

Job, the prophet: the several references are usually illustrative of dignified resignation on the discovery of a new boil.

Jones, the Rev. Alexander: Vicar of Upper Bingley, Glos, well fancied for the Great Sermon Handicap, starts at odds of 3—1 (IJ)

Jonson, Ben: (1572-1637); see **THANK YOU, JEEVES.**

JOY IN THE MORNING: though not published until 1947, had been written, the author tells us, during the German occupation of Le Touquet

> with German soldiers prowling about under my window, plus the necessity of having to walk to Paris Plage every morning to report to the Kommandant (PF)

By one of life's odd quirks, the novel written under such difficulties achieves a joyous distinction. Few in the whole opus are as good, and none is more enjoyable (JM)

Jukes, Rosie: playing fast and loose with the Vicar's rules in the

Girls Egg and Spoon Race, Rosie forfeits her amateur status at Twing school treat (IJ)

Junior Ganymede Club, the: with premises in Curzon Street, W, has a membership restricted to gentlemen's personal gentlemen, together with a few footmen and chauffeurs and a small, fixed quota of butlers. Besides its social amenities the Club's principal activities are bridge and the compilation of the Club Book. By Rule 11 in the constitution, each new member must contribute to this book such details concerning the personal habits, hobbies, pursuits, past history, failings, allergies and idiosyncrasies of his employer as may offer amusing and instructive reading matter to members in their leisure hours. Such data (as Jeeves points out to the young master) are also invaluable to members who may be contemplating taking service with employers who might fall short of the ideal. With consternation Bertie learns that his own entry in the book runs to eleven pages and that most of his more exuberant exploits and trials have been made known to an appreciative public consisting of his friends' valets. In the event Bertie has more reason for gratitude than chagrin, since it is the Club Book's piquant piece of information about Eulalie which saves him from direct action at the gorilla-like hands of Britain's amateur Fuhrer (CW, JFS, *et al.*)

Justices

A Miscarriage of Justices

YOU CAN'T CHOKE A MAN OFF MAGISTRATING, ONCE IT'S IN HIS BLOOD (CW)

The evidence was all in. The machinery of the law had worked without a hitch. And the beak coughed like a pained sheep and slipped us the bad news.

'The prisoner Wooster,' he said—and who can paint the shame and agony of Bertram at hearing himself so described—'will pay a fine of five pounds.'

'Oh, rather!' I said. 'Absolutely. Like a shot!'

I was dashed glad to get the thing settled at such a reasonable figure. I gazed across what they call the sea of faces till I picked up Jeeves, sitting at the back. Stout fellow, he had come to see the young master through his hour of trial.

'I say, Jeeves,' I sang out, 'have you got a fiver? I'm a bit short.'

'Silence!' bellowed some officious blighter.

'It's all right,' I said; 'just arranging the financial details. Got the stuff, Jeeves?'

'Yes, sir.'

'Good egg!'

'Are you a friend of the prisoner?' asked the beak.

'I am in Mr Wooster's employment, Your Worship, in the capacity of gentleman's personal gentleman.'

'Then pay the fine to the clerk.'

'Very good, Your Worship.'

'The beak gave a coldish nod in my direction, as much as to say that they might now strike the fetters from my wrists, and proceeded to hand poor old Sippy one of the nastiest looks ever seen in Bosher Street Police Court.

'The case of the prisoner Leon Trotzky—which,' he said, giving Sippy the eye again, 'I am strongly inclined to think an assumed and fictitious name—is more serious. He has been convicted of a wanton and violent assault upon the police. The evidence of the officer has proved that the prisoner struck him in the abdomen, causing severe internal pain, and in other ways interfered with him in the execution of his duties. I am aware that on the night following the annual aquatic contest between the Universities of Oxford and Cambridge a certain licence is traditionally granted by the authorities, but aggravated acts of ruffianly hooliganism like that of the prisoner Trotzky cannot be overlooked or palliated. He will serve a sentence of thirty days in the Second Division without the option of a fine.'

'No, I say—here—hi—dash it all!' protested poor old Sippy.

'Silence!' bellowed the officious blighter.

'Next case,' said the beak. And that was that. (COJ)

The very first time I set eyes on this Pop Bassett, in the picturesque environment of Bosher Street police court, I remember saying to myself that there sat a man to whom it would do all the good in the world to have hard-boiled eggs thrown at him. One of my crowd on that occasion, a lady accused of being drunk and disorderly and resisting the police, did on receipt of her sentence throw her boot at him, but with a poor aim, succeeding only in beaning the magistrates' clerk (IJ)

'Trying is the *mot juste*, Jeeves. It was an unpleasant experience coming up before Chuffy. A good deal of the awful majesty of the law about old Chuffy. I didn't know he wore horn-rimmed spectacles.'

'When acting as Justice of the Peace, invariably, sir. I gather that his lordship finds that they lend him confidence in his magisterial duties.'

'Well, I got a nasty shock. They change his whole expression. Make him look just like my Aunt Agatha. It was only by reminding myself that he and I once stood in the same dock together at Bow Street, charged with raising Cain on Boat Race Night, that I was able to retain my *sang froid*. However, I must admit he rushed things through nice and quickly. He soon settled Dobson's hash, what? A rather severe reprimand, I thought?'

'Well phrased, sir.'

'And Bertram dismissed without a stain on his character.' (TJ)

A thing about this undersized little son of a bachelor I ought to have mentioned earlier is that he was one of those unpleasant, sarcastic magistrates who get themselves so disliked by the criminal classes. You know the type. Their remarks are generally printed in the evening papers with the word 'laughter' after them in brackets, and they count the day lost when they don't make some unfortunate pickpocket or some wretched drunk and disorderly feel like a piece of cheese. I know that on the occasion when we stood face to face in Bosher Street police court he convulsed the audience with three solid jokes at my expense in the first two minutes, bathing me in confusion (SLJ)

Juvenal: (Decimus Junius Juvenalis, Roman satirist);

> 'The thought filled me,' said Kipper, 'with the righteous fury of a Juvenal.'
> 'Of a who?'
> 'Nobody you know. Before your time.' (JO)

K

Kegley-Bassington, Col. and Mrs: inflict a duologue, 'A Couple of Lunatics', on the village concert audience at King's Deverill (MS)

Kegley-Bassington, George: recitation (MS)

Kegley-Bassington, Muriel: solo (MS)

Kegley-Bassington, Percival: card tricks (MS)

Kegley-Bassington, Poppy: rhythmic dance (MS)

Kegley-Bassington, Watkyn: imitations (MS)

Kegworthy, Mr: can see 'oo—peep-bo! (COJ)

Kegworthy, Bootles: opts for mumps (COJ)

Kegworthy, Tootles: kidnapped by B. Wooster; a fat child, given to smacking jellyfish with a spade in a meditative manner (COJ)

Kilmuir, the Rt. Hon the Earl of, P. C.: see **Lord Chancellor**

King Charles II: the fortunes of Horace Pendlebury-Davenport's ducal house, laid by an ancestress who could not say no to, (UFS); see also **Belfry, Lady Barbara** (RJ)

King Edward the Confessor: (St. Edward of England); Lord Worplesdon, going down for the third time in a sea of dance champagne, sees the monarch plainly, with the naked eye:

> 'and I refuse to believe that Edward looked like that. Lynching parties would have been organised, knights sent out to cope with the nuisance with battleaxes' (JM)

King Edward III: says goodbye to his girl friend in aid of the Distressed Daughters of the Clergy (RHJ)

King Edward VII: possibly the last person to hear a bell in working order at Lord Rowcester's stately home (Though in 'RING FOR JEEVES' they apparently ring for Jeeves. One would like to meet the bell that wouldn't:—*Ed.*) (RJ)

King Edward VIII: (H.R.H. the Duke of Windsor); as Prince of Wales; see **What The Well-Dressed Young Man** (COJ)

King George VI: by a large majority the coffee stall customers agree that his late Majesty did not, as Duke of York, sport a smorl dork moustorche, or any other kind. But when in need of a new top hat, he ankled round to Bodmin's, the Bespoke Hatter of Vigo Street, and said 'Good morning, Bodmin. We want a topper.' (YMS)

King Harold II: experienced the same sort of thing at Hastings as Freddie Widgeon at Bottleton, E. (LEO)

King Henry IV of France and Navarre: see **Vert Galant, le**

King Henry V: when calling on the chaps to close the wall up with their English dead, did not have his spirits damped by hearing a Twistleton say he didn't think he could make it (CT)

King Henry VIII: the bedroom once occupied by him at Rowcester Abbey finds an appropriate tenant (RJ)

King Herod: see **Israelite Mothers**

KING LEAR: the old gentleman's rollicking gaiety is often extolled, and there are wistful references to an England blessed with so equable and mellow a climate as his (*passim*)

King Macbeth of Scots: Shakespeare's play is a popular source, the king being associated esp. with emotions of shocked surprise (Banquo's ghost) or with anxiety and nervous tension. He is identified too with his lady's natural anxiety to have the latest battle report from the spare room (see **Queen Gruoch**) (*passim*)

King Richard I: Lord Ickenham admits that certain Twistleton ancestors, on being ordered by the Lionheart to go and fight the Paynim, were not above using a *nolle prosequi*, as may be verified in the king's despatches from Acre (UD)

King of Ruritania, the: the peripatetic monarch is to be seen ushering guests into their limousines outside several West End hotels, or summarily ejecting other guests from a Soho night spot. But his social life is a round of gaiety (BCE) and he stays at the Hotel Magnifique at Nice (EBC) for the season (*passim*)

King of Scots, the: (unnamed, but the period suggests King James VI); sentences an unruly ancestor of Freddie Chalk-Marshall to an unpleasant end

King Solomon: amounted to little before he started marrying; after that you just sat back and watched his smoke (MS *et al.*)

King William I:

> One doesn't want to make a song and dance about one's ancient lineage, but after all the Woosters did come over with the Conqueror and were extremely pally with him: and a fat lot of good it is coming over with Conqueror if you're simply going to wind up by being given the elbow by Aberdeen terriers (CW)

Kingham Manor: Bertie is induced (in expiation) to cycle 18 miles to and from this Worcestershire seat, along by-lanes, by night, and on toppling from the saddle at journey's end is a very different Bertram from the insouciant boulevardier of Bond Street (RHJ)

Kings of Judah, the: see the interior of Mrs Bingo Little's middy-blouse

Kipling, Old Pop: (Rudyard Kipling, 1865-1936); never said a truer word than when he made that crack about the f. of the s. being more d. than the m. (RHJ)

knitted socks: Jeeves suavely ravels out the Hamlet sleave to produce 'knotted locks', and is equally successful with 'an eye like Mother's', but is not on hand to cope with 'one man's caviar is another man's major general, as the old saw has it.' Bertie, with some slight reserve about Shakespeare's sanity, can usually advance some reason for the poet's many howlers:

> Odd that he should have said porpentine when he meant porcupine. Slip of the tongue, no doubt, as so often happens with ghosts (JO)

Kosy Komfort Kennels: Kingsbridge, Kent; Bingo signs up the family Pekes at the, and totters out to tutor the kid Thos. (VGJ)

Kreisler, the late Fritz: a Drone is rewarded by seeing in a girl's eyes:

> The sort of look which Kreisler beholds in the eyes of the front row of the stalls as he lowers his bow and brushes his forehead with the back of his hand. A look of worship.

Kuala Lumpur and all that

I ONLY WISH THAT I COULD MEET THE RAT IN KUALA LUMPUR (RJ)

Jeeves was his usual helpful self. 'A locality in the Straits Settlements, m'lord, a British Crown Colony in the East Indies including Malacca, Penang and the province of Wellesley, first made a separate dependency of the British Crown in 1853 and placed under the Governor-General of India. In 1887 the Cocos or Keeling Islands were attached to the Colony, and in 1889 Christmas Island. Mr Somerset Maugham has written searchingly of life in those parts.' (RJ)

'I'll give him time,' said the Captain morosely. 'I'll see that he gets plenty. And when he has paid his debt to Society, I shall attend to him personally. A thousand pities we're not out East. They understand these things there. If they know you for a straight shooter and the other chap's a wrong 'un ... Well, there aren't many questions asked.' (RJ)

He had loved this woman from the very moment she had come into his life. How well he remembered that moment. The camp among the acacia trees. The boulder-strewn cliff. Old Simba the lion roaring in the distance. Old Tembo the elephant doing this and that in the *bimbo* or tall grass ... 'Ah, the memsahib,' and he had greeted her with a civil *'Krai yu ti ni ma pay.'*

Naturally, being a white man, he had not told his love, but it had burned steadily, a strong silent passion of such a calibre that sometimes, as he sat listening to the hyenas and gazing at the snows of Kilimanjaro, it had brought him within an ace of writing poetry. (RJ)

Ask any of the chaps out East and they'll say 'Give Bwana Biggar his .505 Gibbs, his eland steak of a night, let him breathe God's clean air and turn his face up to God's good sun, and he asks nothing more.' (RJ)

It is almost impossible to clasp a pendant round its owner's neck without touching that neck in spots, and he touched his companion's in several. And every time he touched it, something seemed to go through him like a knife. It was as though the moon, the nightingale, the breeze, the stock and tobacco plant were calling to him to cover this neck with burning kisses.

Only Tubby Frobisher and the Subahdar, forming a solid bloc in opposition, restrained him.

'Straight bat, old boy!' said Tubby Frobisher.

'Remember you're a white man,' said the Subahdar.

He clenched his fists and was himself again. (RJ)

L

Lacock Abbey: (Wilts); see **Rowcester Abbey**

Lanchester, George: a friend of Sir Roderick Glossop's salad days whose volcanic affections were actively assisted by the alienist (JO)

Larches, the: Wimbledon Common, S.W.; a temporary refuge for the Bassett disaster and a less reliable one for Bertie (MS)

lathered: see **lit A bit**

Lattaker, George (or Alfred): invents an identical twin to cover a bad case of *lèse majesté* (MJ)

Laughing Love God has Hiccoughs

IT WAS ... THE IDENTICAL LOOK WHICH I HAD OB-
SERVED IN THE EYE OF HONORIA GLOSSOP IN THE
DAYS IMMEDIATELY PRECEDING OUR ENGAGEMENT
—THE LOOK OF A TIGRESS THAT HAS MARKED DOWN
ITS PREY (COJ)

I once stayed at the residence of a newly-married pal of mine, and his bride had had carved in large letters over the fireplace in the drawing-room the legend: 'Two Lovers Built This Nest', and I can still recall the look of dumb anguish in the other half of the sketch's eyes, every time he came in and saw it. (CW)

The snag in this business of falling in love is that the parties of the first part so often get mixed up with the wrong parties of the second part, robbed of their cooler judgment by the parties of the second part's glamour. Put it like this. The male sex is divided into rabbits and non-rabbits, and the female sex into dashers and dormice, and the trouble is that the male rabbit has a way of getting attracted by a female dasher (who would be fine for the male non-rabbit) and realising too late that he ought to have been concentrating on some mild, gentle dormouse with whom he could settle down peacefully and nibble lettuce (JO)

'She strikes you as a tender goddess?'
'She does.'
'God bless you,' I said.
'She walks in beauty like the night of cloudless climes and starry skies; and all that's best of dark and bright meet in her aspect and

95

her eyes. Another bit of bread and cheese,' he said to the lad behind the bar (IJ)

You can't get away from it. Love, I mean. Wherever you go, there it is, buzzing along in every class of life. Take newts, for instance. You wouldn't think it, but Gussie Fink-Nottle tells me they get it right up their noses in the mating season. They stand in line by the hour, waggling their tails at the local belles. Starfish too. Also undersea worms. And, according to Gussie, even ribbon-like seaweed. That surprises you, eh? It did me. Just where a bit of ribbonlike seaweed thinks it's going to get by pressing its suit is more than I can tell you, but at the time of the full moon it hears the voice of Love all right and is up and doing with the best of them. I suppose it builds on the hope that it will look good to other bits of ribbonlike seaweed (CW)

You know what engaged couples are like in mixed company, as a rule. They put their heads together and converse in whispers. They slap and giggle. They pat and prod. I have even known the female member of the duo to feed her companion with a fork. There was nothing of this sort between Madeline Bassett and Gussie. He looked pale and corpse-like, she cold and proud and aloof. They put in the time for the most part making bread pills and didn't exchange a word from start to finish. Oh, yes—once, when he asked her to pass the salt, and she passed the pepper, and he said 'I meant the salt', and she passed the mustard (CW)

'As I came to know him, he seemed to have all the marks of a Grade A hammerhead. I wrote him off as a bohunkus. Romantically considered, he seemed to me to be strictly a cigar-store Indian, all wood from the neck up. And now I see that for some reason he was hiding his light behind a bushel. Oh, what shall I do? I love him, I love him, I love him!'

'Well, he loves you, which makes it all square.'

'Yes, but this afternoon he proposed to me, and I turned him down like a bedspread.' (FO)

'Do you think rich women are happy, Captain Biggar?'

The Captain said that all those he had met—and in his capacity as White Hunter he had met quite a number—seemed pretty bobbish.

'They smiled to hide the ache in their hearts,' explained Mrs Spottsworth.

The Captain said he remembered one of them, a large blonde of the name of Fish, dancing the can-can one night in her step-ins, and Mrs Spottsworth said that no doubt she was just trying to show a brave front to the world (RJ)

'When he hears,' said young Bingo, 'that I'm going to marry the daughter of an earl—'

'I say, old man, aren't you looking ahead rather far?'

'Oh, that's all right. She practically told me the other day she was fond of me.'

'What!'

'Well, she said that the sort of man she liked was the self-reliant, manly man with strength, good looks, character, ambition and initiative.'

'Leave me, laddie,' I said. 'Leave me to my fried egg.' (IJ)

She was standing by the barometer which, if it had had an ounce of sense in its head, would have been pointing to 'Stormy' instead of 'Set Fair': and as I hove alongside she turned and gazed at me with a tender goggle which sent a thrill of dread creeping down the spine.

'Oh, Bertie,' she said, 'you remind me of Rudel.'

The name was new to me.

'Rudel?'

'The Seigneur Geoffrey Rudel, Prince of Blaye-en-Saintonge.'

I shook my head.

'Never met him, I'm afraid. Pal of yours?'

'He lived in the Middle Ages. He was a great poet. He fell in love with the wife of the Lord of Tripoli.'

I stirred uneasily. I hoped she was going to keep it clean.

'For years he loved her, and at last he could resist no longer. He took ship to Tripoli, and his servants carried him ashore.'

'Not feeling so good,' I said, groping. 'Rough crossing?'

'He was dying. Of love.'

'Oh. Ah.'

'They bore him ashore into the Lady Melisande's presence on a litter, and he had just strength enough to reach out and touch her hand. Then he died.'

She paused, and heaved a sigh that seemed to come straight up from the cami-knickers. (CW)

'Bingo,' I cried, deeply moved, 'you must act. You must assert yourself. You must put your foot down. You must take a strong stand. You must be master in the home.'

He looked at me. A long, strange, look.
'You aren't married, are you, Bertie?'
'You know I'm not.'
'I should have guessed it, anyway.' (VGJ)

I was standing on the Eden Rock at Antibes, idly watching the bathers, and a girl I knew slightly pointed at a male diver and asked me if I didn't think his legs were about the silliest looking pair of props ever issued to a human being. I replied that I did indeed, and for the space of about two minutes was extraordinarily witty and satirical about this bird's underpinning. At the end of that period I suddenly felt as if I had been caught up in the tail of a cyclone.

Beginning with a critique of my own limbs which, she said justly enough, were nothing to write home about, this girl went on to dissect my manners, morals, intellect, general physique and method of eating asparagus with such acerbity that by the time she had finished the best you could say of Bertram was that, so far as was known, he had never actually committed murder or set fire to an orphan asylum. Subsequent investigation proved that she was engaged to the fellow with the legs and had had a slight disagreement with him the evening before on the subject of whether she should or should not have made an original call of two spades, having seven, but without the ace. That night I saw them dining together, their differences made up and the lovelight once more in their eyes (RHJ)

'There can be no love where there is not perfect trust.'
'Who told you that?'
'Jeeves, I think; it sounds like one of his things.'
'Well, Jeeves is wrong. There jolly well can be love without perfect trust, and don't you forget it. I love Boko distractedly, but at the thought of him going to Hollywood without me I come over all faint. He wouldn't mean to let me down. I don't suppose he would even know he was doing it. But one morning I should get an apologetic cable saying he couldn't quite explain how it had happened, but that he had inadvertently got married last night, and had I anything to suggest. It's his sweet, impulsive nature. He can't say No.' (JM)

'I hope you will be very, very happy. Nice girl, I expect?'
'Yes.'
The response was not what you would call lyrical, but we Woosters can read between the lines. His eyes were rolling in their sockets, and his face had taken on the colour and expression of a

devout tomato. I could see that he loved like a thousand of bricks (JM)

'Jeeves,' I said, 'I don't want to give the impression that I consider myself one of those deadly coves who exercise an irresistible fascination over one and all and can't meet a girl without wrecking her peace of mind.... Nevertheless it is a known scientific fact that there is a particular style of female that does seem strangely attracted to the sort of fellow I am.'

'Very true, sir.'

'I know perfectly well that I've got, roughly speaking, half the amount of brain a normal bloke ought to possess. And when a girl comes along who has about twice the regular allowance, she too often makes a beeline for me with the lovelight in her eyes.'

'It may be Nature's provision for maintaining the balance of the species, sir.'

'Very possibly. It was what happened in the case of Honoria Glossop. She was notoriously one of the brainiest women of her year at Girton, and she just gathered me in like a bull pup swallowing a piece of steak.'

'Miss Pringle, I am informed, sir, was an even more brilliant scholar than Miss Glossop.'

'Well, there you are. At breakfast this morning, when I was eating a sausage, she told me I shouldn't, as modern medical science held that a four-inch sausage contained as many germs as a dead rat. The maternal touch, you understand; fussing over my health.'

'I think we may regard that, sir, as practically conclusive.'

'What's to be done, Jeeves?'

'We must think, sir.'

'You think. I haven't the machinery.' (COJ)

lit a bit: see **off-colour**

Little: family name of Lord Bittlesham, q.v.

Little, Algernon Aubrey: offspring of Richard (Bingo) and Rosie Little, of 39 Magnolia Rd., St. John's Wood, N.8, and a godson of Alexander (Oofy) Prosser; an infant so unprepossessing that, on first catching sight of him in the nursing home, Bingo shies away with a startled 'Oy!' Within a few years, Algernon's homely features call forth from the Rev. Aubrey Upjohn a remonstrance which Freddie Widgeon considers the last word in scholarly invective, though they are financially rewarding when a visiting American cartoonist finds the baby an ideal model for a creature of the underworld:

'That lowering look! Those hard eyes which could be grafted on the head of a man-eating shark and no questions asked! He's a natural!'

Oofy Prosser, waking from a refreshing sleep on the hearth-rug and beholding those eyes peering at him menacingly from six inches away, showers gold in gratitude upon Bingo, for saving him from the ghastly consequences of matrimony. When however Algernon Aubrey is proposed for membership of the Drones, the reaction is austere:

'We don't want infants mewling and puking about the Drones.'
'I say, old boy, keep it clean,' urged a Pieface.
'Shakespeare,' explained the Bean.
'Oh, Shakespeare? Sorry.' (EBC, NS, FO)

Little, Richard (Bingo): (an inverted form perh. of the traditional song 'Little Bingo'); b. in the same village, and 'within a couple of days' of Bertie Wooster, they were at prep school, Eton and Oxford together. Bingo graduated. His 'degree of a sort' stands him in good stead when, having lost his all on an imagined winner, he is forced to tutor unpromising youngsters such as young Thos. We learn next to nothing about his family, save that he is a nephew of Mortimer Little (later Lord Bittlesham, q.v.). On the turf, as in the matrimonial stakes, Bingo is enterprising and optimistic rather than fortunate, until his surprise marriage to Rosie M. Banks, the popular novelist, at Holborn Register Office, after which luck, the occasional judicious intervention of Jeeves and Bingo's inheritance of a fortune and estate in Norfolk from his Uncle Wilberforce, combine to maintain an uneasy but generally happy equilibrium (IJ, COJ, VGJ, EBC, NS, FO)

Little, Wilberforce: hands in his dinner-pail (respected by all) and bequeathes a large fortune and a fine old house, thirty miles from Norwich, to his nephew Richard (Bingo) (VGJ)

Little Chilbury: in a mixed postbag Pongo Twistleton gets a series of strong letters, two telegrams and a picture postcard of the war memorial at, (RHJ)

Lobb's: of St. James's, S.W.; whose shoes, as worn by Oofy Prosser, are a point of local interest pointed out to visitors at the Drones (FO)

Lollobrigida, Gina: the highly individual shape of, (CT)

London Scottish R.F.C.: Bill Shoolbred plays against the, (MJ)

Long Island, N.Y.: a frequent setting for episodes in novels and for short stories. On it we find Bellport, Brookport, Far Rockaway, Goldenville, Hempstead, King's Point, Patchogue and Westbury. And, since on it we also find (at Basket Neck Lane, Remsenburg) the Old Master himself, we need not take too literally the critical note in:

> The days down on Long Island have forty-eight hours in them; you can't get to sleep at night because of the bellowing of the crickets, and you have to walk two miles for a drink and six for an evening paper (COJ)

Longsword, William, Earl of Salisbury: (William Longespée); see Rowcester Abbey (RJ)

Lord Chancellor of Britain, the Rt. Hon. the: within the jurisdiction of, to jug anyone so mistaken as to marry a ward in chancery, unless the Rt. Hon. has hoisted the All Right flag (JM)

At least one former Lord Chancellor is a Wodehouse devotee. On hearing that I was preparing a complete concordance to the opus the Rt. Hon. David Maxwell Fyfe, 1st Earl of Kilmuir, informed me that he had quoted from a Wodehouse book when he was prosecuting at the Nazi War Criminals Trials at Nuremburg, 1945-6. Counsel for one of the prisoners, Dr Rosenberg, had averred that his client, far from being the villain he was alleged to be, was a decent, good-living type who had actually been known to refrain from harming people when he might well have done so.

'When it came to my turn again,' said Kilmuir, 'I remarked that this greatly reminded me of a character in one of Mr P. G. Wodehouse's books, who was such a kindly man that sometimes days would go by during which he would wholly refrain from pulling the wings off flies. His friends would sit down and watch him not doing it.' When this had been translated and relaid to the court, he added, Herman Goering was convulsed and even Ribbentrop was smiling. Later I retailed the anecdote to the Master in a letter. He commented (18th May 1958):

'He got it a little wrong. It wasn't flies. It was lambs. ... In **Piccadilly Jim,** Ch. 17, where Jim is trying to induce Mrs Pett to take Mitchell back (she having fired him for hitting her son Ogden) he says, "I think the heat must have made him irritable. In his normal state he wouldn't strike a lamb. I've known him do it." "Do what?" says Mrs Pett. "Not strike lambs," says Jimmy.'

(A salient point seems to be that during the momentous and un-precedented Nuremberg Trials, with their hundreds of speeches by counsel, the only literary author to be quoted appears to have been P. G. Wodehouse. If there is a moral in this, it seems to be a very English one.—*Ed*.)

Lord Mayor of London, the Rt. Hon. the: about to confer the freedom of the City upon a Drone, changes his mind and takes a swipe at him with the City Mace (YMS)

Lovers' Leap: Esmond Haddock plans to take Gertrude Wink-worth riding about fifteen miles to a spot where there are cliffs and things, to show her the, (MS)

Loyal Sons of Worcestershire, the: as might be expected of a shire whose county town is traditionally the Faithful City, the browsing and sluicing at the annual banquet of the Sons tends to outdo most others—this in face of the competition of e.g. the Hampshire Hogs and the remarkable talent in the neighbouring county of Shropshire, whose Sons include such notable trenchermen as Lord Burslem and Sir Gregory Parsloe. That the loyalty of the flesh is not always equal to that of the spirit is evidenced in the case of Lord Wivelscombe, who is in a highly nervous condition on the morning after the banquet, and in no state to cope with spectres, whether of the White Lady or the Pink Secretary. But Worcester-shire's Sons do not confine their talents to the merely fleshly. Art and culture are encouraged at their gatherings. Sir Reginald Sprockett for instance is cheered to the echo when he recites a saga of his own composition based upon a heroine in local folklore—a certain young lady of Bewdley (YMS, *et al*.)

lulu, a: not (as in later argot) identifiable with gravy. Jeeves, as ever, supplies a precise definition:

'You agree with me that the situation is a lulu?'
'Certainly a somewhat sharp crisis in your affairs would appear to have been precipitated, sir.' (CW)

Lynn, Sir Claude, Bart., M.P.: represents the East Bittlesham parliamentary division. A man of parts, the Bart. would appear to be earmarked for some future Ministry of All the Talents. Is equally adept in debate, in committee, at the hustings, on the links, the tennis court and polo field, and is the original of the handsome Capt. Mauleverer in Lady Wickham's novel *Blood Will Tell*. He is specifically unequal (like so many others) to the authoress's daughter Roberta.

M

McAlpin: Oofy Prosser's obliging turf accountant readily agrees to lay odds against Oofy's nominee in a seaside Bonnie Babies contest. On hearing that the said nominee bears a family resemblance to Oofy, offers fifty to one in tenners (FO)

Macbeth, Lady: see **Queen Gruoch**

McGarry: barman at Bucks, S.W., listens to Bingo Little's latest love problems with flapping ears (IJ)

McGarry: perhaps identifiable with the foregoing, is the talented bartender at the Drones whose gift for accurately estimating the weight of anything placed before him (including fatstock on the hoof) forms the pivotal success of Freddie Widgeon's Fat Uncles Sweepstake (FO)

'M'Grew, Dangerous Dan': Lord Worplesdon, gazing at the portrait of Aunt Agatha over his study door, is in a state of mind to make an unusually jumpy fawn look like, (JM)

Maiden Eggesford: one of the most felicitous village names in the whole opus, carrying overtones of virginal innocence. Six miles from Bridmouth-on-Sea, Somerset. It is entirely fitting that the Vicar's daughter should be Angelica, that she should cause two visiting Drones to feel, on first meeting her, that they have been struck by lightning, and that she should combine the innocence of the dove with the wisdom of the serpent (YMS)

Mainwarings, the: records of this county family are sparse. They live at Stover, Southmoltonshire, and the ménage includes a hypochondriac Peke attended by Jill Wyvern (RJ)

Mainwaring, Peggy: aged 12, daughter of the Professor, achieves fame by being one of the few known to have kissed Jeeves. The occasion is impaired by a sticky sweetmeat (COJ)

Mainwaring, Professor: 'author of the well-known series of philosophical treatises, sir. They have a great vogue, though many of the Professor's opinions strike me personally as somewhat empirical.' (COJ)

Mainwaring-Smith, Colonel: the valet of, has a marital understanding with Rhoda Platt, q.v. (VGJ)

Maloney: one of the Brooklyn Maloneys, contributes to the peculiar pot-pourri of English spoken by the incomparable Anatole, q.v. (RHJ)

Maltravers, Yvonne: stage heroine in popular melodrama, takes umbrage when told she is too plump to play the No. 2 towns (many hold this to be impossible). She trails clouds of glory in her press notices: 'This buxom beauty' (*Leicester Argus*): 'This loyal artiste' (*Wolverhampton Express*): 'As Myrtle in *The Hand of Doom* she is purity personified' (*Bexhill Gazette*). Men in places like Huddersfield have offered her guilty splendour on the strength of a cup of cocoa (YMS)

Malvern, the Most Hon. the Marquess of: f. of Wilmot, Lord Pershore, q.v. Res. Much Middlefold Hall, Shropshire (COJ)

Malvern, the Marchioness of: a crony of Agatha Spenser Gregson and m. of Mottie, Lord Pershore, whom she optimistically entrusts to the care of Bertie Wooster in wildest New York.

> She measured about six feet from o.p. to prompt side, and fitted into my biggest armchair as if it had been built round her by someone who knew that they were wearing armchairs tight about the hips that season (COJ)

Malvern House: the pentitentiary at Bramley-on-Sea, sometimes called St. Asaph's, wears the outward guise of a prep school. The resident Gauleiter is the Rev. Aubrey Upjohn, M.A., whose dossier may be consulted. There is an air of shuddering realism in all Bertie Wooster's references to life at this embryo concentration camp. Over the forty years in which Upjohn has been popping up in the annals like an unforgettable childhood ogre, he has worn a semblance of those rare real life characters who (Wodehouse observes in PF) 'stick out like sore thumbs'. In fact Wodehouse and his elder brother were at a prep school in Guernsey, after which

P.G. was sent to another one at Dover. Richard Usborne, in WAW, notes that 'the Head of the second school lingers on in the person, and in frequent shuddering mentions, of the Reverend Aubrey.' Among other old lags who did their stretch here are Bingo Little, Catsmeat Potter-Pirbright, Freddie Widgeon and Kipper Herring (see **Squaring with Squeers**). Their memories of this abode of desolation dwell feelingly on appointments in the headmaster's study after morning prayers, boiled mutton and caper sauce, margarine and the inevitable Sunday sausages, made from pigs which had expired from glanders, tuberculosis and the botts, all of them a testimony to the lasting impressions made upon their tender minds and elsewhere. Perhaps it is equitable to suppose that such a toughening course, extending over three years, can inure its survivors to the slings and arrows of later life. The resilience with which they accept a night's lodging in the Bosher Street police cells may show that the treatment, though sharp, has been effective (*passim*)

MAN WITH TWO LEFT FEET, THE: published in 1917, marks the start of the Wooster-Jeeves cycle with the short story **Extricating Young Gussie**. Years later the author was to comment a little wryly on Jeeves's modest and undramatic entry into his 'little world', adding that he blushed to think of the offhand way in which he treated the man at their first encounter (Introduction to JOM). More cogent surely is the fact that the ingredients were mixed in correct measure. Jeeves today is still the identical character who slid so smoothly and unobtrusively into our ken, half a century ago. (MT)

Mannering-Phippses, the: and the Woosters. See **Wooster, B. W.** (MT)

Mannering-Phipps, Augustus: Bertie's first cousin, offspring of the late Cuthbert and of Julia Mannering-Phipps, Gussie loses his head, and heart, to a creature, and so is singled out for Treatment A by Aunt Agatha, the Pest of Pont Street (MT)

Mannering-Phipps, Bertram; see **Wooster, B. W.**

Mannering-Phipps, Cuthbert (the late): Bertie's uncle had an expensive thirst, never backed a horse which did not develop housemaid's knee and cherished a bank-beating system that caused the Monte Carlo management to hang out the bunting and ring the joy-bells whenever he was sighted in the offing (MT)

Mannering-Phipps, Julia: Bertie's aunt was originally in vaudeville, but after years of corrective training by that inflexible welldoer Agatha Spenser Gregson, cannot now be distinguished from a dyed-in-the-wool aristocrat (MT)

Maple: butler at Bumpleigh Hall to Lord and Lady Worplesdon, brings a ½-bot from the oldest bin (JM)

Mapleton, Miss: headmistress of St. Monica's College for Young Ladies, Bingley-on-Sea, is a close friend of the redoubtable Lady Wickham and lifelong crony of Aunt Agatha—facts which conduce to Bertie's reflection that a long term of penal servitude would be preferable to his ordeal in trying to return young Prudence Carroway to store, undetected, at dead of night. When he confronts her in her study she has every appearance of a more than usually durable lion-tamer, but in the event she proves a most effective policeman-tamer. Bertie's resource and courage (circumspectly coloured by Jeeves) win him unlooked-for glory and he is even mentioned in despatches to Aunt Agatha. Later we learn that Miss Mapleton's hair is grey. Considering that Prudence Carroway and (in her time) Bobbie Wickham are her pupils, it seems remarkable that she has any (VGJ)

Mario's: fashionable West End restaurant, frequented by all that is best and fairest, and graced by the obbligato ministrations of Leopold and his Band. Normally a sedate place, it suffers illuminated moments, as when Ronnie Fish arrives in a shower of glass (NS, *et al.*)

Market Snodsbury: consequential little Worcestershire town near Droitwich. Tom and Dahlia Travers live about two miles away at Brinkley Court. When the Vicar strains a fetlock (*teste* Aunt Dahlia) Bertie is commanded to give away the prizes at the Grammar School Speech Day. He hands the job to Gussie Fink-Nottle, whose address wins unlooked-for and unwanted fame for the school. The episode (in RHJ) unquestionably ranks as one of the finest pieces of sustained humour in the language. Tourists may like to know that the School was founded *c.* 1416 and still retains the fug of the centuries (RHJ, CW, SLJ, JFS, *et al.*)

Marlborough St. Police Court, W.: Horace Pendlebury-Davenport, that pre-eminent Drone, appears in the dock at, in the full warpaint of a Zulu warrior on the (overnight) charge of jabbing Queen Marie Antoinette in the rear with his assegai at the Bohemian Ball at the Albert Hall. (As reigning darts champion of the Drones Club he was perhaps impelled by *force majeure*) (UFS)

Marsham Manor: Hampshire mise-en-scène of the Fothergill Venus (FO)

Martyn, Algie: like his fellow Drone Ronnie Devereux, can recognise a human tick, even when disguised as a baronet and M.P.

Marvis Bay: Dorset seaside resort favoured for its golf, and enlivened by the periodic descent of Drones *en masse* during their swarming season. Says Bertie:

> While not what you would call a fiercely exciting spot, has many good points. You spend the day there bathing and sitting on the sands, and in the evening you stroll out on the shore with the mosquitoes. At nine p.m. you rub ointment on the wounds and go to bed. It's a simple, healthy life (COJ)

Mary: red-haired parlourmaid at Chuffnell Hall, betrothed to P.c. Dobson, is the sort of girl any red-blooded constable would come leaping into the raspberry bushes to meet (TJ).

Marylebone Cricket Club: the gardener at the Larches, Wimbledon Common, S.W, wears a red and yellow cap suggesting erroneously that he is a member of the, (MS)

Master In Lunacy, the: surprisingly does not make a personal appearance; perhaps because his able lieutenant, Sir Roderick Glossop, is usually ready to contribute distinguished specimens to the Master's collection—even, on one occasion, a Duke. On her own evidence we may assume Aunt Dahlia to be a close chum of the Master. Bertie withholds none of her frankness about his touching faith in the Luminous Rabbit and the Giant Squirt:

> 'Bertie,' she said with a sort of frozen calm, 'listen to me. It's simply because I am fond of you and have influence with the Lunacy Commissioners that you weren't put in a padded cell years ago. Bungle this business, and I withdraw my protection.' (VGJ)

The enterprising pokerwork of noblemen like the Duke of Dunstable, the flaccid vacuity of Clarence, 9th Lord Emsworth, and the height, width and handsomeness of Uncle Fred Ickenham's inspirations suggest that the Peerage are provided at birth with fairy godmothers on the staff of the Commission. There are references to some of the centres of hospitality maintained by the kindly body, notably Colney Hatch which is cited as keeping open doors for deserving cases, and even as being anxious on occasion to lay down the red carpet to welcome them, no questions asked (*passim*)

MATING SEASON, THE: first published in 1949, was written in the birthplace of the Roi Soleil (Pavillion Henri Quatre, St. Germain-en-Laye). In PF the Master notes that he is haunted by the fear that the village concert sequence may fall flat (MS)

Matcham Scratchings: Oxfordshire home of the Prenderby baronets, is the only Stately Home to represent that county. In addition to Sir Mortimer, it houses his lady, a nymphery of sisters, cousins and aunts, a clowder of cats, a Donnybrook of dogs and one anthropoid ape. In one night there (see **Israelite, M.S.S.A.**) Freddie Widgeon experiences cataclysmic disaster.

> As far as the eye could reach there were dogs scratching themselves, cats scratching the furniture, and though he never met it socially, even a tame chimpanzee somewhere on the premises, no doubt scratching away as assiduously as the rest of them (YMS)

Matters & Cornelius Ltd.: leading estate agents at the charming London suburb of Valley Fields, S.E., on whose history and amenities Mr Cornelius is an erudite and fascinating authority (IB, *et al.*)

Maugham, the late W. Somerset:

> When a well-loved mother goes suddenly off her rocker and the tragedy involves the breaking of one's engagement ... one gets something Somerset Maugham could make a three-act play out of without conscious cerebration (YMS)

(see also **Kuala Lumpur**)

Maxton, the late Rt. Hon. James, P.C.: was not normally found dancing in night-clubs (YMS)

Maxwell: an editorial crony of Florence Craye (COJ)

Meadowes: Jeeves's forerunner in the service of Bertie Wooster and a notable collector of silk socks (COJ)

Meadowes: possibly identifiable; Archie Mulliner's valet, a dedicated member of the League for the Dawn of Freedom (YMS)

Me Wang River: is (we need scarcely inform our readers) a tributary of the even more crocodile-infested Wang Me River (RJ)

'**Milady's Boudoir**': in the 300 years long and (moderately) honourable annals of the British Press, few periodicals can have eked out so precarious an existence while 'turning the corner', or taken so many years not to do so. We make its acquaintance in Aunt Dahlia's pre-Brinkley days when (for reasons unexplained) Tom Travers refuses to live in the country and they are established in Charles St., Mayfair. Exiled from fox-hunting, Dahlia finds in weekly journalism an outlet for her surplus energies and for years treads the financial tightrope, leaping from crisis to crisis like a chamois of the Alps, menaced on the one hand by Carey Street and on the other by the Divorce Court. The *Boudoir* subsists on periodical shots in the arm from the wealthy, but dyspeptic and grudging, Uncle Tom, who always refers to it as 'Madame's Nightshirt' and whose valetudinarianism is equalled only by its own. Tom's benevolence in turn depends on Anatole's cooking. Any threat to the outstanding Cordon Bleu is consequently a direct menace to the magazine. Its mechanics become something of a major mystery. Though published weekly ('a weekly for the half-witted woman', Bertie calls it), its proprietor-editor seems to spend all her time in Worcestershire. But it has enjoyed the distinction of publishing the work of some of the most stearine women novelists and has also given to the world the sole journalistic effort ('a piece, we old hands call it') of Bertram Wooster on 'What the Well-Dressed Young Man is Wearing', as he reminds us from year to year. To nobody's great regret and to Uncle Tom's relief the magazine is finally disposed of (JFS) to a Liverpool newspaper proprietor seeking a London foothold (*passim*)

Milky Way, the: see **Via Lactea Galaxy**

Mills, Phyllis: d. of the late Jane Mills, stepdaughter of the Rev. Aubrey Upjohn and god-daughter of Dahlia Travers. Bertie chalks her up as an extremely pretty young prune with a face of the Soul's Awakening type, subsequently raising his bid to 'a pipterino of the first water'. She m. Wilbert Cream, ornament of a great American university (JO)

Moh's Scale of Hardness: Jeeves touches upon, see **Now We Know** (JFS)

Monte Carlo: in the matter of doing down the masses, not even Oofy Prosser has a nastier disposition than the wheel at,

You can play mentally by the hour and never get a losing

spin, but once you put real money up the whole aspect alters (EBC)

Moon, Gwendolen: authoress (for want of a better word) of *'Twas on an English June* and other goo and, as if this were not enough, s. of the gold-ringleted Sebastian. Is united to O.R. Sipperley at the instance of Jeeves (RHJ, VGJ)

Moon, Sebastian: kid brother of Gwendolen Moon, has an appearance calling aloud to any right-minded boy to lure him to a quiet spot, there to wreak violence.

> 'Apart from his curls,' said Jeeves, 'he has a personality which is not uniformly pleasing. He is apt to express himself with a breezy candour.' (VGJ)

Morehead, Daphne Dolores: best-selling American novelist whose latest success is acquired by Dahlia Travers as a means to salt the **Milady's Boudoir** mine before disposing of it. D.D. is not without attributes in other directions. Even devoted husbands, it is reported, are apt to react powerfully when she administers Treatment A. Bertie Wooster, a not inconsiderable judge, classifies her specifically:

> There was a flash of blonde hair and a whiff of Chanel No. 5 and a girl came sailing in, a girl whom I was able to classify at a single glance as a pipterino of the first water. Bertram Wooster is not a man who slops readily over when speaking of the other sex. He is cool and critical. He weighs his words. She could have walked into any assembly of international beauty contestants, and the committee would have laid down the red carpet for her. She had hair the colour of ripe corn and eyes of cornflower blue. Add a tiptilted nose and a figure as full of curves as a scenic railway, and it will not strike you as strange that Stilton should have stood gaping at her dumbly, his aspect that of a man who has been unexpectedly struck by a thunderbolt (JFS)

Moscow's Pride: the unspeakable and unpredictable Brinkley, valet to Bertie Wooster during his banjolele seizure (TJ)

Mottled Oyster Club, W.: leads a chameleon existence, leaping from name to new name after each descent by the C.I.D. Bertie Wooster, a member, escorts Florence Craye thither, to their subsequent discomfiture (JFS)

Much Middlefold: this Shropshire village lays a quiet but lasting spell upon a number of often unrelated characters. It is remembered with nostalgia by, e.g., Wally Mason, Jill Mariner, Freddie Rooke and his fellow Drone R. E. Psmith whose father (while wrestling with County Cricket problems) had his home at nearby Corfby Hall. Lord and Lady Malvern (and the hapless Mottie) live at Much Middlefold Hall (*passim*)

Mull, His Grace the Duke of: bright particular star in that exclusive coterie, the Twelve Jolly Stretcher Cases, at Droitgate Spa (EBC)

Mulliner, Archibald: admittedly one of the less gifted of this ancient and talented family. Even at the Drones, where the intellectual average is not high, it is said of Archie that, were his brain constructed of silk, he would be hard put to it to find sufficient material to make a canary a pair of cami-knickers. Res.: Cork St., W.1. Not surprisingly Archie falls for Aurelia Cammarleigh, q.v., whose potty aunt holds views on the Bacon theory. Their first encounter

> bore an extraordinary resemblance to the famous meeting between the poet Dante and Beatrice Fortinari. ... Dante just goggled at the girl. So did Archibald. The poet's age at the time, we are told, was nine, which was almost exactly the mental age of Archibald Mulliner (YMS, FO)

Mulliner, Lady (Wilhelmina): relict of Sir Sholto Mulliner, M.V.O., lives at Kew, where her son Archie visits her to seek advice on the subject of an aching heart. Few things are less pleasant for a young man in the springtime of life than to have a well-loved mother go suddenly off her rocker.

> There in that sunlit room stood Lady (Wilhelmina) Mulliner, with her tongue out like a dog's, panting in deep gasps. And then, she suddenly stopped panting and began to utter a remark which, even by Archibald's not too exacting standards, seemed noticeably goofy. It consisted of the words 'Q', 'X', repeated over and over again (YMS)

Mundy, Jimmy: social reformer whose views on New York's night life approximate to those of Rocky Todd, q.v. (COJ)

Murgatroyd: quondam butler to Tom Travers at Brinkley Court, is remembered as having the presence of a more than usually respectable archbishop; pinches a fish slice, puts it up the spout and loses the proceeds at the dog races (CW)

Murgatroyd, Mabel: vermilion on top, dimpled and vivacious, brings Oofy Prosser to the verge of the matrimonial precipice (FO)

MY MAN JEEVES: published 1919, is a collection of eight stories, four of them centred on Reggie Pepper (a character later developed as Bertie Wooster) and his manservant. These were later rewritten and republished in **CARRY ON, JEEVES** (MJ)

N

Nannies: 'are not domestics, yet are not quite dictators', though many would aver that they fall well within the category of absolute monarchs. Bertie's own Nanny Hogg has been quiescent in her Bastingstoke villa for years, though few would dare to predict that her forces are spent. Bingo's awe-inspiring Nanny Byles makes a formidable come-back (NS) to establish complete autonomy over his household. That 'Shakespeare himself would have quailed before his Nanny' is no extravagant claim. On the broader scene of the whole opus we have Nannies Bruce, Lippett, Wilks and Ma Price, the last of whom was shared by Freddie Chalk-Marshall of the Drones and his brother Lord Droitwich. None of them can be relied upon for permanent retirement while life lasts.

Nature

Isn't Nature Wonderful?

HE KNEW NOTHING OF ARMADILLOS AT THAT TIME EXCEPT THAT NOBODY HAD EVER CLAIMED THAT THEY WROTE THE PLAYS OF SHAKESPEARE (OS)

'You can tell him,' said Spode, 'that I am going to break his neck.'

'Break his neck?'

'Yes. Are you deaf? Break his neck.'

'I see. Break his neck. Right. And if he asks why?'

'He knows why. Because he is a butterfly who toys with women's hearts and throws them away like soiled gloves.'

I hadn't a notion that that was what butterflies did. Most interesting (CW)

I don't know if you've ever tried detaching a snow leopard of the Himalayas from its prey—probably not, for most people don't find themselves out that way much—but if you did, you would feel fairly safe in budgeting for a show of annoyance on the animal's part (SLJ)

'When he heard I was keeping newts in my bedroom, he said something very derogatory,' said Gussie. 'Under his breath, but I heard him.'

'You've got the troupe with you, then?'

'Of course. I'm in the middle of a very delicate experiment. An American professor has discovered that the full moon influences the love life of several undersea creatures, including one species of fish, eight kinds of worms and a ribbon-like seaweed called *Dictyota*. The moon will be full in two or three days, and I want to find out if it affects the love life of newts, too.'

'But what *is* the love life of newts, if you boil it right down? Didn't you tell me once that they just waggled their tails at each other in the mating-season?'

'Quite correct.'

'Well, all right if they like it. But it's not my idea of molten passion.' (CW)

On these occasions of back-chat between the delicately-nurtured a man should retire into the offing, curl up in a ball, and imitate the prudent tactics of the opossum which, when danger is in the air, pretends to be dead, frequently going to the length of hanging out crepe and instructing its friends to stand around and say what a pity it all is. (VGJ)

Just so might a python at the Zoo have spoken of its keeper, had the latter suddenly started feeding it cheese straws in lieu of the daily rabbit (SLJ)

'Did you know ants can talk?' asked young Edwin. 'They do it by tapping their heads on a leaf. They are characterised by unusual distinctness of the three regions of the body—head, thorax and abdomen—and by the stack or petiole of the abdomen having one or two scales or nodes, so that the abdomen moves very freely on the trunk or thorax.'

'You wouldn't fool me?'

'The female, after laying her eggs, feeds the larvae with food regurgitated from her stomach.'

'Try to keep it clean, my lad.'

'Have you ever seen ants fight? They rise on their hind legs and curve the abdomen' (JM)

'Colour does make a difference,' said Gussie. 'Look at newts. During the courting season the male newt is brilliantly coloured. It helps him a lot.'

'But you aren't a male newt.'

'I wish I were. Do you know how a male newt proposes, Bertie? He just stands in front of the female newt vibrating his tail and bending his body in a semi-circle. I could do that on my head. No, you wouldn't find me grousing if I were a male newt.'

'But if you were a male newt, Madeline Bassett wouldn't look at you. Not with the eye of love, I mean.'

'She would, if she were a female newt.'

'But she isn't a female newt.'

'No, but suppose she was.'

'Well, if she was, you wouldn't be in love with her.'

'Yes, I would, if I were a male newt.'

A slight throbbing about the temples told me that this discussion had reached saturation point (RHJ)

'Doesn't it strike you as odd, Jeeves, that with infant mortality so rife, a girl like Stiffy should have been permitted to survive into the early twenties? Some mismanagement there. What's the tree that does you in if you sit under it?'

'The Upas tree, sir.'

'She's a female Upas tree. It's not safe to come near her. Disaster on every side is what she strews (SLJ)

The swan extended another eight feet of neck and gave us an imitation of steam escaping from a leaky pipe.

'Look out for the swan, Jeeves!'

'I have the bird under close observation, sir.'

The swan had been uncoiling a further supply of neck in our direction, but now he whipped round. The sound of a voice speaking in his rear seemed to affect him powerfully. He subjected Jeeves to a short, keen scrutiny; and then, taking in some breath for hissing purposes, gave a sort of jump and charged ahead.

'Look out, Jeeves!'

'Very good, sir.'

Well, I could have told that swan it was no use. As swans go, he may have been well up in the ranks of the intelligentsia, but when it came to pitting his brains against Jeeves, he was simply wasting his time. Every young man starting life ought to know how to cope with an angry swan. You begin by picking up the raincoat which somebody has dropped; and then, judging the distance to a nicety, you simply shove the raincoat over the bird's head, and taking the boathook which you have prudently brought with you, you insert it beneath the swan and heave. The swan goes into a bush, and starts trying to unscramble itself, and you saunter back to your boat, taking with you any friends who may happen at the moment to be sitting on roofs in the vicinity. (VGJ)

With a snail nothing much ever happens, and, of course, there is no sex angle. An informant on whom I can rely says that they are 'sexless or at least ambivalent'. This means, broadly speaking, that there are no boy snails and no girl snails, so that if you want to write a novel with a strong snail interest, you are dished from the start. Obviously the snail-meets-snail, snail-loses-snail, snail-gets-snail formula will not help you, and this discourages writers from the outset. Almost all we know of snails from English literature is Shakespeare's brief statement that they creep unwillingly to school (OS)

A silver moon was riding in the sky, and a gentle breeze blew from the west, bringing the heart-stirring scent of stock and tobacco plant. Shy creatures of the night rustled in the bushes at her side and, to top the whole thing off, somewhere in the woods beyond the river a nightingale had begun to sing with all the full-throated zest of a bird conscious of having had a rave notice from the poet Keats and only a couple of nights ago a star spot on the programme of the B.B.C. (RJ)

Such was the v. that rose before my e. as I gaped at that closed door, and I wilted like a salted snail. Outside in the garden birds were singing their evensong, and it seemed to me that each individual bird was saying, 'Well, boys, Wooster is for it. We shan't see much of Wooster for the next few years. Too bad, too bad. A nice chap till he took to crime.' (JFS)

Nazi War Criminal Trial: Nuremberg, 1945-46. See **Lord Chancellor**

New York City: the scene of many of the novels and short stories; indeed a pleasant and invigorating dual nationality runs through the whole opus. Wodehouse's dictum of 45 years ago, that

> in their attitude towards America, visiting Englishmen always incline to extremes, either detesting all that therein is, or else becoming enthusiasts on the country, its climate and institutions

remains true today. Most characters are good mixers and are therefore converts and devotees—Bertie, Jeeves, Monty Bodkin, Barmy Phipps, Reggie Havershot and (outstandingly) Freddie Threepwood among them. Lord Ickenham spends a colourful apprenticeship to life in the States and even the Duke of Kirkcudbrightshire only leaves his U.S. hosts (in dudgeon) when the supply of brown sherry runs out. Bertie, though introduced to us in London, is speedily transferred to New York to cope with cousin Gussie's troubles. He finds it embarrassingly hospitable and an enchanting bolt-hole from the flying tomahawks of militant aunts. The sufferings of the exiled New Yorker on the other hand can be extreme. 'They pine away in a country where men say "Well played, sir!" when they mean "Attaboy"!' Finally:

> An American daughter gets it into her head at about the age of six that her word is law, and never loses it. It is always understood that . . . the bird who marries her will roll over and jump through hoops on demand.

Niagara: not so much a town as a heavy downpour, Freddie Threepwood informs his noble father. Freddie should know, since he married it—that is, he married Niagara (Aggie), daughter of Donaldson the Dog-Joy king, who had honeymooned at the Niagara Falls Hotel

Nicholls and Jackson: psychologists may care to ponder the somewhat sadistic flavour of Jeeves's Mikadoesque sense of humour:

> An absurd little story, sir, though I confess I have always thought it droll. According to my Uncle Cyril, two men named Nicholls and Jackson set out to ride to Brighton on a tandem bicycle, and were so unfortunate as to come into collision with a brewer's van. It was discovered that they had been hurled together with such force that it was impossible to sort them out at all adequately. So they collected as much as they

could and called it Nixon. I remember laughing very much at that story when I was a child (RHJ)

Nietzsche: Jeeves, who has taken Nietzsche in his stride, opines that the young master would not appreciate him. 'He is fundamentally unsound, sir.'

Niven, David: 'You hurt and disappoint me, Jeeves. I could understand your argument if the object under advisement were something bushy and waxed at the ends like a sergeant-major's, but it is merely the delicate wisp of vegetation with which David Niven has for years been winning the applause of millions. When you see David Niven on the screen, you don't recoil in horror, do you?'
'No, sir. His moustache is very becoming to Mr Niven.' (JFS)

Nolle prosequi: 'one of Jeeves's gags—it means nuts to you' (*passim*)

NOTHING SERIOUS: published in 1950, is a collection of ten short stories about old and proved favourites. One, **'How's That, Umpire?'** is the only cricketing story to appear since the noble days of **'Mike'**, but it conforms to the book's title as a masterpiece of irreverence (NS)

Notting Hill, W.: under the stimulus of what he conceives to be the lovelight in Dora Pinfold's eyes, Freddie Widgeon finds himself on a platform with the Vicar and a Union Jack behind him and about two hundred Notting Hill mothers in front of him, letting it go like a Crosby (LEO)

'Now We Know' Dept.

THERE IS ONLY ONE REAL CURE FOR GREY HAIR.
IT WAS INVENTED BY A FRENCHMAN. HE CALLED
IT THE GUILLOTINE

He had grown a moustache. I didn't know that clergymen ever did this, but I suppose there is no rule against it. And, of course, for all I knew, he might have been unfrocked, which is a thing they do to the clergy when they catch them bending (JO)

'With a what was that, once again?'

'With a dog-girl,' said Aunt Dahlia. 'One of these dashed open-air flappers in thick boots and tailormade tweeds who infest the rural districts and go about the place followed by packs of assorted dogs. I used to be one of them myself in my younger days, so I know how dangerous they are' (VGJ)

At the school where I was employed, sir, the young ladies had a regular game which they were accustomed to play when a male visitor arrived. They would stare fixedly at him and giggle, and there was a small prize for the one who made him blush first (COJ)

'You remember that fellow you mentioned to me once or twice, Jeeves, who let something wait upon something? You know who I mean—the cat chap.'

'Macbeth, sir, a character in a play of that name by the late William Shakespeare. He was described as letting "I dare not" wait upon "I would", like the poor cat in th'adage.'* (CW)

'You'll be able to give it as your considered opinion that Wilbert is as loony as a coot?' I said.

A pause ensued during which Pop Glossop seemed to be weighing this, possibly thinking back to coots he had met in the course of his professional career, and trying to estimate their dippiness as compared with that of W. Cream.

'Unquestionably his metabolism is unduly susceptible to stresses resulting from the interaction of external excitations,' he said. (JO)

'At least impress on him,' I said resignedly, 'that it is essential, when pinching policemen's helmets, to give a forward shove before applying the upward lift. Otherwise the subject's chin catches in the strap. It was to overlooking this vital point that my own downfall in Leicester Square was due. The strap caught, the subject was enabled to turn and clutch, and before I knew what had happened I was in the dock saying "Yes, your Honour", and "No, your Honour" to your Uncle Watkyn'. (CW)

'It just happens that jewellery is something of a hobby of mine, sir. With diamonds, of course, the test would be different. To ascertain the genuineness of a diamond it would be necessary to take a sapphire-point gramophone needle, which is—as you are no

---

* As all our readers are well aware, the adage in question (in very low latin) is *Catus amat pisces sed non vult tingere plantas*, or as in Heywood's '*Proverbs*', 'The cat would eat fyshe but would not wet her feete'—*Ed.*

doubt aware—corundum having a hardness of nine, and make a small test scratch on the underside of the suspect stone. A genuine diamond, I need scarcely remind you, is the only substance with a hardness of ten—Moh's scale of hardness. Most of the hard objects we see about us are approximately seven in the hardness scale. But you were saying, sir?' (JFS)

'My name's Wooster. I'm a pal of your nephew, Oliver.'
'Oh?' she said. 'When I heard your voice I thought you were someone else.'
'No, that's who I am.' (COJ)

Mr Wooster being one of those easy-going young gentlemen who will drive a car but never take the trouble to study its mechanism, I felt justified in becoming technical.
'I think it is the differential gear, sir. Either that, or the exhaust.' (COJ)

'I'm a Rotationist, you know.'
'Ah, yes. Elks, Shriners and all that. I've seen pictures of them, in funny hats.'
'No, no. You're thinking of Rotarians. I'm a Rotationist, which is quite different. We believe that we are reborn as one of our ancestors every ninth generation.' (RJ)

'Mrs Trotter, sir, being socially ambitious, is extremely anxious to see Mr Trotter knighted.'
I was rather surprised. 'Do they knight birds like him?'
'Oh yes, sir. A gentleman of Mr Trotter's prominence in the world of publishing is always in imminent danger of receiving the accolade.'
'Danger? Don't these bozos like being knighted?'
'Not when they are of Mr Trotter's retiring disposition, sir. He would find it a very testing ordeal. It involves wearing satin knee-breeches and walking backwards with a sword between the legs, not at all the sort of thing a sensitive gentleman of retiring habits would enjoy. And he shrinks, no doubt, from the prospect of being addressed for the remainder of his life as Sir Lemuel.'
'His name's not Lemuel?'
'I fear so, sir.'
'Couldn't he use his second name?'
'His second name is Gengulphus.'
'Golly, Jeeves, there's some raw work pulled at the font from time to time, isn't there?' (JFS)

'You see it on all sides,' said Nelson. 'Something very serious has gone wrong with girls nowadays. There is lawlessness and licence abroad.'

'And here in England, too,' said Percy.

'Well, naturally, you silly ass,' said Nelson with some asperity. 'When I said abroad, I didn't mean abroad, I meant abroad.' (YMS)

'Jeeves, I wish I had a daughter. I wonder what the procedure is?'

'Marriage is, I believe, considered the preliminary step, sir.' (COJ)

O

Oaker, Freddie: of the Drones, composes tales of pure love for the women's weeklies under the pen name Alicia Seymour. He estimates that flowery meadows in springtime alone are worth at least a hundred pounds a year to him (TJ)

Oakshott: butler to Bertie's Uncle Willoughby at Easeby Hall, Shropshire (COJ)

Oates, P.c. Eustace: guardian of the peace at Totleigh-in-the-Wold, Glos, at whose trousers every self-respecting village dog conceives it his duty to have a go. 'Is zurled from his bersicle, your Worship, by the animal Bartholomew Byng, this being the second occasion on which he has been assaulted verlently, your Worship, by a savage animal not under proper control' (CW)

Obiter Dicta

IN AN EMPLOYER BRAINS ARE NOT DESIRABLE (COJ)

No good (said Aunt Dahlia) can come of association with anything labelled Gwladys or Ysobel or Ethyl or Mabelle or Kathryn. But particularly Gwladys (VGJ)

It has been my experience, sir, that no lady can ever forgive another lady for taking a really good cook away from her (COJ)

A fellow with fifty millions in his kick doesn't have to wear the mask (TJ)

Jill had that direct, honest gaze which many nice girls have, and as a rule Bill liked it. But at the moment he could have done with something that did not pierce quite so like a red-hot gimlet to his inmost soul. A sense of guilt makes a man allergic to direct, honest gazes (RJ)

'You don't mean he's scared of Aunt Agatha? A tough bird like him? Practically a bucko mate of a tramp steamer?'
'Even bucko mates stand in awe of the captains of their vessels, sir.' (JM)

It is never immediately that the ordinary man, stunned by some revelation of genius, is able to find words to express his emotion. When Alexander Graham Bell, meeting a friend one morning in the year 1876, said 'Oh, hullo, George, heard the latest? I invented the telephone yesterday', it is probable that the friend merely shuffled his feet in silence (RJ)

My experience, sir, is that when the wife comes in at the front door the valet goes out at the back (COJ)

The modern young man (said Aunt Dahlia) is a congenital idiot and wants a nurse to lead him by the hand and some strong attendant to kick him regularly at intervals (VGJ)

The thought crossed his mind that this must be his guardian angel, buckling down to work after a prolonged period of negligence. Then he saw that the other had no wings. He had spoken, moreover, with an American intonation, and the guardian angels of members of the Drones Club would have had an Oxford accent (FO)

Never give a sucker an even break (EBC)

It seems to be the rule in this world that though you may have goose, it is never pure goose. In the most apparently Grade A ointment there is always a fly (EBC)

'She once tipped me half-a-crown.'
'You will generally find women loosen up less lavishly than men. It's something to do with the bone structure of the head. (UD)

Say what you like against civilisation, it comes in dashed handy in a crisis. It may be a purely artificial code that keeps a father from hoofing his daughter's kisser when they are both fellow-guests at a house, but at this moment I felt I could do with all the artificial codes that were going (TJ)

He is one of those men of whom one feels instinctively that they need a brazil nut in the topper; for while there is sterling stuff in them, it requires some sudden shock to bring it out (CT)

Average adjustors are like chartered accountants. When they love, they give their hearts forever (LEO)

occiput, the: the normal target for the stuffed epidermis of the soft-finned osseous fish *anguilis* (very well, eelskin) with which fate waits round the corner, especially on those days when all seems for the best in the best of all possible worlds (*passim*)

odalisques: not aunts, find a watery grave in Turkey (CW)

off-colour: see **oiled**

Ogpu, the: prepare to search Stiffy Byng's bedroom (CW)

'Oh, look!': Madeline Bassett is a confirmed Oh-looker. Bertie reports that at Cannes she called his attention in this way to a French actress, a Provençal filling-station, the sunset over the Estorels, Michael Arlen, a man selling coloured spectacles, the deep velvet blue of the Mediterranean and the last Mayor of New York in a striped one-piece bathing suit (RHJ)

oiled: see **ossified**

Old Austinians R.F.C.: devotees of the Wodehouse school stories find a stimulating example of the Master's readiness to make a cockshy of every sacred cow in the world—even, in this case, in the Sporting Calendar. His own devotion to Rugby football is patent to everyone who has read PF, and his descriptions of rugger matches in the school novels have hardly been bettered. The burlesque version in VGJ came nearly thirty years later, its effect being heightened by the fact that to Bertie, as narrator, the game is incomprehensible since rugger is not played at Eton. The match, too, is the annual blood-bath between two rival Hampshire villages, than which there is no whicher. Tuppy Glossop, burgeoning with hopes of glory under the eyes of his idol-of-the-moment, is ill-advised enough to wear his Old Austinian colours, a translucent light blue picked out with bold transverse orange stripes:

> Tuppy wiped a fair portion of Hampshire out of his eye, peered round in a dazed kind of way, saw the mass meeting and ran towards it, arriving just in time for a couple of heavy-

weights to gather him in and give him the mud-treatment again. This placed him in an admirable position for a third heavyweight to kick him in the ribs with a boot like a violin-case. The red-haired man then fell on him. It was all good brisk play and looked fine from my side of the ropes. I saw now where Tuppy had made his mistake. On such occasions it is best not to be too conspicuous, and that blue and orange shirt rather caught the eye. A sober beige was what his best friends would have recommended. (VGJ)

As an after-thought on club colours, what are the Drones? When Bingo Little, lunching Valerie Twistleton at Mario's, is humiliated by the public arrival of his former Nannie, bringing him his woollen comforter in the Drones Club colours, it would be instructive to know just what those colours are. Something, perhaps, on the lines of the 'Balmoral tartan' evolved for Queen Victoria, with a lavender base tastefully augmented with stripes in orange, heliotrope and carmine?

Old Battling Daphne: see **Winkworth, Dame Daphne, D.B.E.** (MS, JO)

Old Dr Gordon's Bile Magnesia: (Acts Like Magic and Imparts an Inward Glow); Bertie applies its psychological counterpart to Reggie Herring. The faithful will be mindful of its U.S. equivalent —Old Dr Murphy's Tonic Swamp Juice (JO)

Old Sureshot: England's Answer to Annie Oakley, visits the Drones and shows what can be done with a catapult and a brazil nut (CT)

Old Vic, the: London S.E. Bertie Wooster, under amital duress, conveys young Thos. thither on several occasions, to attend stimulating performances of *King Lear* and the Russian tragedies (*passim*)

Old Wrykinians: most former alumni of the famous school flourish outside the Wooster scene (the cricketing Jacksons, Corky Corcoran and the egregious Ukridge are among them) but J. G. (Looney) Coote represents them at the Drones

Orators Corner: Hyde Park, W., is the mise for the public exposure of Lord Bittlesham and Bertie by Bingo Little, filibustering from the rostrum of the Heralds of the Red Dawn (IJ) as well as for the pulling off of some good, ripe stuff by Meadowes, Archie Mulliner's valet, speaking for the League for the Dawn of Freedom at the third soap-box from the left as you enter by the Marble Arch gate (YMS)

ossified: see pie-eyed

Othello: his press notices usually encompass travellers tales (antres vast, Anthropophagi etc.) or illustrate an apogee of the green-eyed. Stilton Cheesewright is 'a chap who could give Othello a couple of bisques and be dormy one at the eighteenth' (JM, *passim*)

P

Paddington Station, W.2.: as point of departure for Market Snodsbury, Market Blandings and the coloured names of so many West Midland villages, Paddington's antres vast are a treasure-house of memories. It is painted (with some lingering justification even today) as a stronghold of the old leisured order as compared, e.g., with Waterloo, q.v. Many of its pleasing inspirations are found in the Blandings saga, but Rosie and Bingo have leading parts in one. Bingo is facing a critical reunion with his wife, who is bringing her aged mother back to town from Droitwich. Bingo has blued the ten-pound note sent to him with instructions to open a wee bank account for Algernon Aubrey, and Rosie's return leaves him no time to make up the deficit. It is therefore with delight that, on her arrival, he hears her say:

> 'I've got to take Mother to the flat. She's not at all well.'
> 'No, I noticed she seemed to be looking a bit down among the wines and spirits,' said Bingo, casting a gratified glance at the old object, who was now propping herself up against a passing porter.

Which gives Bingo the necessary ten minutes in which to collect fifty pounds from (of all people) an Oofy Prosser stirred up by gratitude for having been saved from the consequences of matrimony (EBC *et al.*)

Palladium, the London: Bingo enjoys the show *Cuddle Up* at, (IJ)

Parker, Jane: loses her amateur status in the Girls Egg and Spoon Race at Twing School Treat (IJ)

Parker, Julia: not normally moved to poetic metaphor, the enraptured Pongo Twistleton describes her as a pippin of about 19 with large lustrous eyes and a face like a dewy rosebud seen at daybreak on a June morning. She is for him the sole, and temporary, mitigating factor in the ordeal he suffers in **'Uncle Fred Flits By'** (YMS)

'Parnassus': an *avant garde* publication for which Percy Gorringe dashes off a little thing in the modern idiom called *Caliban at Sunset* (JFS)

'Patience': Bertie, cajoled into taking Thos. to see Gilbert and Sullivan opera, thinks it not a bad little show, though a bit high-brow (SLJ)

Patterson, Sam: writes a novelette, three short stories and 10,000 words of a magazine serial, every month (MJ)

Peabody & Simms: defying Jeeves's judgment, the young master orders six soft silk evening shirts from, (COJ)

Peasmarsh: family name of the Earl of Bodsham, q.v. (NS)

Peasmarsh, Lady Mavis: Lord Bodsham's attractive daughter, defers to the prior claims of a lady in a pink negligée picked out with ultramarine lovebirds, and returns Freddie Widgeon to store (NS)

Peasmarsh, the Hon. Wilfred: y.s. of Lord Bodsham and a discerning critic of headgear (NS)

Peckham, the Most Hon. the Marquess of: a prominent member of that exclusive coterie, the Twelve Jolly Stretcher Cases (EBC)

Pen and Ink Club, the: meets at the Lotus Rooms, Knightsbridge, a barrack-like building which seems to exist only for these sad affairs (*passim*)

Pendlebury, Gwladys: a Chelsea artist who, driving her Widgeon Seven at 60 m.p.h. through the Park (speed limit 10 m.p.h.) impresses the susceptible heart of B. W. Wooster. The younger male reader is earnestly advised to consult Aunt Dahlia (in **Obiter Dicta**) on the perils latent in certain Christian names, Gwladys heads the list (VGJ)

Pendlebury-Davenport: family name of his Grace the Duke of Dunstable

Pendlebury-Davenport, Horace: nephew and heir pres. to the Duke of Dunstable, q.v., Res. Bloxham Mansions, Park Lane W. This engaging Drone looks like a meridian of longitude, and was probably the thinnest Zulu ever to appear in full war paint in Marlborough St. police court. On seeing him approach, Euclid might nudge a friend and indicate that here was an example of his definition of a straight line as having length but no thickness. Like his fellow Drones, Pongo Twistleton and Freddie Widgeon, suffers sorely from uncles. Is the Club darts champion. He m. Valerie Twistleton, q.v. (UFS *et al.*)

Penworthy, Mrs: village students of form consider her a cinch for the Mothers Sack Race at Twing School Treat (IJ)

Percival: resident porker at Miss Mapleton's Academy for Young Ladies. Prudence Carroway transfixes him through the ear with an arrow after setting fire to the school (YMS)

Perkins: cook at Chuffnell Hall, provides a black-faced Wooster with a repast which he rapidly converts into four skeletonised kippers and an empty toast-rack (TJ)

Perkins, George: betrothed to the billowy blonde who leaps into Freddie Widgeon's life and two-seater at Bramley-on-Sea (NS)

Perkins, Honest Patch: a 9th Earl is transformed into, with walrus moustache and patch on left eye (see **Rowcester, Earl of**):

> 'Back your fancy and fear nothing, my noble sportsmen,' he said. 'Walk up. Walk up. Roll, bowl or pitch. Ladies halfway and no bad nuts returned,' he said. So I put my double on him (RJ)

Perkins' Digestine: Maudie Wilberforce's preferred emollient in all matters touching the lining of the stomach (VGJ)

Pershore, Lord: e.s. and heir to the Marquess of Malvern, Motty is thin and meek looking. His chin has given up the struggle and he has no eyelashes. But these are merely the concomitants of his enforcedly sheltered life in a Shropshire village. Delivered into

Bertie's care in New York, he makes up for the lost years with the best of them. The sole glimpse of him which Bertie catches in the ensuing weeks is when he flies gracefully through the air from the door of a night club (MJ)

Petherick-Soames, Major-General Sir Masterman: the euphonious brasshat holds conservative ideas about the reputations of the younger ladies of his family and, befitting his profession, is a believer in direct action. He horsewhips Capt. Walkinshaw on the steps of the Drones Club for trifling with the affections of his niece Hester, horsewhips Rupert Blenkinsop-Bustard on the steps of the Junior Bird Fanciers for slighting the affections of his niece Gertrude, and has a few stern words with a Mulliner:

'By the way, what is your club?'
'The United Jade Collectors,' quavered Osbert.
'Has it steps?'
'I—I believe so.'
'Good. Good.' A dreamy look came into the General's eyes. 'Well, the announcement of your engagement to my niece Mabel will appear in tomorrow's *Morning Post*. If it is contradicted . . . well, good morning, Mr Mulliner, good morning.'

Petite, Pauline: heart-shattering and world renowned film star. idol of Freddie Threepwood and heroine of such epics as *Passion's Slaves, Silken Fetters, Purple Passion, Bonds of Gold, Seduction*, and other masterpieces of which Clarence, 9th Earl of Emsworth, has never heard (BCE)

Philibert, George: of 32 Acacia Rd., Cricklewood, tries to remove himself from a bright and breezy world (BCE)

pie-eyed: see **plastered**

Piggott, Lester: rides Escalator in the Derby (RJ)

Piggott, Mrs Mary Jane: Lord Rowcester's gifted cook, who contrasts so favourably with her pigtailed counterpart at Wyvern Hall (RJ)

Pikelet, Charles ('Charles Always Pays'): on one occasion does not. Wheeling his infant daughter in the Park, he is accosted by his client Bingo Little who, on taking a quick look into the perambulator, winces like one who has seen some fearful sight, but politely avers that Arabella is almost pretty, compared with the contents of his own pram, Algernon Aubrey. Charlie offers odds of 5/1 against such a slander and a passing constable is called on to adjudicate:

Just as the policeman stood vacillating, there peeped through the clouds a ray of sunshine. It fell on Arabella's face, causing her to screw it up in a hideous grimace. And at the same instant, with the race neck and neck, she suddenly started blowing bubbles out of the corner of her mouth. The judge took Miss Pikelet's hand and raised it. 'The winnah!' he said. 'But you ought to see the one I've got at home!' (EBC)

Pim, Lucius: Chelsea artist, victim of Gwladys Pendlebury's charms and driving habits, elects to spend his convalescence *chez* Wooster (VGJ)

Pinker, the Rev. Harold (Stinker): kindly if muscular Christian, is one of the finest of the Master's long series of splendid men of God. At Magdalen with Bertie, he got a Rugger Blue and was capped for England; also boxed for Oxford. Now has a cure of souls at Totleigh-in-the-Wold, Glos, and is devoted, and secretly engaged, to Stephanie Byng, the ward of Totleigh's squire, Sir Watkyn Bassett, and owner of the saurian-toothed, Gaelic-speaking Aberdeen, Bartholomew. Urged on by the unprincipled Stiffy, he reluctantly pinches the local constable's helmet, and in a brief but homeric contest, metes out justice to the gorilla Spode. Persistently deprived of parochial preferment by the intransigent Bassett, he owes to Jeeves's kindly intervention the gift of the neighbouring living of Hockley-cum-Meston which, we like to think, he now invests with otium-cum-dig, or cum as much dig as is likely in a vicarage shared by the effervescent Stiffy (SLJ, CW, JFS)

Pinfold, Lady: relict of Sir Ramsworthy Pinfold, the period of her sentence, as prospective mother-in-law to B. Wooster, is the normal couple of days (LEO)

Pinfold, Dora: a virulent do-gooder, is selected by Lord Bliecester as bride for Freddie Widgeon. Unlike Bertie, Freddie needs no help from the master-mind in eluding the matrimonial trap. He is inevitably returned to circulation by his own unaided efforts (LEO)

pipterino, a: origin obscure, but perhaps a grandiose form of slang exp. pippin. An object or person excelling in relation to its (but more usually her) species. cf. Freddie Threepwood's forebodings that a fifth telegram from his bride may be an absolute, since even her fourth was good, juicy stuff; for the human variety see e.g. Daphne Dolores Morehead (*passim*)

Pitt-Waley, Mr: one of the very few East Anglican characters, flits fleetingly across the scene as Bertie's host at a shooting party in Norfolk (IJ)

plastered: see **polluted**

Platt, Rhoda: of Wistaria Lodge, Kitchener Rd., East Dulwich, S.E., a waitress at his club, is ardently wooed by Lord Yaxley, q.v., Bertie's elderly uncle. The young master is despatched by Aunt Agatha to buy her off, but Jeeves arranges matters more equitably (VGJ)

Plimsoll, Eustace H.: would live at the Laburnums, Alleyn Road, West Dulwich, S.E., were he not a timely figment of Bertie Wooster's imagination in the police dock on the morning after the Boat Race. But how did Bertie dream up the apposite 'Alleyn'? (TJ)

Pliny the Younger: the inspired words of, are consigned to a simian larder, with the nuts, by Bill Rowcester.(RJ)

Plomer, the Rev. William: Vicar of Market Snodsbury, Worcs, strains a fetlock and cancels his fixture to present the prizes at the town's grammar school. Gussie Fink-Nottle steps into the breach with resounding results (RHJ)

Poe, Edgar Allan: (1809-1849) is cited in instances stimulating terror:

> In his works it was always tough going for those who stayed in country houses, the visitor being likely at any moment to encounter a walking corpse in a winding sheet with blood all over it (JO)

Elsewhere (CW) his maxim that 'what is obvious is easily overlooked' is cited as a solution for the problem of finding a hiding place for a purloined cow creamer (*passim*)

polluted: see **primed**

Pomeroy: an undignified fate (lightly glossed over in the annals) overtakes this stately butler (resembling a saintly Anglican bishop) to Tom and Dahlia Travers. He finds himself venially exchanged with the Bassington-Copes for an oviform silver chocolate-pot on three scroll feet (CW)

Popjoy, P.c.: tireless guardian of the Queen's lieges at Lower Smattering-on-the-Wissel, Worcs, is unexpectedly beaned by a Russian nuclear missile in the course of its orbit and his duty (FO)

Pott, Claude (Mustard): a stout, bald, round, pursy little man of about fifty who might have been taken for a Silver Ring bookie or a minor Shakespearian actor and who has, in fact, been both in his time. Befriended by Lord Ickenham, he founds a private-eye business and soon finds himself unknowingly shadowing his benefactor's niece Valerie at the behest of her fiancé, Horace Davenport. It is as a club guest at the Drones that Mustard is able to display his full range of talents. The members have just returned from their annual weekend at Le Touquet, where the dingy gods who preside over the chemin-de-fer tables have been extraordinarily kind. When Mustard organises a Clothes Stakes for all comers the response is gratifying and so (for Mustard) are the rewards. But this is before he mistakenly sits down to teach the Duke of Dunstable the simple game of Persian Monarchs (UFS)

Potter-Pirbright, Cora (Corky): Hollywood film star better known to millions as Cora Starr, is a lissom girl constructed on the lines of Gertrude Lawrence, the general effect being that of an angel who eats lots of yeast. If you were called upon to pick something to be cast away on a desert island with, Hedy Lamarr might be your first choice, but Corky would be high in the list of hon. mentions. Bertie tells us that she habitually wears gowns of some clinging stuff which accentuates rather than hides her graceful outline if we see what he means. Sharing with her brother Catsmeat much of the talent of their famous mother, Corky is endowed also with a species of built-in super-charger mechanism, impelling her to step high, wide and handsome in the well-known Bobbie-Stiffy-Terry-Nobby manner:

> Though differing from my Aunt Agatha in almost every possible respect, Corky has this in common with that outstanding scourge, she is authoritative. When she wants you to do a thing, you find yourself doing it. This has been so from her earliest years. I remember her, at our mutual dancing class handing me an antique orange, a blue and yellow mass of pips and mildew, and bidding me bung it at our instructress ... I did it without a murmur, though knowing full well how bitter the reckoning would be.

A girl of spirit and discernment may demand certain qualities from the man she wants to marry. Corky steadfastly refuses to wed the eligible Esmond Haddock, squire of King's Deverill, until he puts his house in order by dealing summarily with the surging sea of aunts who infest his home (MS, et al.)

Potter-Pirbright, Claude Cattermole (Catsmeat): 'brilliant but unsound' was the verdict of the Rev. Aubrey Upjohn in one of Catsmeat's prep school reports, and Bertie is ready to confirm the verdict after an interval of fifteen years:

If ever a headmaster with a face like a cassowary rang the bell and entitled himself to receive a cigar or a coconut, this headmaster was that headmaster. And if in walking about London one comes upon one of those bent, haggard figures who look as if they have recently been caught up in some powerful machinery, they are probably those fellows who got mixed up with Catsmeat when he was meaning well.

Catsmeat is a West End actor of considerable talent. By common consent and despite Oofy Prosser's shoes by Lobb, he is regarded as a modern Brummel and the *Arbiter Elegantiae* of the Drones, and he is the obvious first choice as producer of the annual Club smoker (UFS, *et al.*)

Potter-Pirbright, the Rev. Sidney: tall but drooping, and looking as if he had been stuffed by an inexperienced taxidermist, the Vicar of King's Deverill, Hants, earns much sympathy. Already plagued by the atheistical village rozzer (ever ready to jump out from some gateway with awkward questions as to where Cain got his wife, and what price Jonah and the Whale) the good man is called on to act as host to Gussie Fink-Nottle, to his incandescent niece Corky and her odiferous castaway from the Battersea Dogs Home and, in the event, to Thos. Spenser Gregson. It is not surprising that, on seeing the latter in his midst, the good man looks as if he were on the point of saying some of the things he gave up saying when he took Orders (MS)

Prenderby, Sir Mortimer, Bart.: of the *ferae naturae* which Freddie Widgeon discovers infesting Matcham Scratchings, the Prenderbys' home in Oxfordshire, Sir Mortimer is perhaps the third fiercest specimen, ranking below Wilhelm the cat-eating wolfhound and the Pekinese puppy which ejects Wilhelm from Freddie's bedroom. The Bart's natural talents are stimulated, though, by his accidentally receiving (at Freddie's hands) a tortoiseshell cat in the back of the neck (YMS)

Prenderby, Lady: tall, rangy, Tudoresque type with blancmange eyes (YMS)

Prenderby, Dahlia: is fleetingly impressed by Freddie Widgeon's talents, but has a fixation (probably pre-natal) for her mother's private zoo (YMS)

primed to the sticking point: see scrooched

Pringle, Professor: in the urgent interests of the imprisoned Oliver Sipperly, Bertie agrees to impersonate him on a visit to the Pringle menage, a mile or two out of Cambridge on the Trumpington Road. The Prof. is thinnish, baldish and dyspeptic, with an eye like a haddock (COJ)

Pringle, Mrs: has the aspect of one who had bad news about the year 1900 and has never really got over it (COJ)

Pringle, Mrs (Sen.): one of a couple of elderly females with shawls all over them:

> 'No doubt you remember my mother?' said Professor Pringle mournfully, indicating Exhibit A (COJ)

Pringle, Miss Jane: 'And my aunt,' sighed the Prof., as if things were getting worse and worse. The whole strength of the company gazed at me like a family group out of one of Edgar Allan Poe's less cheery yarns.

'I remember Oliver,' said Exhibit A. She heaved a sigh.

'He was such a pretty child. What a pity! What a pity!'

Tactful, of course, and calculated to put the guest completely at his ease.

'I remember Oliver,' said Exhibit B, looking at me in much the same way as the Bosher St. beak had looked at Sippy before putting on the black cap. 'Nasty little boy! He teased my cat.'

'Aunt Jane's memory is wonderful, considering that she will be eighty-seven next birthday,' whispered Mrs Pringle with mournful pride.

'What did you say?' asked the Exhibit suspiciously.

'I said your memory was wonderful.'

'Ah!' the dear old creature gave me another glare. 'He chased my Tibby all over the garden, shooting arrows at her from a bow.'

At this moment a cat strolled out from under the sofa and made for me with its tail up. Cats always do take to me, which made it all the sadder that I should be saddled with Sippy's criminal record. I stooped to tickle it under the ear, and the Exhibit uttered a piercing cry.

'Stop him! Stop him!'

She leaped forward, moving uncommonly well for one of her years, and having scooped up the cat, stood eyeing me with bitter defiance, as if daring me to start anything. Most unpleasant. And conversation was at a low ebb when the door opened and a girl came in.

'My daughter Heloise,' said the Prof. moodily, as if he hated to admit it. (COJ)

Pringle, Heloise:

I suppose everybody has had the experience of suddenly meeting somebody who reminded them frightfully of some fearful person. Heloise Pringle, in the most ghastly way, resembled Honoria Glossop. And her voice put the lid on it. I backed away convulsively and sprang into the air as my foot stubbed itself against something squashy. A sharp yowl rent the air, followed by an indignant cry, and I turned to see Aunt Jane, on all fours, trying to put things right with the cat, which had gone to earth under the sofa.

As Jeeves later reveals, Heloise and Honoria are first cousins. Mrs Pringle, née Blatherwick, is Lady Glossop's younger sister. For the sickening denouement, see **Aunts** (COJ)

Pringle, Muriel: one of those drips who hope to qualify as wifie's best friend because they don't miss much. When the husband under review is Bingo Little, such snoops have hardly a dull moment (EBC)

Prosser, Alexander (Oofy): of tight-wads, the annals are generous in their examples. Many noblemen (Lord Blicester is one) raise large colonies of moths in their wallets. Others, like the Duke of Chiswick (who owns half London and several northern counties) complain bitterly about the price of taxis. The Drones point with justifiable pride to Oofy. He is not prepossessing; there is general agreement that he has more pimples than most men would want to be seen about with. Bertie believes he has bequeathed the collection to the nation. He is also considered to be the nearest thing to a piece of cheese yet produced by the human race. But he is the Club's wealthiest property and has the stuff in stacks; therefore he is, like Pooh Bah, ever on the look-out for the stray halfpenny lying in the gutter:

We said earlier that he did not need the cash, but it was we who said it, not Oofy. His views on the matter were sharply divergent. Whenever there was cash around, he wanted to get it. It was well said of him at the Drones that despite his revolting wealth he would always walk ten miles in tight boots to pick up twopence. Many put the figure even lower (FO)

In his efforts to grind the faces of the poor, Oofy's reverses have been many and hilarious. He is now (IB) married to Myra Shoesmith, daughter of Freddie Widgeon's last employer and a girl of considerable but extremely severe beauty. As an exponent of the one-way pocket system, Oofy's day, we feel, is over (*passim*)

Prosser, the late Hildebrand: senior uncle of the Drones Club plutocrat, d. of apoplexy, 1947 (FO)

Prosser, Horace: displaces even Lord Blicester as favourite for the Fat Uncles Sweepstake:

> an elderly man in a bathing suit, so rotund, so obese, so bulging in every direction, that Shakespeare, had he beheld him, would have muttered to himself 'Upon what meat doth this our Horace feed that he is grown so great?' One wondered how any bathing suit built by human hands could contain so stupendous an amount of uncle without parting at the seams (FO)

Prosser, the late Stanley: junior uncle of Oofy Prosser, died of cirrhosis of the liver, 1949 (FO)

Psmith, Rupert Eustace Ronald: The 'Ronald' was a late addition of the author's—a substitution, rather—for Rupert. An autobiographical note may be permissible here. I was fortunate enough to read the Mike-and-Psmith books at school. Thirty years went by before I re-read **LEAVE IT TO PSMITH,** when it occurred to me that 'Ronald' struck a strange note. From the mists of school memories I roused a pungent phrase of Psmith's father: 'I fear for my Rupert among these wild undergraduates'. So, on preparing the complete concordance, I wrote to consult the Master himself. Replying from Long Island (May 18, 1958) he noted:

> Psmith. I remember what happened there. I called Baxter in Ch. 1 Rupert Baxter and when I got to that scene where Psmith tells Eve his name I felt it was a question of either going right back through the book and changing Baxter's name—which I didn't want to do, as Rupert Baxter seemed so right—or assuming that nobody would remember 'Mike' and giving Psmith another name. I think Rupert Eustace Ronald Psmith would be okay!

His membership of four London clubs (two more to follow shortly) for which he was put down in the moneyed days, are about all Psmith's assets on his father's death. The happy accident that the

Drones is one of those clubs is the reason for his inclusion here, since his bright particular star has its own separate and brilliant orbit. To the Drones, indeed, he has cause to be grateful for the accident of his meeting with Eve Halliday. The *point d'appui* is the best umbrella the Drones cloakroom can provide. It belongs to the Hon. Hugo Walderwick (LIP)

Pulbrook, Eustacia: announcing her violin solo, the Vicar conveys the impression that while he knows as well as the audience that she will be as corny as they come, they had better make the most of her, as after that they will have the Kegley-Bassington gang at their throats (MS)

Punter, Lady: of Berkeley Square, W., m. of Diana, understandably retires to bed with a digestive tablet, a sex novel and (presumably) the *obbligato* of the Square nightingale (YMS)

Punter, Diana: is that half of the crosstalk act in Bruton Street which makes grooves in the pavement with her heel (N.B.: we have verified the grooves—*Ed.*) (YMS)

Punting, Willie: a non-starter in the Choirboys Bicycle Race won by Bertie Wooster at the age of 14 (RHJ)

Purvis: odds-on starter in the Jobs-We-Don't-Envy Stakes, is butler to Agatha Spenser Gregson at Woollam Chersey, Herts (VGJ)

Purvis, Miss: school-teacher at Lower Smattering-on-the-Wissel (FO)

Purvis, Annabel: charming assistant to the illusionist, the Great Boloni, enchants Freddie Fitch-Fitch of the Drones, who worships the very rabbits she lifts from the Boloni top-hat (EBC)

Purvis, P. K.: of Market Snodsbury Grammar School, steps up to the Speech Day platform to receive his prize for spelling and dictation at the hands of Gussie Fink-Nottle; about three foot six in his squeaking shoes, he has a pink face and sandy hair:

> Gussie patted his hair. He seemed to have taken an immediate fancy to the lad.
> 'You P. K. Purvis?'
> 'Sir, yes, sir.'
> 'It's a beautiful world, P. K. Purvis.'
> 'Sir, yes, sir.'
> 'Ah, you've noticed it, have you? Good. You married, by any chance?'

'Sir, no, sir.'

'Get married, P. K. Purvis,' said Gussie earnestly. 'It's the only life . . . Well, here's your book. Looks rather bilge to me, from a glance at the title page, but, such as it is, here you are.'

P. K. Purvis squeaked off amidst sporadic applause, but one couldn't fail to note that the sporadic was followed by a rather strained silence. It was evident that Gussie was striking something of a new note in Market Snodsbury scholastic circles. Looks were exchanged between parent and parent. The bearded bloke had the air of one who has drained the bitter cup. As for Aunt Dahlia, her demeanour now told only too clearly that her last doubts had been resolved and her verdict was in. I saw her whisper to the Bassett, who sat on her right, and the Bassett nodded sadly and looked like a fairy about to shed a tear and add another star to the Milky Way (RHJ)

Purvis, the late Rupert: Annabel tells the infatuated Sir Aylmer Bastable that her father was a colonel. She does not add that his regiment was the Salvation Army, or that before getting his commission he was a Silver Ring bookie known widely as Ratface Rupert the Bermondsey Twister (EBC)

Pyke, Laura: if Rosie M. Little could be said to harbour one small failing (which Bingo, one feels, would warmly deny) it is her odd disposition to kow-tow to authoritative females such as former nannies or, in this case, the Old School Chum. An unexpected trait in one so versed in the matter of retaining the love of one's husband-baby; one foredoomed to failure, too, as if the invader is not jostled out of place at the Canal Turn of Rosie's disillusionment, she comes a complete purler at the Becher's Brook of Jeeves' suave diplomacy (VGJ)

Pytchley Hunt, the: patronised in hot youth, and even hotter middle-age, by Dahlia Wooster (now Travers). Chivvying the fox in all weathers has left her face brick-red and has lent amazing power to her voice and vocabulary. Seasoned followers of the Hunt have been known to leap convulsively in their saddles at her comments, even when heard across a couple of ploughed fields and a spinney (*passim*)

Q

'Q' ... and 'X': see 'X' ... and 'Q' (YMS)

Queen Boadicea: (Boudicca, fl. c. A.D. 50) Queen of the Iceni;
unaccountably wears a ruff at the Wembley Exhibition (COJ) but
is usually a prototype of tough and potentially powerful femininity,
esp. on the regal plane and in association with dominion over palm
and pine. See particularly those ladies whose tents on shikar (or
safari) whether erected on the pampas, the steppes, the Deccan,
the tundra, the prairie, the desert, the high or low veldt or in the
Australian outback, are invariably a rendezvous for lonely wilde-
beeste, rhinos, lions, boa constrictors and other wildfowl. The
unfortunate animals rarely emerge undamaged. Boadicea is
impersonated by Agatha Spenser Gregson (RHJ) at a village
pageant, and probably was never portrayed more faithfully (*passim*)

Queen Cleopatra: (60-30 B.C.) Queen of Egypt: performs ju-jitsu
with a snake at Wembley (COJ); would not have liked Gussie Fink-
Nottle (RHJ); usually as an apogee of the languorously sensuous.
Her classic entry is outside the saga, when the exotic Gloria Salt,
entering Mario's Restaurant, looks so like a Serpent of Old Nile
that a nervous host might be excused for wondering whether to
offer her a cocktail or an asp (*passim*)

Queen Elizabeth I: (1533-1603); must, in Bertie's view, have been
something like Aunt Agatha (COJ); Catsmeat Potter-Pirbright
points out (MS) that the stiffish nymphery of maiden aunts sur-
rounding the object of his devotion at King's Deverill would be at
one with Queen Elizabeth in classing actors as rogues and vaga-
bonds (*passim*)

Queen Elizabeth: (H.M. Queen Elizabeth the Queen Mother);
Her Majesty, as Queen Consort, is implicitly depicted as handling
with royal tact an incident at a Buckingham Palace banquet when
an Irish guest, surmising that soup is all, consumes four or five
helpings:

> 'Perhaps,' said Gussie, 'you can explain what their social
> position is, for it is frankly beyond me. Pat, for instance,
> appears to move in the very highest circles, for he describes
> himself as dining at Buckingham Palace, and yet his wife
> takes in lodgers. Is it credible that a man of his class would be
> invited to dinner at Buckingham Palace, especially since he is

apparently completely without social *savoir-faire?* He relates how the Queen asked him if he would like some mulligatawny and he, thinking that there was nothing else coming, had six helpings with the result that, to quote his words, he spent the rest of the evening sitting in a corner full of soup' (MS)

Queen Gruoch (fl. 1050); 'Lady Macbeth', Queen Consort of Scotland; an archetype of all that is bloody, bold and resolute in the female of the species. Her readiness in dealing with a crisis, her firmness and executive ability, and her surpassing talents as a hostess are touched upon, together with her sporadic curiosity for the latest information from the spare room. Nobby, e.g., comes leaping towards Bertie like Lady Macbeth coming to get first-hand news from the guest-room (*passim*) [Hist. Queen Gruoch nighean Bode, in whose right of succession her husband the Mormaer of Moray claimed the Sc. throne in 1040—*Ed.*]

Queen Guinevere: usually (like Caesar *vis-à-vis* Brutus) as connotation of reproach when faced by King Arthur (*passim*)

Queen Jezebel:

> 'Eaten by dogs, wasn't she?'
> 'Yes, sir.'
> 'Can't have been pleasant for her.'
> 'No, sir.'
> 'Still, that's the way the ball rolls' (JO)

Queen Mary I: (r. 1553-9): in contexts of the well-known chagrin. Bill Rowcester feels his own heart is as deeply engraved as that of, with the words, in his own case, 'Three thousand and five pounds, two and six' (RJ, *et al.*)

Queen of Sheba, the: frequently perceives (as, e.g., on beholding the 9th Earl of Emsworth in LEO) that the half was not told unto her. Catsmeat Pirbright confesses to similar reactions on coming face to face with Charlie Silversmith:

> 'If it hadn't been for Queenie buoying me up with a quick cooking sherry I might have swooned in my tracks' (MS)

Queen Victoria: (1819-1901) the Good and Great makes few appearances:

> what counts with these old-style females who have lived in the country all their lives is the exhibition of those little politenesses which were all the go in the reign of, (YMS)

Queenie: lovable and charming, as are almost all Wodehouse's female domestics, she is parlourmaid at Deverill Hall—a testing ordeal for any girl with human limitations; is affianced to the atheistic P.c. Dobbs, but finds time to administer general comfort to Catsmeat Pirbright (MS)

Quintin, Dante Gabriel: next-door neighbour to the Bingo Littles in Magnolia Road, St. John's Wood, takes strong exception to his water barrel's conversion into a refuge for escapees from a raided gambling den (FO)

Quorn Hunt, the: ranks equally with the Pytchley in Aunt Dahlia's affections, and has likewise had its formative influence upon her voice and vocabulary. Students of venery, despite deep research as to whether her richer expletives are traceable to the one Hunt or the other, have confessed themselves foxed. It would seem though that neither can vie, in one sentimental particular in Aunt Dahlia's memory, with the York and Ainsty, q.v. (*passim*)

R

Racing Intelligence

ONE LIKES TO KEEP *AU COURANT* IN THESE MATTERS, SIR. IT IS, ONE MIGHT SAY, AN ESSENTIAL PART OF ONE'S EDUCATION (RJ)

ALEXANDRA PARK: Bingo Little has a hot tip for (IJ); Freddie Widgeon meets misfortune with Marmalade at (YMS); Bingo shows a mistaken confidence in Sarsaparilla at (NS)

ASCOT: Jeeves has a most agreeable, and wins quite a satisfactory sum, thank you, sir (RHJ); Monty Bodkin, as a schoolboy, cleans up on the Gold Cup to the extent of eleven bob plus a bag of bananas, two strawberry ice-creams and a three-cornered Cape of Good Hope stamp

CATTERICK BRIDGE: Bingo buys Rosie a diamond brooch as the result of an inspired speculation at (EBC)

CAMBRIDGESHIRE, THE: Dahlia Wooster marries Tom Travers (under an archway of hunting horns?) the year Bluebottle wins (VGJ)

CESAREWITCH, THE: Shining Light disqualified for boring (RHJ); Monty Bodkin urged to put his shirt on Whistling Rufus

DERBY, THE: Rory Carmoyle fancies Oratory for (RJ); Escalator, ridden by Lester Piggott, later commends itself to Rory (RJ); Bill Rowcester hears about the Irish horse Ballymore, which has been kept as dark as a moonless night has but twice secretly broken the record for the course (RJ); Rory avers that you can't go by Guineas form in, as there are too many outsiders (RJ); in a photo-finish for the first time, in the history of the classic, Moke the Second wins from Ballymore with Escalator third (RJ)

DONCASTER: Lord Rowcester, turning bookmaker, amasses £420 at, only to lose £3,000 at the Oaks (RJ)

EPSOM: Bwana Biggar doubles Lucy Glitters with Whistler's Mother at, winning £3,000, but Honest Patch Perkins belies his name and welshes (RJ)

GATWICK: Bingo fancies Pink Pill at, (IJ)

GOODWOOD CUP: Bingo advises Bertie to put his last dollar on Lord Bittlesham's Ocean Breeze for the (IJ)

GRAND NATIONAL STEEPLECHASE: Jack Guffington finishes third in the (YMS) Bingo finishes the jumping season on the right side (IJ)

GUINEAS, THE: Taj Mahal, in Rory Carmoyle's view, is the only horse running (RJ)

HAYDOCK PARK: Bingo slaps his ten on Hot Potato at (FO); Bingo comes unstitched at (IJ); Bingo dreams that he sees his Uncle Willoughby dancing a rumba in the nude on the steps of the National Liberal Club, and consequently loses his all on Bounding Beauty (EBC)

HURST PARK: Claude Wooster goes to, prudently wearing whiskers (IJ); Bingo has a snip for the two o'clock at (EBC); Pongo Twistleton comes unstuck at (COJ); Bingo is lucky at (COJ)

JUBILEE CUP, THE: Looney Coote collects £500 on Crazy Jane, a week after his Aunt Jane is certified

KEMPTON PARK: Looney Coote cleans up £750 on Stolen Goods the day after his car is stolen; Emerald Stoker loses her chemise and foundation garments on Sunny Jim (sixth in a field of seven) and takes a job as cook (SLJ)

LEWES: Bingo likes Musk Rat for the one-thirty at (IJ)

LAKENHAM: The Bingo Littles are luncheonless at, and forgo tea (VGJ)

LINCOLNSHIRE HANDICAP, THE: Pongo Twistleton comes a bit of a mucker at; Algy Wetherby cannot pay for his wedding breakfast as a result of,

NEWMARKET: Barmy Phipps loses his shirt at (CW); Lord Biskerton tries to touch his noble father for a tenner at,

NOVEMBER HANDICAP, THE: Yorkshire Pudding wins (VGJ)

OAKS, THE: Whistler's Mother wins at 33–1, bringing very different reactions to Bwana Biggar and the waiter at the Goose and Gherkin, who have both backed it (RJ)

PLUMPTON: Gargoyle fails to finish in the first six (EBC); Bounding Bertie wins the 2.30 at 100–8

PRIX HONORÉ SAUVAN: Oofy Prosser advises (naturally) Spotted Dog (EBC)

SANDOWN: Lord Biskerton has something pretty juicy for; Looney Coote fails to collect on My Valet, although his valet has just broken his leg.

The bookie pursed his lips. 'It's silly to be superstitious,' he said, 'but I can't help remembering that every single bloke that's ever done me down for money has had a nasty accident occur to him. Almost seems like some kind of fate. Only the other day there was a fellow with a ginger moustache, named Wotherspoon. Owed me fifty for Plumpton, and pleaded the Gaming Act. And would you believe it, less than a week later he was found unconscious in the street—must have got into unpleasantness of some kind—and had to have six stitches.'

'Six!' croaked Bingo.

'Seven. I was forgetting the one over his left eye. Makes you think, that sort of thing does. Hoy, Erbut,' he called.

A frightful plugugly appeared from nowhere, as if he had been a Djinn and the bookie had rubbed a lamp.

'Erbut,' said the bookie, 'I want you to meet Mr Little, Erbut. Take a good look at him. You'll remember him again?'

Erbut drank Bingo in. His eye was cold and grey, like a parrot's.
'Yus,' he said. 'Yus, I won't forget im.'
'Good,' said the bookie. 'That'll be all, Erbut. Then about that money, Mr Little, we'll say Friday without fail, shall we?' (EBC)

'Jeeves,' I said, for I am fond of the man and like to do him a good turn when I can, 'if you want to make a bit of money, have something on Wonderchild for the Lincolnshire.'
He shook his head. 'I'd rather not, sir.'
'But it's the straight goods. I'm going to put my shirt on him.'
'I do not recommend it, sir. The animal is not intended to win. Second place is what the stable is after.'
Perfect piffle, I thought, of course. Still, you know what happened. Wonderchild led till he was breathing on the wire, and then Banana Fritter came along and nosed him out. I went straight home and rang for Jeeves.
'After this,' I said, 'not another step for me without your advice. From now on consider yourself the brains of the establishment.'
'Very good, sir. I shall endeavour to give satisfaction.' (MJ)

I instructed Eustace to put a tenner on the Twing flier at current odds for each of the syndicate, and after lunch he rang me up to say he's done business at a snappy seven to one, the odds having lengthened owing to a rumour that the Rev. was subject to hay fever, and was taking big chances strolling in the paddock behind the Vicarage in the early mornings. And it was dashed lucky that we had managed to get the money on in time, for on the Sunday morning old Heppenstall fairly took the bit between his teeth, and gave us thirty-six solid minutes on Certain Popular Superstitions. I was sitting next to Steggles in the pew, and I saw him blench visibly (IJ)

'The Derby. Know anything, Jeeves?'
'I fear not, Sir Roderick. It would seem to be an exceptionally open contest. Monsieur Boussac's Voleur is, I understand, the favourite. Fifteen to two at last night's callover and the price likely to shorten to sixes or even fives for the S.P. But the animal is somewhat small and lightly boned for so gruelling an ordeal; though we have, to be sure, seen such a handicap overcome. The name of Manna, the 1925 winner, springs to the mind, and Hyperion, another smallish horse, broke the course record previously held by Flying Fox, accomplishing the distance in two minutes, thirty-four seconds.'

Rory regarded him with awe. 'By Jove, you know your stuff, don't you?' (RJ)

'If you were a married man, Bertie, you would be aware that the best of wives is apt to cut up rough if she finds that her husband has dropped six weeks housekeeping money on a single race. Isn't that so, Jeeves?'
'Yes, sir. Women are odd in that respect.' (VGJ)

Rainsby, the Viscount: 'Dogface' at the Drones; an earnest candidate for the Seekers Club when at Oxford (IJ)

Ramfurline, his Grace the Duke of: see **Lord Alastair Hungerford** (IJ)

Ranelagh, Lord Frederick: former employer of Jeeves, is swindled by Soapy Sid at Monte Carlo (IJ)

RIGHT HO, JEEVES: published in 1934, had been serialised in the *Saturday Evening Post* in December 1933, so clashing with the serialised **THANK YOU, JEEVES** in *The Cosmopolitan* which had delayed its publication for two years. The *Post* paid 40,000 dollars for RHJ and it was later published in book form in the U.S. as **BRINKLEY MANOR** (in all British versions the Travers ménage is **Brinkley Court**). Dedicated to 'Raymond Needham, K.C., with affection and admiration'. The novel is outstanding as containing the famous prizegiving sequence which must rank as one of the best passages of sustained humour in all literature. Its rivals, in the Wodehouse opus, would perhaps number **'Uncle Fred Flits By,' 'The Great Sermon Handicap,' 'The Amazing Hat Mystery'** and one or two Mulliner stories (RHJ)

RING FOR JEEVES: published 1953, appeared in the U.S. the following year as **THE RETURN OF JEEVES.** The story was adapted from a play by Guy Bolton called *Derby Day* (a title already used by Sir Alan Herbert for a well-known operetta). It is the only Jeeves story in which Bertie makes no personal appearance, and the only one in which Jeeves sinks his pride and becomes a butler and (an unusual improbability) a bookie's assistant (RJ)

Ripley: Oofy Prosser declines to communicate details of a miracle to the Believe-It-Or-Not expert (EBC)

Roberts, the Rev. J. J.: Vicar of the euphonious village of Fale-by-the-Water, Glos, receives 10 minutes in the Great Sermon Handicap (IJ)

Robinson: sagacious cloakroom attendant at the Drones, smoothly re-establishes the reputation of a famous hatter (YMS)

Rockmeteller, Cora Rita: causes a pukka sahib to exclaim 'Howki wa hoo!' (RJ)

Rockmeteller, Isabel: Rocky Todd's aunt, like Lochinvar, suddenly comes out of the Middle West, unbelievably bent on scattering goodness and light:

> 'I read a poem about a young man who had longed all his life for a certain thing and won it in the end only when he was too old to enjoy it. It was very sad and it touched me.'
> 'A thing,' interpolated Rocky bitterly, 'that I've not been able to do in ten years.' (MJ)

Rogers, Tuppy: one of several Drones cited as being likely to indulge in profane, ungentlemanly emphatics on learning that Bingo Little, in cold print, has been referred to by his wife as 'half god, half prattling, mischievous child' (COJ)

Rosherville Gardens, S.W.3.: see **Sir Stanley Gervase Gervase, Bart.** (COJ)

Rowbotham, Charlotte Corday: a Herald of the Red Dawn:

> There was too much of her. Billowy curves. And while she may have had a heart of gold, the first thing you noticed was that she had a tooth of gold. I know that when in form young Bingo could fall in love with practically anything, but this time I couldn't see any excuse for him at all (IJ)

Rowcester, the 2nd Earl of: 17th century Royalist who, evincing a debonair courage on mounting the scaffold at Tower Hill, nodded affably to the headsman and waved a suave, gloved hand to friends and admirers in the front row of the stalls (RJ)

Rowcester, the 3rd Earl of: an uninhibited nobleman in the days of the Glorious Restoration of his Majesty King Charles II of Blessed Memory. At a Court which could hardly be called prim or straitlaced he won a reputation for gallantry which earned, from discerning ladies-in-waiting, the sobriquet 'Tabasco' Rowcester (RJ)

Rowcester, the 8th Earl of: haughty peer of Edwardian vintage and uncle of the present holder of the title. With awe, his impoverished modern posterity recollect that the 8th Earl, in the course of a long life, was never known to put on his own boots and, when desirous of summoning domestic help, was wont simply to raise his head and howl like a timber wolf (RJ)

Rowcester, the Rt. Hon. the Earl of: William Egerton Bamfylde Ossingham Belfry, 9th of his line, s. his uncle the 8th E., q.v. Is D.L. and J.P. for Southmoltonshire. Res. Rowcester Abbey, Southmolton. Club, the Drones. (pron. 'Roaster')

The basic trouble is summed up by Bill Rowcester's sister, Monica ('Moke') Carmoyle, in the pregnant words 'We Rowcesters aren't easy to place. All the Rowcester men have been lilies of the field'. Good-looking, amiable and popular, Bill is not a mental giant. At the Drones his intellect is held to lie somewhere between those of Freddie Widgeon and Pongo Twistleton. Some indeed hold it to be lower even than that of Barmy Phipps. In addition he is saddled with a mouldering abbey which no one will buy and an exchequer so empty that he turns bookmaker, failing within a fortnight to the tune of £3,000. When fortune at length decides to smile on him, she pulls no punches. He acquires the services of Jeeves as butler (Bertie having prudently joined a boarding school where gentlemen are instructed in elementary economics) with the customary desirable, if momentous, results. We leave the Earl supervising the demolition of the abbey for its transit to America and preparing for his coming nuptials to the attractive Jill Wyvern, q.v. (RJ)

Rowcester Abbey: the facts are impressive. It was built *c.* 1250, about the time of Sir Caradoc Belfry ('Caradoc the Crusader') and would appear to lay claim to being one of the oldest inhabited houses in the country, and possibly the longest-inhabited by one family. Records of its foundation (as of its disestablishment) are lost. The well-attested ghost of the Lady Agatha, Sir Caradoc's spouse, leads to the tenable theory that she founded the abbey on her husband's death.* The Belfrys' ancestral home stands (such portions as have not fallen down) near the county town of Southmolton. Its basic Early English design has notable Decorated and Tudor additions. Its dilapidation is 20th century post-World War Two. In the summer months the river is at the bottom of the garden. In the winter the position is reversed. The Abbey was offered for a song to the Government as a home for Reclaimed

---

* cf. Lacock Abbey, Wiltshire, which was founded by the Countess Ela following the death of her husband William Longsword, Earl of Salisbury, natural son of King Henry II and Fair Rosamund. Ela became first Abbess—*Ed.*

Juvenile Delinquents, but refused on the grounds that it would give the delinquents rheumatic fever. It has recently been acquired by a wealthy American visitor who intends to dismantle it and re-erect it in California. Presumably the Ghost, too, will Go West (RJ)

Royal Albert Hall, the: falls on the Crystal Palace (COJ); Bohemian Ball at the, see **Marlborough St. Police Court** (UFS); the All In Wrestling Championship at (FO)

Rugby football: in the Wooster-Jeeves cycle neither football nor cricket win the attention given them elsewhere. For lively, realistic and pithy comment the *aficionado* must turn to the early school stories and especially to the annals of the cricketing Jacksons. There is a twenty-seven years hiatus between St. Austin's and the only sustained reportage of a Rugger game in the Wooster-Jeeves books. Its central figure, Tuppy Glossop, is (it turns out) an Old Austinian and wears the old school colours (light blue with broad orange stripes) for the blood-boltered annual match between Upper Bleaching and Hockley-cum-Meston. To Bertie, who was at Eton (a non-Rugger school) the game is something of a mystery:

> I can follow the broad, general principles, of course. I know that the main scheme is to work the ball down the field somehow and deposit it at the other end, and that, in order to squelch this programme, each side is allowed to put in a certain amount of assault and battery and do things to its fellow-man which, if done elsewhere, would result in fourteen days without the option, coupled with some strong remarks from the Bench (VGJ)

The merit of the comment is that, as usual, Bertie's direct and deceptively simple mind has gone right to the root of the matter in pointing a fact unperceived by most of us. *Rem*, as Jeeves would say, *acu tetigit*

Rumbelow, the Rt. Hon. Lord: though a mere baron, whose Coronation robes have only two rows of spots on each shoulder, wins distinction as a sufferer from that rare and exotic disease telangiectasis, and is consequently elected to the exclusive Twelve Jolly Stretcher Cases (EBC)

S

St. Asaph's Preparatory School: Bramley-on-Sea, see **Malvern House**

St. Cecilia: contemplating Mary Burgess, Bingo is reminded of (IJ)

St. Crispin: looking back on the martyrdom and wounds which he and Kipper Herring shared at Malvern House, Bertie feels they are a couple of old sweats who, like his famous ancestor, the Sieur de Wocestre, have fought shoulder to shoulder on Crispin's Day (JO)

St. George's, Hanover Square, W.: B. W. Wooster is slated to walk down the aisle at, with Lady Florence Craye on his arm (JFS)

St. James's, S.W.: an area where festive old gentlemen may be seen on most days, wheezing a little as they make the grade, on their way from one water-hole to the next. Various Wooster uncles are among its prominent sights, some of them growing more prominent each year, especially when seen sideways.

St. Monica's College: for Young Gentlewomen, Bingley-on-Sea; Principal Miss Mapleton. Scene of one of Bobbie Wickham's more outrageous misprisions (VGJ)

St. Peter's, Eaton Square, S.W.: stages the nuptials of Oliver Randolph Sipperley and Gwendolen Moon, 11 a.m., 1st June. Presents should be delivered before the end of May (VGJ)

St. Sebastian: Lord Chuffnell looks like, on receipt of about the fifteenth arrow (TJ)

sabbatical: Wilbert Cream is on his. Every seventh year, in American universities, members of the faculty are given leave of absence for travel or study (JO)

Sargent, Sir John S., R.A.:

> 'My private impression is that I've worked that stunt that Sargent and those fellows pull. I've put the child's soul on canvas.'
> 'But could a child of that age have a soul like that? I don't see how he could have managed it in the time.' (MJ)

Saviours of Britain, the: national movement founded and led by Roderick Spode, q.v., popularly (and otherwise) known as the Black Shorts:

'When you say "shorts" you mean "shirts", of course.'

'No. By the time Spode formed his association, there were no shirts left. He and his adherents wear black shorts.'

'Footer bags, you mean? Bare knees?'

'Yes.'

'How perfectly foul.'

'Yes.' (CW, JFS, FO)

Scholfield, Mrs: Bertie's married sister, domiciled in India for some years, arrives in England with her three young daughters, thereby implanting strange ideas in what may loosely be called Bertie's mind (COJ)

School Prize-Givings:

the bearded bloke stepped to the footlights and started making a speech. From the fact that he spoke as if he had a hot potato in his mouth without getting the raspberry from the lads in the ringside seats, I deduced that he must be the headmaster. With his arrival in the spotlight, a sort of perspiring resignation seemed to settle on the audience. The speech was on the subject of the doings of the school during the past term, and this part of a prize-giving is always apt rather to fail to grip the visiting stranger. I mean, you're told that J. B. Brewster has won an exhibition for classics at Cat's, Cambridge, and you feel that it's one of those stories where you can't see how funny it is unless you know the fellow. And the same applies to G. Bullett being awarded the Lady Jane Wix Scholarship at the Birmingham College of Veterinary Science (RHJ)

Schopenhauer: typifying the negative outlook (*passim*); would have slapped Bill Rowcester on the back and told him he knew exactly how he felt (RJ)

scrooched: see **sozzled**

Seabury: s. of Lady Chuffnell, is something the Dowager picked up in the course of a previous marriage, and consequently is not Issue within the meaning of Burke and Debrett. The annals are silent in the matter of his surname. Has aeroplane ears and a habit of looking at you as if he had picked you up during a slumming trip. In Bertie's view not quite so bad as young Thos. or Mr Blumenfeld's Junior, but well ahead of little Sebastian Moon, Aunt Dahlia's

Bonzo or the field. (Does Homer nod, or is that inveterate well-doer Edwin Craye unplaced? (TJ)

Senator J. Freylinghusen Botts, the S.S.: the liner in which Adolphus Stiffham's ripe, fruity but ill-timed letter to Lord Wivelscombe crosses the Atlantic. In hot pursuit of it, on the same ship, goes Stiffy (YMS)

Senior Liberal Club, S.W., the: feeling like inmates of a displaced persons camp, Bertie and Bingo encounter each other in the vasty halls of, under arrangements made by the Secretary of the Drones during the Club's annual renovation. We have it on B. Wooster's evidence that the youngest member of the Senior Liberals is about 87, and that it is not considered good form to address a fellow member unless you were through the Peninsular War together. Bingo however finds considerable consolation in the staff* (IJ)

Seppings: the post of butler at Brinkley Court, Worcs, is surely one which demands diplomatic gifts. Consider the household; the dyspeptic and pessimistic Tom Travers, the extrovert and unpredictable Dahlia, the hot Provençal passions of a chef well aware that England cannot boast his like, the hell-instructed Bonzo. . . . These are, as it were, the army of occupation; they are augmented frequently and at short notice (if indeed any) by guests of the calibre of Gussy and his travelling newts, and Tuppy Glossop. Seppings, we are told is a cold and unemotional man. He has need to be; yet even he is seen to gasp and practically reel when Tuppy, under love's influence, waves aside Anatole's famed *nonettes de poulet Agnès Sorel*, while the footman, standing by with the *pommes Duchesse*, stares like one seeing visions. Nor are these all. Seppings can hardly dismiss the constant reflection that, like one of his predecessors, he may at any moment find himself bartered to some neighbouring collector in exchange for a *vinaigrette*, a cow creamer, or an oviform silver chocolate pot on three scroll feet (CW, RHJ, JFS *et al.*)

Seymour, Alicia: alias Freddie Oaker, q.v.

Shrewsbury clock: Aunt Dahlia has been hanging on to this damned telephone receiver a long hour by, (JO)

---

* The chronicles are silent as to whether the exchange arrangement is reciprocal. The spectacle of the Senior Liberals seeking hospitality at the Drones is one at which the imagination boggles. (We have inspected the Editorial imagination and we were right. It is boggling.)

shy creatures of the night: despite their shyness pop up habitually. Usually they 'rustle in the undergrowth', and often include members of the order Coleoptera (beetles to you) which tend to nest in the small of the back; occasionally also nightingales (*daulias luscinia*, Linn.) who are fully conscious of having earned a rave notice from the poet Keats, not to mention a star spot on the B.B.C. the night before.

Sidcup, the Rt. Hon. Lord: Roderick Spode, leader of Britain's Black Shorts, succeeds to the barony on his uncle's demise. See **Spode.** See for that matter **Eulalie** (JFS)

Sidney, Sir Philip: (1554-86) is remembered as having been given a big build-up by the Rev. Aubrey Upjohn:

> because when wounded at the battle of somewhere and offered a quick one by a companion in arms, he told the chap who was setting them up to leave him out of that round and slip his spot to a nearby stretcher-case whose need was greater than his. This spirit of selfless sacrifice, said the Rev. Aubrey, was what he would like to see in you boys—particularly you, Wooster, and how many times have I told you not to gape at me in that half-witted way. Close your mouth, boy, and sit up (MS)

Silversmith, Charlie: Jeeves's respected uncle, butler to the Haddock-Winkworth-Deverill ménage, is, as might be expected, a majestic man, having in his deportment a suggestion of the ambassador who is about to deliver important State papers to a reigning monarch. He is also, as Catsmeat Pirbright is to discover, a Roman father. It takes a good deal, we imagine, to shake a popular West End actor of Catsmeat's natural resilience:

> 'What effect does that bloke have on you, Bertie?' he asked in a hushed voice. 'He paralyses me. I don't know if you are familiar with the works of Joseph Conrad, but there's a chap in his *Lord Jim* of whom he says "Had you been the Emperor of the East and West you could not have ignored your inferiority in his presence." That's Silversmith. He shrivels my immortal soul to the size of a parched pea' (MS)

Similes

YOU GET ABOUT AS MUCH CHANCE TO TALK IN THIS
HOUSE AS A PARROT LIVING WITH TALLULAH
BANKHEAD

Joy had made him the friend of all the world. He was more like something out of Dickens than anything human (SLJ)

She was one of those girls you're always meeting on the stairs and in passages. It's a peculiar thing in life that the people you want most particularly to edge away from always seem to cluster round like a poultice (COJ)

She was breathing emotionally, like the dog Bartholomew just after he had finished eating the candle (CW)

He spun round with a sort of guilty bound, like an adagio dancer surprised while watering the cat's milk (JM)

Her face was shining like the seat of a bus-driver's trousers (JFS)

His map was flushed and his manner distraught. He looked like Jack Dempsey at the conclusion of his first conference with Gene Tunney, the occasion, if you remember, when he forgot to duck (JO)

'Is this Wembley?' says chap. 'No, Thursday,' says deaf chap. Ha, ha, I mean, what?
The merry laughter froze on my lips. Sir Roderick just sort of waggled an eyebrow in my direction and I saw that it was back to the basket for Bertram. I never met a man who had such a knack of making a fellow feel like a waste product (COJ)

The fiend that slept in Aunt Dahlia was also up on its toes. She gave Upjohn a look which, if directed at an erring member of the Quorn or Pytchley hound ensemble, would have had that member sticking his tail between his legs and resolving for the future to lead a better life (JO)

He spoke in a throaty growl, like a Bengal tiger snarling over its breakfast coolie (JFS)

His demeanour was that of an Assyrian who, having come down like a wolf on the fold, had found in residence not lambs but wild cats, than which, of course, nothing makes an Assyrian feel sillier (JFS)

Simpson, Enoch: obliges with *Dangerous Dan M'Grew* at an East End concert (VGJ)

Simpson, Oofy: ousts Oofy Prosser (in **'Big Money'**) temporarily as the richest property in the Drones.

Singer, Muriel: a shrinking menace with liquid eyes who does not, however, shrink from the prospect of marriage with Bruce Corcoran or failing him (one shrewdly suspects) Bertie Wooster. Bertie never bates his enthusiasm in describing his feelings during the half-dozen affairs which have come nearest to robbing him of his bachelordom; he has never been so candid as when speaking of this modest violet:

> one of those very quiet, appealing girls who have a way of looking at you with their big eyes as if they thought you were the greatest thing on earth and wondered why you hadn't got on to it yet yourself. She sat there in a sort of shrinking way, looking at me as if she were saying to herself 'Oh, I do hope this great, strong man isn't going to hurt me.' She gave a fellow a protective kind of feeling, made him want to stroke her hand and say 'There, there, little one!' or words to that effect. She made me feel that there was nothing I wouldn't do for her.

The Wooster student who does not see the red light here does not know his Bertie. And to point the moral, there are Bertie's own musings on dashers and dormice (see **Laughing Love God**) (MJ)

Sipperley, Oliver Randolph: draws the short straw when, partnering Bertie in a Boat Race Night expedition, he mishandles the delicate matter of lifting a policeman's helmet in Coventry Street, and is gaoled without the option. Sippy is twice extracted from the bottom of the tureen by Jeeves's inventive intellect; first by the judicious expenditure of £5 on a Yorkshire P.c., and second through the agency of a vase which had been the apple of its owner's eye (COJ, VGJ)

Sipperley, Vera: of The Paddock, Beckley-on-the-Moor, Yorks, on whom (when not editing the *Mayfair Gazette*) her nephew Oliver is dependent. By a masterstroke of Jeeves, is persuaded to approve actively her nephew's assault on a Metropolitan policeman (COJ)

Slingsby, Alexander: Hill St., Mayfair, W., is the imperious tycoon who makes a fortune from Slingsby's Superb Soups (VGJ)

Slingsby, Beatrice: consort of the Soup King and s. of Lucius Pim (VGJ)

Slingsby's Superb Soups: it is on coming off the boat train that Bertie, driving through Sloane Square, first notices the enormous coloured poster:

pasted on a blank wall and measuring about a hundred feet each way ... mostly red and blue. At the top of it were the words SLINGSBY'S SUPERB SOUPS, and at the bottom SUCCULENT AND STRENGTHENING. And in between, me. Yes, dash it, Bertram Wooster in person (VGJ)

smeller, a: a purler, cropper, crash or precipitous descent. To ride a bicycle, e.g., without benefit of hands, especially if one is a not too popular village rozzer, spells a, (CW)

Smethurst: Col. Mainwaring-Smith's valet, has an understanding with Rhoda Platt, q.v., to the (mistaken) relief of Aunt Agatha:

> 'Your uncle has been speaking to me ... He is not going to marry that girl. Apparently he sees how unsuitable it would have been. But what is astonishing is that he *is* going to be married!'
> 'He is?'
> 'Yes, to an old friend of his, a Mrs Wilberforce. A woman of a sensible age, he gave me to understand. I wonder which Wilberforce that would be? There are two main branches of the family—the Essex Wilberforces and the Cumberland Wilberforces. I believe there is also a cadet branch somewhere in Shropshire.'
> 'And one in East Dulwich.'
> 'What did you say?'
> 'Nothing,' I said (VGJ)

Snettisham, the Rt. Hon. Lord and Lady: turf acquaintances of Dahlia Travers, stay at Brinkley, where they cast covetous eyes on her *cordon bleu* Anatole. In the matter of the Good Conduct competition between Bonzo Travers and young Thos., they show a blackness of soul sufficient to get themselves barred from every racecourse in the country:

> 'Only yesterday,' said Aunt Dahlia, 'it came to my knowledge that Jack Snettisham had been urging Bonzo to climb on the roof and boo down Mr Anstruther's chimney' (VGJ)

Society of Psychical Research, the: standing in the haunted chapel at the witching hour, Rosalinda Spottsworth holds Jeeves spellbound with an account of the recent investigations of, (RJ)

Song of Songs, the: is the one with that bit about the Angels being lonely:

I fancy, sir, that if Mr Glossop were to sing 'Sonny Boy' directly after you, too, had sung 'Sonny Boy', the audience would respond satisfactorily. By the time Mr Glossop began to sing, they would have lost their taste for that particular song and would express their feelings warmly (VGJ)

South American Joe: in the greensickness of love Catsmeat Pirbright sees in Esmond Haddock a Grade-A louse and a raw Home Wrecker, a flitting butterfly and a sipping bee, a public menace who ought to be kept on a permanent chain, and the nearest thing to a, (MS)

sozzled: see **squiffy**

Spelvin, Dr: peremptory Worcestershire medico, forbids Lord Wivelscombe to drink champagne (YMS)

Spettigue, the Rev. Mr: Rector of Gandle-by-the-Hill, Glos, is presented to that living following the incumbency of the Rev. James Bates (IJ)

Spettisbury: family name of the Earl of Wivelscombe, q.v.

Spettisbury, Lady Geraldine: the superlative d. of the Earl of Wivelscombe, who separates her (by eleven feet, two inches in the first instance) from Adolphus Stiffham. When later the Earl, in a nervous state after an overnight engagement, sees Stiffy's wraith on the terrace, Geraldine, a resourceful maiden, foregoes breakfast in order to contact her beloved on the ouija board. She is eventually successful in persuading the Earl that a corporeal son-in-law is preferable to a disembodied Drone (YMS)

'Spindrift': Lady Florence Craye's purposeful novel (Book Society Choice) was written, Bertie surmises, to take the author's mind off Aunt Agatha, who has just become her stepmother. Well received by the intelligentsia (who notoriously enjoy the most frightful bilge) it is even dramatised by Percy Gorringe. It is also, and unwisely, picked up in a bookshop by Bertie, who is not to know that the author, standing behind him, will persuade herself that this is the point at which his long deferred education must begin (JM, JFS)

Spode, Roderick: founder and leader of the Saviours of Britain (the Black Shorts) whom, in fact, we never see in action; is 'about seven feet in height, and swathed in a plaid ulster which made him look about six feet across. It was as if Nature had intended to make a gorilla, and had changed its mind at the last moment'. Thus he is introduced to us and the introduction is symbolic. The character is remarkably interesting and illuminating. No one will pretend that Spode represents all that his creator might have to say about Fascism. Wodehouse is a writer with no conscious messages and is blessedly free from prejudice. He is incapable of hate, and his evil-doers usually suffer little worse than a little condign indignity. In the Wodehouse world, the ambitious would-be Dictator takes the form of a sub-human, elementary force, an anthropoid being with amoral, animal motivations, who on no single occasion is allowed to put them into effect. Chance—and Jeeves—are ever at hand to frustrate his most murderous plans. Needless to add that the effects are gratifyingly diverting, especially that sequence in which the Eulalie pea-shooter transforms the raging ogre instantly to an apprehensive Caliban (CW, JFS, JO, SLJ)

Spottsworth, the late A. B.: a confusion of ideas between this millionaire and a lion he was hunting in Kenya caused A.B. to make the obituary columns. He thought the lion was dead; the lion thought it wasn't. He placed his foot on the lion's neck for photographic purposes and a rather nasty brawl ensued. Bwana Biggar's bullet, though unerring, was too late. Nothing remained to be done save pick up the pieces and transfer A.B.'s vast fortune to his widow, adding it to the sixteen million she had already inherited from her first husband (RJ)

Spottsworth, Rosalinda: at mention of whose name the blood-sucking leeches of the United States Internal Revenue Department raise their filthy hats with a reverent intake of the breath, exudes wealth. She was b. Banks, of the Chilicothe, Ohio, Bankses, with no assets beyond a lovely face, superb figure and some talent for *vers libre*. With these modest assets she met Clifton Bessemer, pulp paper magnate, at a party in Greenwich Village, married him, was at once widowed, married the millionaire A. B. Spottsworth, was re-widowed and now has the stuff in sacks. As Monica Carmoyle's guest at Rowcester Abbey she is able to indulge her twin talents for ghost-hunting and husband-spotting (RJ)

squaring with Squeers: it falls into a category which Jeeves would label as injudicious when an unpopular headmaster takes pen in hand and subsequently publishes a thoughtful belle-lettre on the subject of how to conduct a preparatory school. It is even more impolitic if he takes no steps to discover whether one of its reviewers once served a sentence at the school. And if the said reviewer's unminced comments are privily augmented by those of a singularly uninhibited fiancée, the effects may be expected to engender a certain amount of strontium fall-out. One passage which subsequently causes pursed lips in Lincoln's Inn Fields is:

> We have not forgotten the sausages on Sunday, which were made not from contented pigs but from pigs which had expired, regretted by all, of glanders, the botts and tuberculosis (JO)

squiffy: see stewed

Starkie, the Rev. Leonard: the loquacious incumbent of Stapleton, Glos, is a scratch entry in the Great Sermon Handicap (IJ)

Starr, Cora: see **Potter-Pirbright, Corky**

**Stately Homes and Their Owners
(Temporal and Astral)**

A SIGH OF RELIEF WENT UP FROM A DOZEN STATELY HOMES AS IT BECAME KNOWN THAT THE SHORT STRAW HAD BEEN DRAWN BY BLEACHING COURT (VGJ)

Biddleford Castle, Norfolk	Earl of Havershot	traditionally haunted by a Wailing Lady
Binghampton Hall, Sussex	Viscount Binghampton	houses the Curse of the Southern Counties and a clowder of Siamese cats
Blandings Castle, Market Blandings, Shropshire	Earl of Emsworth	periodically haunted by errant nieces with gyves upon their wrists
Bleaching Court, Upper Bleaching, Hampshire	Sir Reginald Witherspoon, Bart.	haunted by a Giant Squirt and a Luminous Rabbit

Blicester Towers, Blicester Regis, Kent	Earl of Blicester	
Branstead Towers, Sussex	Miss Cammarleigh	
Bumpleigh Hall, Steeple Bumpleigh, Hampshire	Earl of Worplesdon	its chatelaine conducts human sacrifices at the time of full moon
Brinkley Court, Market Snodsbury, Worcestershire	Thomas Portarlington Travers, Esq.	
Chuffnell Hall, Chuffnell Regis, Somerset	Lord Chuffnell	suffers a visitation by the Devil in person
Corfby Hall, Much Middlefold, Shropshire	R. E. Smith, Esq.	
Deverill Hall, King's Deverill Hampshire	Esmond Haddock, Esq.	is awash with a surging sea of aunts
Ditteredge Hall, Hampshire	Sir Roderick Glossop	
Easeby Hall, Shropshire	Willoughby Wooster, Esq.	
Edgeling Court, Tonbridge, Kent	Earl of Hoddesdon	
Ickenham Hall, Bishop's Ickenham, Hampshire	Earl of Ickenham	houses a record collection of nude Venuses
Ilsworth Hall, Shropshire	R. E. Smith, Esq.	
Kingham Manor, Pershore, Worcestershire	Sir Percival Stretchley-Budd, Bart.	

Langley End, Worcestershire	Earl of Droitwich	
Marsham Manor, Marsham-in-the-Vale, Hampshire	Miss Cornelia Fothergill	houses the Fothergill Venus
Matcham Scratchings, Oxfordshire	Sir Mortimer Prenderby, Bart.	infested by a Donnybrook of dogs, a clowder of cats and an anthropoid ape
Much Middlefold Hall, Shropshire	Marquess of Malvern	
Rowcester Abbey, Southmolton, Southmoltonshire	Earl of Rowcester	haunted by mildew, mice and the ghost of the Lady Agatha, proto-martyr to its dampness
Rudge Hall, Rudge-in-the-Vale, Worcestershire	Lester Carmody, Esq.	
Skeldings Hall, Hertfordshire	Lady Wickham	periodically haunted by a red-haired Jezebel
Smattering Hall, Lower Smattering-on-the-Wissel, Worcestershire	Reginald Watson-Watson, Esq.; later Sir Murgatroyd Sprockett-Sprockett, Bart.	
Totleigh Towers, Totleigh-in-the-Wold, Gloucestershire	Sir Watkyn Bassett, J.P.	with Aberdeen terriers in the bedrooms and newts in the bath, little better than a lazar house
Tudsleigh Court, Worcestershire	Lady Carroway	
Twing Hall, Twing, Gloucestershire	Earl of Wickhammerseley	

Wivelscombe Court, Upton Snodsbury, Worcestershire	Earl of Wivelscombe	haunted by a White Lady and a pink secretary
Woollam Chersey Place, Hertfordshire	Spenser Gregson, Esq.	
Wyvern Hall, Southmoltonshire	Col. Aubrey Wyvern	

Steggles, Rupert: leading snake, dreams up the Great Sermon Handicap and (unbelievably) is given a second chance to show his expertise when running the book at the Twing School Treat (IJ)

stewed to the gills: see **stinko**

STIFF UPPER LIP, JEEVES: written when the author was 81, sparkles as iridescently as ever. The star cast includes (besides Bertie and Jeeves) Gussie, Aunt Dahlia, Madeline, Sir Watkyn, Spode, Old Uncle Tom Travers and all. Published 1963 (SLJ)

Stiffham, Adolphus (Stiffy): secretary to Lord Wivelscombe, whom he assists (in the role of projectile) to break the Midland Counties record for the standing place-kick (11 ft. 2 ins.)* when the Earl discovers his (reciprocated) penchant for the fair Geraldine Spettisbury. Stiffy goes to America where he amasses £30,000 in three hours at a curious local pastime known as craps. Returning to claim his bride, he finds himself converted into a cautionary projection of a distant personality (YMS)

stinko: see **tanked**

Stoker, Dwight: not only refuses to pay protection money to Seabury, but causes that young squirt to wish he had protection himself (TJ)

Stoker, Emerald: y.d. of Old Pop Stoker, pride of the Spanish Main, studies at the Slade. Unquestionably has a heart of g. but looks like a Pekinese with freckles. Losing her foundation garments on a horse which comes in sixth, she takes a job as cook to Sir Watkyn Bassett and administers salutary justice to the demon Spode with a bean-basin. Elopes to Brinkley with Gussie Fink-Nottle and competently deputises for Anatole when he develops *mal au foie* (SLJ)

* Inquiries show that the record, like the victim, still stands—*Ed.*

Stoker, the late George: second cousin of J. Washburn S., after a lifetime spent in doing down the widow and orphan, begins to feel the strain. When he begins to walk on his hands, is gathered in by the public-spirited neurologist Sir Roderick Glossop. The disposal of his millions depend on the validity of his will, and this rests largely on the looney-doctor's evidence (TJ)

Stoker, J. Washburn: of East 67th St., New York City, was b. at Carterville. Whether this is the place in Mass. or its namesake in Ky. becomes a matter of moment to the continued survival of B. Wooster, as southern gentlemen are known to have odd ideas concerning their daughters' honour. Bertie, who has every opportunity to view him at close range, says he is reminiscent of a pirate of the Spanish Main, a massive blighter with piercing eyes to boot. He throws Bertie into irons aboard his private yacht and proposes to keep him there until he can forcibly marry him to the (supposedly) wronged Pauline (TJ)

Stoker, Pauline: e.d. of the Pride of the Main, has been previously (for 48 hours) engaged to Bertie Wooster. This is broken off at the instance of Sir Roderick Glossop who touches on the incidence of cats and fish in Bertie's bedroom. In the legion of his acquaintance, the highly attractive Pauline probably shares with Aunt Dahlia the deepest insight into Bertie's complex make-up. There is an intuitive depth in her summing-up: 'There is a sort of woolly-headed duckiness about you.' The young prune ranks high among the rabble-rousers. In particular she achieves uniqueness in being the only girl ever discovered in Bertie's bed—wearing moreover Bertie's mauve pyjamas with the old-gold stripe. She carries the incident off with an artlessness recalling the charm and innocence of the Elizabethan lovers' song, 'and innocent as she was yonge, she dreamèd not of guile'. Jeeves takes buccaneers, like Nietzsche, in his stride, and engineers Pauline's marriage to Lord Chuffnell without conscious cerebration (TJ)

Stretchley-Budd, Sir Percival, Bart.: Res. Kingham Manor, Pershore, Worcs, has one fair daughter (RHJ)

Sturridge, the Rt. Hon. the Earl of: f. of the Hon. and Rev. Hubert Wingham, q.v. (IJ)

Surrey County Cricket Club: Hilda Gudgeon touches briefly on the prospects of the, (MS)

Sycamore, Beau: once the star of the Army class at Uppingham, has now become Hobo Sycamore:

'Once made 146 in a house cricket match before being caught low down in the gully off a googly ball that dipped and swung away late. On a sticky wicket too,' added Captain Biggar (RJ)

T

tanked: see **tight**

Tennyson, Reginald: of the Drones, designated by his family as Idle Apprentice, does his best to fulfil their gloomiest expectations. In a Mayfair containing such leading exponents as Hugo Carmody and the pustule Pilbeam, none is more heartily devoted to other people's business (LB)

THANK YOU, JEEVES: published 1934, was written at the author's new home at Auribeau, Provence, and is his first full-length novel in the first person. It was sold to the *Cosmopolitan* magazine for 50,000 dollars, his best payment to date. Of its preparation, he noted in PF:

> I went off the rails and had to rewrite three times. That is the curse of my type of story. Unless I get the construction absolutely smooth, it bores the reader. ... Still, I'll bet the plot of **Hamlet** seemed just as lousy when Shakespeare was trying to tell it to Ben Jonson in the Mermaid Tavern. ('Well, Ben, see what I mean, the central character is this guy, see, who's in love with this girl, see, but her old man doesn't think he's on the level, see, so he tells he—wait a minute, I'd better start at the beginning. Well, so this guy's in college, see, and he's coming home because his mother's gone and married his uncle, see ...') (TJ)

Thompson, Fred: evanescent member of Buck's, S.W. (IJ)

Thorpe & Briscoe, Ltd.: coal merchants whose premises confront the Drones Club in Dover St., W. Their somewhat commercial frontage is improved beyond measure when Eve Halliday shelters from a sudden shower under their awning, enabling Psmith to inaugurate a lifetime's happiness by dashing from the Drones to lend her someone else's umbrella (LIP)

Thorpe & Widgery Ltd.: the popular grocers of Bridmouth-on-Sea, where two Drones are struck by lightning on beholding Angelica Briscoe buying five pounds of the best streaky (YMS)

Thistleton: family name of Lord Bridgworth, q.v.

Threepwood: family name of the Earl of Emsworth, q.v.

Threepwood, the Hon. Frederick: y.s. of the Earl of Emsworth, Freddie is one of the three links which join the Wooster and Blandings sagas. His own story lies largely, alas, outside the Drones, of which he is a member. Bertie recollects that Freddie once told him there had been trouble down at Blandings about a cousin of his who wanted to marry a curate, and the fact does not brace him with regard to Stiffy Byng and the Rev. Stinker Pinker (CW)

'Thursday Review, The': the sober and respected weekly review in whose book columns Reggie Herring, with unsuspected help from Bobbie Wickham, levels the score against Aubrey Upjohn (JO)

tight as an owl: see **under the sauce**

Tinkler-Moulke, the Hon. Mrs: Bertie's neighbour at C6 Berkeley Mansions, W., swells the chorus of complaint about the banjolele phase (TJ)

Todd, Montague: a resilient financier, and one of the small but distinguished band who have been Jeeves's employers. Now in the second year of his sentence, he is held up by Jeeves as a paradigm of those gifted in the art of dealing with the critical situation:

> I have known men call upon Mr Todd with the express intention of horsewhipping him and go away half-an-hour later laughing heartily and smoking one of his cigars (COJ)

Todd, Rockmeteller: an early beneficiary of Jeeves's genius, Rocky is an indigent artist who detests the city lights, but whose wealthy aunt forces him at chequebook-point to act as her cicerone on an endless sojourn among the fleshpots and flash joints of New York (MJ)

Todd, Smiler: prop forward, gets his Blue at Cambridge (SLJ)

Tomlinson, Miss: headmistress of the girls' school near Brighton whom Jeeves uses as a means of curbing Bertie's paternal yearnings:

> 'Do you know, Jeeves, I've never been inside a girls' school

in my life. Ought to be a dashed interesting experience, what?'
'I fancy that you may find it so, sir.'

The story **'Bertie Changes His Mind'** is the only one told, not by
Bertie, but by Jeeves. It also has the distinction of recording the
one and only indisposition of the euphoric Bertie—a slight attack
of influenza. (COJ)

Townend, William: lifelong friend of Wodehouse (they were at
Dulwich together) and editor of **PERFORMING FLEA.**

to touch Horace: [*]

The door of the Drones Club swung open, and a young
man in form-fitting tweeds came down the steps and started
to walk westwards. An observant passer-by, scanning his
face, would have fancied that he discerned on it a keen,
tense look, like that of an African hunter stalking a hippo-
potamus. And he would have been right. Pongo Twistleton—for it was he—was on his way to try to touch Horace
Pendlebury-Davenport for two hundred pounds.

To touch Horace Pendlebury-Davenport, if you are coming
from the Drones, you go down Hay Hill, through Berkeley
Square, along Mount Street and up Park Lane to the new
block of luxury flats which they have built where Bloxham
House used to be ... (UFS)

Tottie: a thing which adds years to the conscientious historian is
life's bad habit of throwing up the occasional hero (heroine in this
case) with no details other than a mere Christian name. The culprit
is once again an elderly raconteur recalling his exuberant youth.
It was so with Gally Threepwood and the girl who unhinged the
programme at a Buckingham Palace garden party by getting a
beetle down her back. In the present instance it is Lord Worplesdon
the shipping magnate. For it was Tottie, that all but unsung heroine,
who changed the course of maritime marine history by postponing
his marriage to Aunt Agatha (then Miss Wooster) by a matter of
thirty years. Not that this prevented the poor mutt from taking

[*] On unimpeachable authority we are told that this is a certain American
devotee's favourite opening paragraph. Though not known to us personally, the
gentleman in question is not only a University Professor but an Admiral in the
U.S. Navy, a historian, and the father of a charming daughter. Further excuses for
its inclusion would seem to be pragmatical, but if any demur, the Editor calls upon
the sacrosanct claim of Anglo-American solidarity.

the Gadarene slope in the long run. There are men who simply won't take a hint:

> You mightn't think it to look at me now, but there was a time when no Covent Garden ball was complete without me. I used to have the girls flocking round me like flies round a honey pot. Between ourselves, it was owing to the fact that I got thrown out of a Covent Garden ball and taken to Vine Street Police Station in the company of a girl who, if memory serves me aright, was named Tottie that I escaped—that I had the misfortune not to marry your aunt thirty years earlier than I did.... We had just got engaged at the time, and she broke it off within three minutes of reading my press notices in the evening papers. ... Your aunt is a wonderful woman, Bertie, but—well, you know how it is.'
>
> I said I knew how it was (JM)

traumatic symplegia: Augustus suffers from; see ~~Dumbchummery~~ (JO)

Travers, Angela: o.d. of Tom and Dahlia, and first cousin to Bertie, who had been her childhood idol. After a certain amount of in-and-out running on Tuppy Glossop's part and of amusing mishandling of her own affairs, she is booked for the holy moment with Tuppy, whose summing up is probably apt:

> 'I'm not saying I don't love the little blighter. I love her passionately. But that doesn't alter the fact that I consider that what she needs most is a swift kick in the pants.' (RHJ, et al.)

Travers, Bonzo: o.s. of Tom and Dahlia Travers, makes sporadic but always welcome appearances. Visits the Bijou Dream Cinema at Market Snodsbury to see an old film featuring Lillian Gish. Comes out with a pale, set face, resolved to live a finer, better life:

> 'Heaven knows I have no illusions about my darling Bonzo,' said Aunt Dahlia. 'He is, and has been from the cradle, a pest. But to back him to win a Good Conduct contest with Thos. seemed to me simply money for jam. When it comes to devilry, Bonzo is just a good, ordinary selling-plater. Whereas Thomas is a classic yearling.' (VGJ)

Travers, Dahlia: brick-faced, large, exuberant, sagacious and shrewd, she swam (charged would be apter) into our lives as long ago as 1925, and a new Wooster novel which numbers her among its treasures has always made one walk a little faster to the bookstall. If I were asked to draw up the specifications for a new relative in my family, Aunt Dahlia would be my model. As with Bertie and others, her family background was indeterminate at first, though her personal qualities were fixed and changeless from the beginning. But though her Wooster parentage and her rather astonishing sisterhood with Aunt Agatha were later established, that of their younger sister Katherine was not. Bertie's references to 'Aunt Dahlia's younger sister' and 'my Aunt Dahlia's late father' should accurately read 'my Aunt Katherine' and 'my grandfather'. She m. Uncle Tom Travers 'the year that Bluebottle won the Cambridge-shire'. At that time she was, as she tells us, a dog-girl:

> One of these dashed open-air flappers in thick boots and tailor-made tweeds who infest the rural districts and go about the place followed by packs of assorted dogs. I used to be one of them myself in my younger days, and I know how dangerous they are (VGJ)

She was then also, and for years after, an assiduous yoickser and hark-forrarder with the Berks and Bucks, the Pytchley, the Quorn and the York and Ainsty Hunts. Uncle Tom, for unexplained reasons, refused to live in the country, and their earlier home was at their Mayfair home at 47 Charles St., W.1. It was then that Dahlia acquired the magazine *Milady's Boudoir*, q.v., published in Covent Garden, and our first sight of her is when she receives the copy ('the piece, we old hands call it') on What the Well Dressed Young Man Is Wearing for the husbands and brothers section of the magazine, which she has cajoled Bertie into writing. To him she is 'my good and deserving aunt', 'the old relative', 'the old flesh and b.' and 'the only decent aunt I've got'; to her, he is 'my favourite nephew'. She is under no illusions as to his i.q., and is even ready to spend time and energy in describing the minutest details (RHJ) of the steps he should take in ridding the world of his unwanted presence; but she is equally ready to leap to his defence against the enraged Spode, and she shows an early and remarkable percipience of Jeeves's true role. Mothers are rarer than fathers in the Wodehouse world. Bertie barely mentions his own mother. In Aunt Dahlia he possesses a mother figure incorporating the most volatile brouhaha of a mature and experienced Bobbie Wickham, and the relationship is unique in fiction (COJ, VGJ, RHJ, CW, JFS, FO, SLJ)

Travers, Thomas Portarlington: of Brinkley Court, Market

Snodsbury, Worcs, and 47 Charles St., W., m. Dahlia (née Wooster); 1 s., 1 d.; made a large fortune in the Far East, for which his liver is now paying the price. Only the ministrations of Anatole are competent to prevent the feeling that Old Home Week in Moscow has broken out under the third waistcoat button. On his well-being depends his reluctant quarterly cheque to keep *Milady's Boudoir* off the rocks. But Anatole's continued service depends in turn on Aunt Dahlia's perilous disposition to wager him against her own baccarat debts—a vicious circle which becomes a series of flaming hoops through which these engaging people leap. Tom has a yacht, an impressive collection of old silver and an intermittent fixation about income-tax, the coming revolution and general damnation. He also has (*teste* Gussie) a face like a walnut (Bertie suggests 'a pterodactyl with a secret sorrow') (RHJ *et al.*)

Trelawney, Evangeline: post-war cook to Col. Wyvern, q.v., like her colleague Bulstrode the butler, is one of the younger set. She is 15 (RJ)

Tressider, Squire: of Twing, Glos, a fairly mauve old sportsman with white whiskers, declines to join in the refrain of a ripeish ballad at Bingo Little's Christmas show at the village hall, and marches out at the head of his family (IJ)

Trevelyan, the Rt. Hon. the Viscount: is not specifically named as a member of the Drones, yet it seems unlikely that any other forcinghouse could have produced the dexterity with which he picks off six waiters with six successive rolls at Mario's Restaurant, W. (BCE)

Tucker, B. B.: Bingo Little's bespoke hosier and shirtmaker (EBC)

Tucker, the Rev. Joseph: once in the pulpit, the Vicar of Badgwick, Glos, is prone to take the bit between his teeth, and is therefore a scratch starter in the Great Sermon Handicap (IJ)

Twistleton-Twistleton: family name of the Earl of Ickenham, q.v.

Twistleton, Beau: celebrated Regency dandy who, like his descendant Pongo, had good reason to imagine spiders were walking up his spine when he heard faint, rustling sounds from a cupboard (UD)

Twistleton-Twistleton, Lady Brenda: a great-aunt of Pongo's who, as related in a classic passage by Lord Ickenham (alas, off the present canvas), laid the foundations of the late Sir Thomas Lipton's fortunes while airing her pug dog Jabberwocky in Grosvenor Square (UFS)

Twistleton, Sir Gervase: a supine blot on Pongo's otherwise (fairly) unstained escutcheon, fl. c. 1180. On being invited by King Richard Lionheart to do his stuff at the siege of Joppa, curled up in bed and remarked 'Some other time'.

Twistleton-Twistleton, the Hon. Marmaduke: Pongo's late great-uncle, owned the Mitching Hill estate in south-east London which is the setting for the classic 'Uncle Fred Flits By'. The Hon.'s whiskers were, on Uncle Fred's authority, of a plenitude which no-one with a pure mind would credit (YMS)

Twistleton-Twistleton, Reginald (Pongo): nephew and heir to the Earl of Ickenham, q.v. Is some four years junior to Bertie Wooster (it is at Pongo's 21st birthday party that Bertie proposes to wear the white evening mess jacket with brass buttons with which he has lately been enlivening the Cote d'Azur). Pongo, though a practising Drone, is at heart a modest and conventional soul with some regard for social niceties and the quiet life. It is his cross that fate has given him as uncle the devastation-spreading Lord Ickenham. Pongo's main occupations are on the normal two-dimensional plane of preserving body and soul in a highly competitive world peopled by beings with a higher i.q. than his own (which at the Drones is estimated as little, if any, above that of Barmy Phipps) and of pursuing the current object of his affections. He is seen joyously thus, partnering Barmy, in 'Tried in the Furnace' (YMS). It is when Uncle Fred is allowed off the chain by a reluctant Aunt Jane, and invades the Metropolis that Pongo becomes the suffering sounding-board for his uncle's excesses, especially when, as in UFS or YMS, he is suborned into gatecrashing someone's castle or suburban villa under some ghastly pretence as that he has come, e.g., to assist the vet to cut the parrot's claws. When such pleasing inspirations visit Lord Ickenham's mind, we are told, prudent men make for the nearest bomb-proof shelter. It is in Pongo's ever-frustrated efforts to reach such a shelter that half the fun lies. He is possibly the most misused nephew on the whole canvas, though Horace Davenport and Freddie Widgeon would bitterly dispute the claim. For the record, Pongo, despite a chronic mendacity, manages to live in Albany, W. He finally comes into his long-awaited inheritance, and weds the charming Sally Painter (YMS, UFS, UD, et al.)

Twistleton-Twistleton, Valerie: Pongo's sister is the earliest recorded victim of the susceptible Bingo Little. On Nannie Byles's authority, which is considerable in a double sense, Bingo and Valerie broke the record for mistletoe kisses at the age of six when attending the Wilkinsons' children's party. One feels that Uncle Fred, in hailing her as his favourite niece, is actuated rather by the reflection that she is also his only one. For Valerie, we feel, is a tough baby, a maiden with few illusions about her world and still fewer about her uncle. Her dewy eyes are fixed on the ducal coronet she will one day wear as the wife of Horace Davenport. Their affection seems sincere, but neither heart, it would seem is over-frangible (NS, UFS, JFS)

U

uncles: if they do not always achieve the draconic absolutism assumed by most aunts, it is not for want of trying. In one's childhood they can even, sometimes, be human enough to send one the odd mid-term subsidy (cf. Bertie's Uncle Henry); thereafter they all too often become heavy or even Dutch uncles, raising successive colonies of moths in their pocket-books and generally contributing to overcast one's sky like stig tossed full of doodle gammon. They may furthermore run to avoirdupois, becoming encumbrances who have to be accompanied to the more dismal spa resorts, or worse, entertain feelings towards the other sex (Lord Yaxley) which they ought to have forgotten long ago. It is when they are in the unassailable position of guardian however that they tend (Lord Blicester, Lord Emsworth, Lords Bittlesham and Bodsham and the Duke of Dunstable) to fill young men's minds (young women's in Lord Emsworth's case) with thoughts of emigration:

> 'No, sir,' said the man, 'Mr Davenport has been entertaining his uncle, the Duke of Dunstable, to luncheon, and over the coffee his Grace broke most of the sitting-room furniture with the poker.'
> To say that Pongo was astounded would be going too far. His Uncle Alaric's eccentricities were a favourite theme of conversation with Horace Davenport, and in Pongo he had always found a sympathetic confidant, for Pongo had an eccentric uncle himself. Though hearing Horace speak of his

Uncle Alaric, and thinking of his own Uncle Fred, he felt like Noah listening to someone making a fuss about a drizzle (UFS)

under the sauce: see **whiffled**

unfrocked: see **Now We Know Dept.**

Union Castle Line, the: one of the weightier Sunday newspapers recently mentioned that the well-known steamship company had a notable record in the transporting of celebrities. Sir Winston Churchill as a young war correspondent, as well as Prime Ministers Gladstone and Macmillan, have been among its passengers. To complete the record, the Union Castle also served its country in an outstanding peace-saving mission by removing (for their country's good) those incandescent twins Claude and Eustace Wooster from a Metropolis which was fast growing too hot to hold them. The operation as conceived and executed (by Jeeves, naturally) was a masterpiece of diplomacy which any of the three Premiers would have applauded (IJ)

Union League Club, the: J. Chichester Clam, owner of the Clam Line, sitting in a potting shed and listening to Boko Fittleworth's view-halloos, feels this must be the Collapse of Civilisation, of which he has so often spoken at, (JM)

Upas tree: Stephanie Byng little better than a female variety of the, disaster on every side being what she strews (JM)

Upjohn, the Rev. Aubrey, M.A.: headmaster (and pres. proprietor) of Bertie Wooster's prep school Malvern House, q.v. He m. in middle-age the wealthy widow Jane Mills. On retirement he is spoken of as a prospective candidate for the Market Snodsbury division of Worcs (an unusual step for the cloth). Publishes a belle lettre on the management of preparatory schools which receives hot treatment by Reginald Herring, a former pupil, in a weekly review. His behaviour and general arrogance cause Dahlia Travers to sack him from a house party at Brinkley Court, when Bertie is fittingly selected by fate to convey him to exile in the village inn.

The facts are remarkably brief considering the penumbra cast by the character. Students of psychology would probably find him a rewarding study. His entrances have been scattered over forty years of novels and short stories, a remarkable record for a minor figure. Such entrances are brief but potent. He dominates them as they, in turn, dominate the subconscious mind of the narrator, Bertie Wooster. It is true that for Bertie, whose age is pegged at about

25, school memories are fairly recent; the author's seeming pre-occupation with the character is a different matter. Against the handful of realistic headmasters, remote and stately, of Beckford, Wrykin and St. Austin's, he stands out like a feral creature of the jungle night. There is a suggestion that even the author hesitates (for thirty-seven years) to let us see Upjohn in, as it were, full daylight—cassowary eye, bare upper lip (now clothed in an un-clerical moustache), scrawny neck and all. By that time, for us as for Bertie, the years have shrunk him to a little less than lifesize. Some might suppose a fate of draconic dimensions might overtake him in the end. That is not the Wodehouse way. Indignity is the just reward of the evildoer, and the funnier the indignity, the better everyone is pleased. Aubrey therefore is made to share the fate of those Assyrians who, coming down like wolves on the fold, found it full not of lambs but of wildcats; than which (as we are reminded) nothing is liable to make an Assyrian look more foolish (*passim* and esp. NS, JO)

> those get-togethers in his study, when with a sinking heart I had watched him reach for the whangee and start limbering up the shoulder muscles with a few trial swings at that period he had been an upstanding old gentleman about eight feet six in height with burning eyes, foam-flecked lips and flame coming out of both nostrils. He had now shrunk to a modest five foot seven or thereabouts, and I could have felled him with a single blow
>
> I used to sneak down to Aubrey Upjohn's study at dead of night in quest of the biscuits he kept there in a tin on his desk, and there came back to me the memory of the occasion when, not letting a twig snap beneath my feet, I had entered his sanctum in pyjamas and a dressing-gown, to find him seated in his chair, tucking into the biscuits himself. The What-does-this-mean-Woostering that ensued and the after-math next morning—six of the best on the old spot—has always remained graven on the tablets of my mind, if that's the expression I want (JO)

Upper Bleaching: Hampshire village celebrated for its annual battle (officially termed a football match) with Hockley-cum-Meston. The village squire is Bertie Wooster's uncle by marriage (VGJ)

Uppingham School: Rutland, among former alumni are Bimbo (later Bwana) Biggar and Beau (later Hobo) Sycamore (RJ)

Usborne, Richard A.: author of **WODEHOUSE AT WORK** (1961), the first considerable assessment of the opus. Not very much more could be said about Wodehouse the worker. A fan from boyhood, Usborne co-relates the musings of years in a manner at once shrewd and stimulating. His analyses of Wodehouse's characters, both great and small, are a treasury. The chapters on Bertie and Jeeves should be read and re-read. Like other students (Anthony Powell, Nigel Dennis, George Orwell, R.B.D. French), Usborne gives much thought to the determined caprice which characterises what has come to be known as 'vintage' Wodehouse, and does it in a manner at once scholarly, sparkling and therapeutic in the sense that Wodehouse himself is therapeutic (WAW)

V

Van Alstyne, Mr: South Africa has had its unpopular moments, but all Britain has cause to praise the name of this Johannesburg businessman who found employment there for the Wooster twins Claude and Eustace (IJ)

Vert Galant, le: takes the Dover Street air in full view of the Drones Club:

> The door of the Demosthenes Club had swung open and there had come down the front steps a tall, stout, florid man of middle age, who wore his top hat like the plumed helmet of Henry of Navarre (CT)

Verulam, Lord: 1st Baron (Francis Bacon, Viscount St Albans, 1561-1626). Whilst not (quite) going to the ingenious lengths of the late Mgr. Ronald Knox, who showed conclusively that the Baconian 'Cipher' proved that Queen Victoria wrote the works of Lord Tennyson, the Master has fun with the Bacon theory in his own fashion. Bertie is an occasional, if woolly, Baconian but (a perceptive point, this) always visits Shakespeare's supposed sins on the Bard himself:

> Bacon, as you no doubt remember, wrote Shakespeare's stuff for him and then, possibly because he owed the latter money

or it may be from sheer good nature, allowed him to take the credit for it (JM)

His fellow Drone Archie Mulliner gets into deep waters when he dines as the guest of his girl friend's aunt in the Sussex Weald:

What this woman needed was a fluid ounce of weed-killer . . . After the coffee was over she threw off all restraint. Scooping him up and bearing him off into the recesses of the west wing, she wedged him into a corner of a settee and began to tell him all about the remarkable discovery which had been made by applying the Plain Cipher to Milton's well-known epitaph on Shakespeare.

'Oh, that one?' said Archibald.

' "What needs my Shakespeare for his honour'd bones? The labour of an Age in piled stones? Or that his hallowed Reliques should be hid under a star-ypointing Pyramid?" ' said the aunt.

Archibald, who was not good at riddles, said he didn't know.

'As in the Plays and Sonnets,' said the aunt, 'we substitute the name equivalents of the figure totals . . .'

'All right,' said Archibald, 'let it go. I dare say you know best.'

The aunt inflated her lungs.

'These figure totals,' she said, 'are always taken out in the Plain Cipher, A equalling one to Z equals twenty-four. A capital letter with the figures indicates an occasional variation in the name count. For instance, A equals twenty-seven, B twenty-eight, until K equals ten is reached, when K, instead of ten, becomes one, and R or Reverse and so on, until A equals twenty-four is reached. The short or single digit is not used here. Reading the Epitaph in the light of this Cipher, it becomes, "What need Verulam for Shakespeare? Francis Bacon England's King be hid under a W. Shakespeare? William Shakespeare. Fame, what needest Francis Tudor, King of England? Francis. Francis W. Shakespeare. For Francis thy William Shakespeare hath England's King took W. Shakespeare. Then thou our W. Shakespeare Francis Tudor bereaving Francis Bacon Francis Tudor such a tomb William Shakespeare".'

The speech was unusually lucid and simple for a Baconian, yet Archibald, his eye catching a battle-axe that hung on the wall, could not but stifle a wistful sigh. How simple it would have been, had he not been a Mulliner and a gentleman, to spit on his hands and haul off and dot this doddering old ruin one just above the imitation pearl necklace.

VERY GOOD, JEEVES: published in 1930, is a collection of eleven stories. It is dedicated to E. Phillips Oppenheim, on whom there is a passage in PF. In the brief preface to **VERY GOOD, JEEVES** the Master observes:

> It is now some fourteen summers since, an eager lad in my early thirties, I started to write Jeeves stories; and many people think that this nuisance should now cease. Carpers say that enough is enough. Cavillers say the same. They look down the vista of the years and see these chronicles multiplying like rabbits, and the prospect appals them. But against this must be set the fact that writing Jeeves stories gives me a great deal of pleasure and keeps me out of the public-houses (VGJ)

Via Lactea Galaxy, the: most branches of learning are explored by the Master. His only astronomical expert however is Madeline Bassett. On calm reflection Bertie finds he is unable to subscribe to her theory connecting the appearance of new heavenly bodies in the Milky Way with the incidence of lachrymation in the fairy world (RHJ)

Vickers, Elizabeth: is reunited to her Freddie through the agency of a chunk of toffee resembling the Albert Memorial. (COJ)

vieux regime: it took a lot to make them chuck people out of music halls in 1887 (COJ)

Village England: see **Gazetteer**

Vine St. Police Station: a popular rendezvous for young gentlemen and occasionally (see **Tottie**) young ladies on the morrow of festive occasions as, e.g., the annual aquatic contest, sir, between the Universities of Oxford and Cambridge. Stirring legends are handed down to the younger gendarmerie by their elders about the brave days of old, when, for instance, Gally Threepwood, uncle of the impressionable Drone, was a regular habitué. With pride, they recollect that in his prime it took two, and sometimes three policemen to remove him thither from the Alhambra or the old Oxford music-hall, plus one more following behind, to carry his hat (*passim*)

Vinton St. Police Station: an alternative overnight rest-home for tired revellers, especially too for those who neglect the forward tilt before the upward lift when relieving rozzers of their headgear.

Bertie is presented in court there, having formerly, he tells us, taken his custom to the rival establishment at Bosher St. He finds that Barmy Phipps has understated the facts in describing the presiding beak at Vinton St. as a twenty-minute egg with many of the less endearing qualities of some high-up official in the Spanish Inquisition (JFS)

violin solos: there are several ways of classifying this form of entertainment. Bertie takes an austere line:

> It was loud in spots and less loud in other spots, and it had that quality which I have noticed in all violin solos of seeming to last much longer than it actually did (MS)

Voules, Police Sergeant Edward: Dorset County Constabulary, stationed at Chuffnell Regis. Is built rather on the lines of the Albert Hall, round in the middle and not much above. Holds strong views on shackling the rural police in their ceaseless war against the wrongdoer (TJ)

W

Walderwick, the Hon. Hugo: is that rare product, a toffee-nosed Drone. He earns fame in the Raleigh Stakes. Sir Walter sacrificed his cloak to keep dry a Maiden Queen. Hugo unwittingly sacrificed his umbrella to keep dry a queen among maidens. See **Psmith** (LIP)

Walkinshaw, Douglas: the hapless Pongo Twistleton is constrained to become a vet's anaesthetist and assistant under this name when his unquenchable uncle calls at a strange house on the pretext of cutting the parrot's claws (YMS)

Walkinshaw, Capt. J. G.: a dark and monocled Drone, held in some regard for his saxophonic prowess, is (a little improbably) horse-whipped on the steps of the Club. See **Petherick-Soames**

Waterloo Station, S.E.: of London's main rail termini it is second in popularity to Paddington. Its stir and bustle are contrasted with the leisurely, aristocratic air of Paddington where (is there a faint hint of it still left today?) you get only the best people—women in two-piece tweeds with faces like horses and men who obviously mix with only the best type of basset-hound:

> The march of progress has robbed Waterloo Station of its mysteries. Once, it used to be a quaint, dim Wonderland in which bewildered Alices and their male counterparts wandered helplessly, seeking information of officials as naïvely at sea as themselves. But now it is orderly and efficient. (*passim*)

Waterbury, Mr: Oliver Sipperley's former prep school headmaster was once in a position to direct small malefactors to come into his study in the manner of lions roaring at early Christians; but on trying to cajole the adult Sippy into publishing his dreary articles he is discomfited.

Watson, Jane: is the surpassing cook employed by Bingo Little's uncle, Mortimer Little, before his ennoblement as Lord Bittlesham. Jeeves has 'an understanding', amounting to an engagement, with her. After seven years of rearguard actions to prevent covetous friends from luring her away, Mortimer marries Jane, to Jeeves's undisguised relief and to Bingo's chagrin (IJ)

WEEK-END WODEHOUSE: First Edition, 1939. An Anthology with the notable introduction by Hilaire Belloc which hailed Wodehouse as the best living writer of English, 'the head of my profession'. It contains two Jeeves stories, two Drones stories and two extracts from Wooster novels (WEW)

'Wee Nooke': Bertie feels that this cottage on the Worplesdon estate, placed at his disposal by his uncle, should be renamed 'Oompus Boompus' (JM)

Wee Tots: this popular and influential organ, which does so much to mould public opinion in the nursery, is owned by H.C. (who occasionally signs himself P.P.) Purkiss. It is through the chance exposure of some of H.C.'s (or P.P.'s) personal foibles that Bingo Little contrives to insinuate himself into the editorial chair. One by-product of this is the extraordinary era of literary renascence which sets in at the Drones. Scarcely an Egg or Bean, a Pieface or Crumpet, fails to take pen in hand with the feeling that here is where he cashes in and recoups some of the stuff that has gone down the drain at Ally Pally and Kempton Park (EBC, NS, FO)

Wellbeloved, Mrs Clara: of High Street, King's Deverill, Hants is one of the Rev. Sidney Pirbright's needy parishioners, to whom Corky Pirbright, that bedizening Hollywood star, pursuing her role of Little Mother to the parish, conveys a bowl of strengthening soup. The old lady proves so well-informed on the population of Beverly Hills that she is able to add to Corky's stockpile of Hollywood folklore (MS)

Wellbeloved, Percy: what England needs, we feel, to make it perfect is more Wellbeloveds. This unit in the prolific family is gardener to the Earl of Rowcester at Rowcester Abbey. An interesting point arises. Only in summer (we are told) is the river at the bottom of the garden. In winter the position is reversed. What does Percy do in the winter? Perhaps he grows watercress? (RJ) On the indubitable authority of Jeeves, it is pleasant to record that Percy has Shropshire connections. He may then, with near certainty, be equated with that notable family which has produced the erratic George Cyril (quondam guide and mentor to the Empress of Blandings), his father Orlando, whom so many people don't want to hear about, and his grandfather Ezekiel, who took off his trousers one snowy afternoon in the High Street and gave them to a passer-by, observing that he would not need them as the world was coming to an end at 5.30 sharp. (RJ)

West, Rex: pen-name of Percy Gorringe, an ambivalent soul who composes avant-garde verse with titles like *Caliban At Sunset* with equal facility as such esoteric and improving works as *The Mystery of the Pink Crayfish* and others frequently consulted by Bertie Wooster and that other whodunit specialist, Freddie Threepwood (JFS)

> **What the Well-Dressed Young Man is not Wearing**

'WHAT DO TIES MATTER, JEEVES, AT A TIME LIKE THIS?'
'THERE IS NO TIME, SIR, AT WHICH TIES DO NOT MATTER'

Just then the waitress arrived. Rather a pretty girl.

Bingo was goggling. His entire map was suffused with a rich blush. He looked like the Soul's Awakening done in pink.

'Hullo, Mabel!' he said, with a sort of gulp.

'Hallo,' said the girl.

'You see I'm wearing the tie,' said Bingo.

'It suits you beautiful,' said the girl.

Personally, if anyone had told me that a tie like that suited me, I should have risen and struck them on the mazzard, regardless of their age and sex, but poor old Bingo simply got all flustered with gratification, and smirked in a most gruesome manner (IJ)

I went straight back to my room, dug out the old cummerbund and draped it round the old tum. I turned round and Jeeves shied like a startled mustang.

'I beg your pardon, sir,' he said in a sort of hushed voice, 'you are surely not proposing to appear in public in that thing?'

'The cummerbund?' I said in a careless, debonair way. 'Oh, rather!'

'I should not advise it, sir. Really, I shouldn't. The effect, sir, is loud in the extreme.'

'You know, the trouble with you, Jeeves, is that you're too— what's the word I want—too bally insular. You can't realise that you aren't in Piccadilly all the time. In a place like this a bit of colour and a touch of the poetic is expected of you. Why, I've just seen a fellow downstairs in a morning suit of yellow velvet.'

'Nevertheless, sir—'

'Jeeves, my mind is made up. This cummerbund seems to me to be called for. I consider it has rather a Spanish effect. Sort of Vicente y Blasco What's-his-name stuff. The jolly old hidalgo off to the bullfight.'

'Very good, sir,' said Jeeves coldly (IJ)

I reached for the umbrella and hat, and was heading for the open spaces, when I heard Jeeves give that soft cough of his, and saw that a shadow was about to fall on what had been a day of joyous reunion. In the eye he was fixing on me I detected the aunt-like gleam which always means that he disapproves of something, and when he said in a soupy sort of voice 'Pardon me, sir, but are you proposing to enter the Ritz Hotel in that hat' I knew that the time had come when Bertram must show that iron resolution of his which has been so widely publicised. Right from the start I had been asking myself what his reaction would be to the blue Alpine hat with the pink feather in it which I had purchased in his absence. Now I knew. I could see at a g. that he wanted no piece of it.

I, on the other hand, was all for this Alpine lid. It unquestionably lent a *diablerie* to my appearance, and mine is an appearance that needs all the *diablerie* it can get. In my voice, therefore, as I replied, there was a touch of steel.

'Yes, Jeeves, that, in a nutshell, is what I am proposing to do. Don't you like this hat?'

'No, sir.'

'Well, I do,' I replied rather cleverly, and went out with it tilted just that merest shade over the left eye which makes all the difference (SLJ)

'Jeeves,' I said, 'you don't read a paper called *Milady's Boudoir*, do you?'

'No, sir. The periodical has not come to my notice.'

'Well, spring sixpence on it next week, because this article will appear in it. Wooster on the Well Dressed Man, don't you know.'

'Indeed, sir?'

'Yes, indeed, Jeeves. I've rather extended myself over this little bijou. There's a bit about socks that I think you will like.'

He took the manuscript, brooded over it, and smiled a gentle, approving smile.

'The sock passage is quite in the proper vein, sir,' he said.

'Well expressed, what?'

'Extremely, sir.'

I watched him narrowly as he read on and, as I was expecting, what you might call the love-light suddenly died out of his eyes. I braced myself for an unpleasant scene.

'Come to the bit about soft silk shirts for evening wear?' I said carelessly.

'Yes, sir,' said Jeeves in a low, cold voice, as if he had been bitten in the leg by a personal friend, 'and if I may be pardoned—'

'You don't like it?'

'No, sir. I do not. Soft silk shirts with evening costume are not worn, sir.'

'Jeeves,' I said, looking the blighter diametrically in the eyeball, 'they're dashed well going to be. I may as well tell you now that I have ordered a dozen of those shirtings from Peabody and Simms, and it's no good looking like that, because I am jolly well adamant.'

'If I might—'

'No, Jeeves,' I said, raising my hand, 'argument is useless. Nobody has a greater respect that I have for your judgment in socks, in ties and—I will go further—in spats; but when it comes to evening shirts your nerve seems to fail you. Hidebound is the word that suggests itself. It may interest you to learn that when I was at le Touquet the Prince of Wales buzzed into the Casino one night with soft silk shirt complete.'

'His Royal Highness, sir, may permit himself a certain licence which in your own case—'

'No, Jeeves,' I said firmly, 'It's no use. When we Woosters are adamant, we are—well, adamant, if you know what I mean.'

'Very good, sir.' (COJ)

'You remember the day I lunched at the Ritz, Jeeves?'

'Yes, sir. You were wearing an Alpine hat.'

'There is no need to dwell on the Alpine hat, Jeeves.'

'No, sir.'

'If you really want to know, several fellows at the Drones asked me where I had got it.'

'No doubt with a view to avoiding your hatter, sir.' (SLJ)

'One of your best and brightest, Jeeves,' I said, refilling the glass. 'The weeks among the shrimps have not robbed your hand of its cunning.'

He did not reply. Speech seemed to have been wiped from his lips, and I saw, as I had foreseen would happen, that his gaze was riveted on the upper slopes of my mouth. It was a cold, disapproving gaze, such as a fastidious luncher who was not fond of caterpillars might have directed at one which he had discovered in his portion of salad, and I knew that the clash of wills for which I had been bracing myself was about to rear its ugly head.

'Something appears to be arresting your attention, Jeeves. Is there a smut on my nose?'

His manner continued frosty. There are moments when he looks just like a governess, one of which was this one.

'No, sir. It is on the upper lip. A dark stain like mulligatawny soup' (JFS)

'Jeeves,' I said, 'you stand alone. I wish there was something I could do to repay you.'

He coughed that sheep-like cough of his.

'There does chance to be a favour it is within your power to bestow, sir.'

'Name it, Jeeves. Ask of me what you will, even unto half my kingdom.'

'If you could see your way to abandoning your Alpine hat, sir.'

I ought to have seen it coming. That cough should have told me. But I hadn't, and the shock was severe.

'You would go as far as that?' I said, chewing the lower lip.

'It was merely a suggestion, sir.'

I took the hat off and gazed at it. The morning sunlight played on it, and it had never looked so blue, its feather so pink.

'I suppose you know you're breaking my heart?'

'I am sorry, sir.'

I gave him the hat. It made me feel like a father reluctantly throwing his child from the sledge to divert the attention of the pursuing wolf pack, as I believe happens all the time in Russia in the winter months, but what would you? (SLJ)

What Tiny Hands Can Do For Nannie: Bingo Little composes a thoughtful editorial on, for Wee Tots (NS)

What Jeeves doesn't know: 'They can't get it into their nuts' said Catsmeat, 'that the modern actor is a substantial citizen who makes his sixty quid a week and salts most of it away in sound Government securities. Why, dash it, if I could think of some way of doing down the income-tax people, I should be a rich man. You don't know of a way of doing down the income-tax people, do you, Bertie?'

'Sorry, no. I doubt if even Jeeves does.' (MS)

whiffled: see **woozled**

Whistler's Mother: Jeeves has grave misgivings on noticing the long legs and the powerful rump of,

'Who the dickens *was* Whistler, anyway?'

'A figure, landscape and portrait painter of considerable distinction, m'lord, born in Lowell, Massachusetts, in 1834. His "Portrait of My Mother", painted in 1872, is particularly esteemed by the cognoscenti and was purchased by the French Government for the Luxembourg Gallery, Paris, in the year 1892. His works are individual in character and notable for subtle colour harmony.' (RJ)

White House Wonder: the headgear as worn by President Coolidge is specifically preferred by Jeeves to the Broadway Special (COJ)

White Hunter, the: see **Brabazon-Biggar** (RJ)

Wibbleton-in-the-Vale: Freddie Widgeon is fortunate in finding a scarecrow at this Worcestershire village, and borrows its trousers (YMS)

Wickham, the late Sir Cuthbert, Bart.: of Skeldings Hall, Herts. 'Father of Roberta' might be held more than enough for any man's epitaph, yet with Roberta in mind we should like to know more about the deceased Bart. The *brio* and *empressement* of the Mulliners is not evident in her mother. Was it then from Cuthbert that Bobbie acquired those talents which can even bring a shudder into the voice of Jeeves? If so, the Baronet must have been blood brother to Gally Threepwood and Uncle Fred (JO)

Wickham, Lady: relict of the foregoing, lives at the picturesque Skeldings Hall, Herts. Author of *Agatha's Vow, A Strong Man's Love, Meadowsweet, A Man for a' That, Fetters of Fate* and other goo. She is not only a close buddy of the Pest of Pont Street but also a practising member of the Pen and Ink Club. If a solitary fact may be advanced in her favour, it is that she and she only, on the whole Wooster canvas, is able to exert firm, and even drastic control over the squirt Roberta. It is no mean achievement (BCE, *et al.*)

Wickham, Miss: s. of the late Sir Cuthbert and aunt, therefore, to the carrot-topped saboteuse, lives in Eaton Square, S.W. Tel.: SLOane 8090 (VGJ)

Wickham, Roberta: o.d. of the late Sir Cuthbert and of Lady Wickham, Skeldings Hall, Herts, has figured (always sensationally) in six short stories and one novel and, perhaps on these grounds alone, may be accepted as archetype of her genre—that of the glorious, young female fire-raisers whom Wodehouse has evolved from the most shadowy and sporadic beginnings in the story of English fiction, or indeed of history itself. His well-versed readers will recollect a clergyman who, thoughtfully composing tomorrow's sermon, spends time and effort in trying to think of a single-syllabled word meaning Supralapsarianism. The best we can do in Bobbie's case is the three-syllabled 'catalyst', as suggesting an agent capable of producing dissolution, ruin, gloom and destruction on all sides whilst itself undergoing no apparent change. They rank among the Master's evergreens. They will live in literature among his greatest and best known creations.

There is a sharp distinction between the Stiffy-Nobby-Pauline-Bobbie-Corky type of Wodehouse girl and the predictable, dependable Joan-Terry-Sally-Jill-Kay coterie whose prototype perhaps (a personal choice) is Sue Cotterleigh (Brown) of **'Heavy Weather'**. Bobbie and her sodality of mischief-ripe maidens have been generating fizz for the vintage stories for thirty years. In a restricted sense they have no male counterparts, since their female gender is an essential part of their formidable armoury. There is though an essential relationship with some of the more enterprising Drones and an even closer one with the senior firebrands. Perhaps Claude and Eustace Wooster, Fred Ickenham, Psmith and (in youthful prime) Gally Threepwood approach them most nearly. These 'spirited damsels, human ticking-bombs', as he calls them, are traced back by Richard Usborne to the young raggers of the early school stories. In WAW he notes:

> These festive young female squirts, androgynous mischief-makers, are a sore trial to their mothers (Bobbie), guardians (Stiffy and Nobby) and uncles (Corky). They are charming, unscrupulous, quarrelsome, mettlesome, demanding, quick to tears, quick to wrath (especially with their loved ones) and always apt to 'start something'.

If we seek even further back, I suspect we might find their historic origins amongst the ice-down-the-dress-collar lady guests of the high society Edwardian boulevardiers and the Pelican Club companions of Fruity Biffen, Plug Basham, Tubby Parsloe and Stiffy Bates. In maturity, they are seen, and gloriously, in Aunt Dahlia. In embryo they are typified by Prudence Carroway, who sets fire to the school by dropping the lamp with which she is impersonating Florence Nightingale, and has her clothes kicked into the river by the horse on which she is emulating Lady Godiva.

It may seem pragmatical to stress the importance of their sex. Armed as fully as their male counterparts with a fertility of inventive enterprise, they have an additional offensive-defensive weapon of devastating effect and power. If they are loved, the unfortunate goop is made to jump through flaming hoops. If they have the gorgeous opportunity of two men on a string simultaneously, these are played off against each other for the sheer hell of it. And even when they return their swain's devotion, they contrive a series of Herculean labours for him. They are, above all, ever ready to seek refuge and a recruitment of devilry in that highly artificial but ingeniously effective code of chivalry on which the world of Dronery depends. It is this above all which to my mind seems to assume an even earlier genesis for them. For me there was a stab of recognition on reading:

> The visitor, who walked springily into the room, was a girl of remarkable beauty. She resembled a particularly good-looking schoolboy who had dressed up in his sister's clothes.

That is Bobbie Wickham; but substitute 'schoolgirl who had dressed up in her brother's clothes' and you have Viola in *Twelfth Night*. You may safely take the suggestion much further by observing the close parallel between the idiomatic, rapier cut and thrust dialogue of these young moppets of misrule and that of their Shakespearian counterparts, especially Beatrice and Rosalind.

Bobbie, we are told, has been 'pretty extensively wooed for years, with no business resulting'. Bertie is perennially attracted to her, and twice engaged to her—the second time without his own knowledge. Jeeves, of course, is aware of, and able to cope with, the menace *ab initio*. The only man, save Jeeves, who has no illusions about her is Kipper Herring, and that in itself constitutes a happy ending to a saga when they are booked for the holy moment. By way of panache for Bobbie's legend, it is reserved for her to crown the discomfiture of Simon Legree Upjohn in the dictation of surrender terms, which she begins with a curt 'Listen, Buster . . .' (VGJ, BCE, MMS, JO)

Wickham, Wilfred: schoolboy cousin of Bobbie Wickham, and a pretty ghastly specimen, with an offensive habit of regarding a well turned out Drone like a biologist examining some lower organism under a microscope (MMS)

Wickhammersley, the Rt. Hon. the Earl of: once a close friend of Bertie's father, owns Twing Hall, Glos, where Bertie is always a welcome guest (IJ)

Wickhammersley, Lady Cynthia: y.d. of Lord Wickhammersley, whose family name is not specified. Bertie confides that he was once in love with her. 'A dashed pretty and attractive girl, but full of ideals and all that . . . so the jolly old frenzy sort of petered out. . . . I think she's a topper and she thinks me next door to a looney, so everything's nice and matey' (IJ)

Widgeon: family name of the Earl of Blicester, q.v.

Widgeon, Cyril: a cousin of the enterprising Freddie, joins the police force via Hendon Training College and starts his new career auspiciously by pinching Freddie at Hurst Park (JM)

Widgeon, Frederick Fortescue: perhaps the most likeable of all Drones—save, of course, Bertie. Is nephew, and perh. heir, to the Earl of Blicester, on whose grudging quarterly pittances Freddie subsists. He is also (and one has the claims of Bingo Little and Pongo Twistleton well in mind) probably the most susceptible young man in the W.1. postal district. It is notorious at the Drones that the girls who have returned him to store, if placed end to end, would stretch from Piccadilly to Hyde Park Corner—probably farther, because some of them were pretty tall. In fact Freddie should really be chronicled in **Collectors' Corner,** were it not for the fact that he invariably loses his pieces. Among them may be mentioned Mavis Peasemarch, Dahlia Prenderby, Dora Pinfold, Helen Christopher, Drusilla Wix, Hildegarde Watt-Watson and

Vanessa Vokes. His reverses are not uneventful. No Jeeves stands by to ease him from his entanglements or predicaments with dignity and ease. Rather is his path beset with dog-ridden bed-rooms, morning milk-trains, scarecrows' trousers, militant Army officers and barrages of tomatoes and bad eggs in the expert hands of East End costermongers. It was both welcome and fitting that after almost thirty years' pacemaking Freddie should blossom out as central character of a full length novel (ICE IN THE BED-ROOM) in which he wins both financial independence and the hand of the attractive Sally Painter, who is at last prepared to revise her first judgment:

> 'You stand revealed as a cross between a flitting butterfly and a Mormon elder' (IB)

Freddie's future now lies on his Kenya coffee plantation. England is the loser (*passim* and IB)

Wiffin, Ambrose: when at the height of his fever, would probably have looked askance at Royalty itself, had Royalty been so inconsiderate as to interrupt his tête-à-tête with Bobbie Wickham, for whose sake he willingly would (and inevitably does) suffer the plagues reserved for the Egyptians (MMS)

Wilberforce, Maudie: graced the bar of the Criterion in the brave days of old, and is now a buxom widow with orange hair living at Wistaria Lodge, Kitchener Road, East Dulwich, S.E. She lives, too, to prove that the Gibson Girls and the Old Gaiety had no monopoly of marriage into the Peerage. Girls of the old Cri. may have to wait forty years, but they get their man in the end—in this case Bertie's uncle, Lord Yaxley (VGJ)

> There are some people who don't seem intended to be seen close to, and this was one of them. Billowy curves, if you know what I mean. Also the orange hair and the magenta dress.
> 'So you're here at last!' she said. 'We needn't waste time. You can be taking a look at my knee.'
> I'm all for knees at their proper time and, as you might say, in their proper place, but somehow this didn't seem the moment.
> 'What do you think of that knee?' she asked, lifting the seven veils. Well, of course one has to be polite.
> 'Terrific!' I said. (VGJ)

Willoughby, Old Scrubby: fast wing three-quarter, would never learn to give the reverse pass:

He had said enough to show me that this Willoughby must have been a pretty dubious character, and when he went on to tell me that poor old Scrubby had died of cirrhosis of the liver in the Federated Malay States I wasn't really surprised (SLJ)

Wimbolt, Percy: of the Drones, dreams he is standing in morning dress on the steps of London Guildhall, and is about to receive the Freedom of the City, when the Lord Mayor suddenly reaches for the City Mace and takes a swipe at him (YMS)

Wimsey, Lord Peter Death Bredon: younger b. of his Grace the Duke of Denver. Res. 100A Piccadilly, W. Is conjectured by Freddie Widgeon as wondering what to make of a kid's frock, no kid inside it, floating on the river (YMS). Boko Fittleworth is advised by Nobby Hopwood to consult Lord Peter on the dubious value of an alibi, or alternatively to refer to Reggie Fortune, M. Poirot, Inspector French or Nero Wolfe (JM)

Winchell, Walter: references to the playboy son of Homer and Adela Cream, usually under the sobriquet 'Broadway Willie', are frequent in the column conducted by, (JO)

Wingham: family name of the Earl of Sturridge, q.v.

Wingham, the Hon. and Rev. Hubert: 3rd s. of the Earl of Sturridge, has a cure of souls at Twing, Glos, and is Bingo Little's successful rival for the hand of Mary Burgess after the ill-fated village concert (IJ)

Winkworth, Dame Daphne, D.B.E.: widow of the historian, is the gauleiter of the nymphery of aunts who hold Esmond Haddock in thrall at King's Deverill; also conducts a girls' school, and is a rugged light-heavyweight whose make-up and general forthrightness suggest a sort of unpleasant amalgam of Nellie-Wallace-Beery:

the thought crossed my mind that life for the unfortunate moppets who had drawn this Winkworth as a headmistress must have been like Six Weeks on Sunny Devil's Island (MS, JO)

Winkworth, the late P. B.: noted historian, m. Daphne Deverill and understandably became the late (MS)

Wintergreen, Mrs: of Pont St., S.W., widow of Col. H. W. Wintergreen, is not only an aunt of Roderick Spode, Leader of

Britain's Black Shorts, but is engaged to wed Sir Watkyn Bassett. Having in mind her neighbour Agatha Spenser Gregson, it seems that the scales have been unduly weighted against this inoffensive Chelsea thoroughfare (CW)

Witherspoon, Sir Reginald, Bart.: m. Katherine Wooster. He res. at Bleaching Court, Upper Bleaching, Hants., where Bertie has a standing invitation (VGJ)

Witherspoon, Lady: is (though the point is never clarified) younger sister to Agatha and Dahlia and is therefore Bertie's aunt (CW)

Witherspoon, Chief Inspector, C.I.D.: of New Scotland Yard promises to fling the prisoner Wooster into a cell with dripping walls and to see that he is well gnawed by rats (SLJ)

Wivelscombe, the Rt. Hon. the Earl of: Ferdinand James Delamere Spettisbury, 6th E., res. at Wivelscombe Court, Upton Snodsbury, Worcs. Hobbies: oenology, the standing place-kick (his lordship holds the Midland Counties record) and spiritualism. A prominent member of the Loyal Sons of Worcestershire. (See also **Ballindallochs** and **Spettisbury, Geraldine**) (YMS)

Wivelscombe, the late Dowager Countess of: m. of the present peer, was by birth a Ballindalloch and, like her Highland forebears, had the gift of the sight. Some of her sights got her disliked in the County (YMS)

Wix, Drusilla: transient lodestar of Freddie Widgeon, flashes like a meteor across his firmament. She comes of a long line of bishops and archdeacons, but looks like a blend of Tallulah Bankhead and a policewoman (YMS)

WODEHOUSE AT WORK: see **Usborne, Richard A.** (WAW)

Wodehouse Country, the: is appropriately of dual nationality with occasional French extensions—mainly Provence and the Cote d'Azur. No one will advance any pretentious claim that P. G. Wodehouse has attempted to appropriate any territories in the sense of 'the Hardy country', the 'Brontë country' or the Shropshire of Mary Webb and A. E. Housman. Yet his repeated returns to certain settings does (one believes) imply a personal preference and even an addiction to those scenes. Something has been said (see **New York City**) about the American settings. The French ones are confined to the short stories and to **FRENCH LEAVE.** This brief note therefore deals with the England of the Wooster-Jeeves stories, an England, indeed, which includes all the others with home settings.

With Wodehouse, whose instincts (as he tells us in PF) in planning a novel are to set in advance a series of scenes, in the stage sense, the settings are never obtrusive and play no major role. Their influence, if any, is mildly beneficent, or at least benedictory. Nature tends to take the current mood of the story. The weather too falls into line. There are exceptions to this when characters, staggering beneath the bludgeonings of chance or malignity, feel that the indecent sunshine ought, if it had any conscience, to give way to the weather conditions of *King Lear*, Act III, Sc. 2; but in general the weather has the sanguine element of, e.g., Blandings Castle, which basks in sempiternal sunshine and is regaled by the choirings of the best bird music obtainable, save for the short summer storm which echoes the human drama inside its walls. Wodehouse's England is neatly parcelled out. It has three well-defined areas; the Welsh Marcher counties of Worcestershire, Shropshire and Gloucestershire; the county of Hampshire; and London, including parts of Greater London. Perhaps (though one isn't sure) its heart, in the emotive sense, is in the three West Midland counties, and especially Worcestershire. One of England's smallest counties, it rates more village names than any other in the opus (see **Gazetteer**) and is third out of 19 counties in the Stately Homes industry. In one of his forewords the Master says he likes to pop down to Shropshire and look in at Blandings; he obviously feels the same sentiment for Worcestershire and Brinkley Court. Indeed, this genuine attachment for the upper Severn Vale goes much further back. If you take an Ordnance map and draw a straight line northwards from the city of Gloucester to a point four miles west of Wolverhampton (significantly enough, through a village named Rudge) that line will pass through the very heart of Wodehouse England. On either side of it, and within a few miles of it, are names redolent of characters in the stories, generally used as they appear on the map, occasionally (Wooster is a classic example) slightly altered. Many of them go back to the early school stories, others are of later usage. Among them are Ackleton, Stableford, Claines, Snodsbury, Tewkesbury, Eckington, Rudge, Beckford, Malvern, Alcester, Preston, Droitwich, Powick, Davenport, Wick, Kidderminster, Storridge and Pershore. Wrykin School has obvious Shropshire roots. Moreton-in-the-Marsh becomes the Earl of Marshmoreton. The site of Blandings Castle can be pinpointed. The River Skirme, the brook Wopple, joining the River Wipple, lead us to Rudge-in-the-Vale.

The village names are usually felicitous (purists would cavil at the -by suffix in shires outside the Danelaw) and are often inspired. Their very extravagance is a mere echo of English place nomenclature. As with life itself, nature constantly chases his most fantastic names, and occasionally overtakes them. He gives us the delightful names of Higglesford, Gandle-by-the-Hill, Little Wigmarsh, Old Crockford and Twing. The Ordnance Survey for his own chosen area counters with Flyford Flavell, Much Marcle, Neen Savage, Dymock and Quatt. He comes back with Maiden Eggesford, Pondlebury Parva, Fale-by-the-Water, Lower Smattering-on-the-Wissel and Briskett-in-the-Midden. The map quenches him with Ainderby Quainhow, Mamble, Mousehole, Much Birch, Margaret Roding, Leonard Stanley, Nether Wallop, Styrrup and Barton-in-the-Beans. In case of further extravagances it holds in reserve Archdeacon Newton, Toller Porcorum, Huish Champsfleurs and Quy.

His American appellatives are equally satisfying. Carterville (Ky.), Chilicothe (Ohio), Carbondale (Ill.), Duboque (Iowa), Cooden Beach (Long Island), Snakebite (Mich.) and Skewasset (Maine) are as plausible as the inspired Cogwych (Cheshire), Rising Mattock (Hants) or Dovetail Hammer (Berks).

London should have its own detailed section. I have a list of London addresses, clubs, churches, hotels, pubs, streets and institutions of all kinds which fills fourteen foolscap pages. The devotee can hardly pass down a single Mayfair street without mentally affixing blue plaques to hallowed landmarks. In that window of the Berkeley Grill, overlooking the corner of Berkeley Street and Piccadilly, Ronnie, last of the Fishes, entered the seventh heaven when Sue consented to be his wife. In nearby St. James's Street, his uncles Clarence and Galahad ran into each other outside the Senior Conservatives, and Bertie's Uncle George is a prominent sight—especially when seen sideways. Round the corner in Burlington Arcade is Blucher's, famed for gentlemen's ties and socks and Vigo Street has its occasional Royal visitor in search of a new topper. But the associations are as endless as the ghosts are real—more real by far than the anonymous drifting crowds; in a sense more real, too, than those places with personal Wodehouse links— Onslow Square where Jeeves was conceived, and the King's Road where the Master once lived.

Woollam Chersey Place: Hertfordshire home of Aunt Agatha during her first marriage (not to be confused with Woollam Chersey Manor, Bill Bannister's shack in **Doctor Sally**) and one of only three stately homes figuring in that county. It is the thought of being booked for a three weeks stay there that prompts Bertie's purple passage:

> Jeeves uncovered the fragrant eggs and b., and I pronged a moody forkful (VGJ)

It is when her husband, Spenser Gregson, cleans up to an amazing extent in Sumatra Rubber that Aunt Agatha lashes out impressively by buying Woollam Chersey with its 'miles of rolling parkland, trees in profusion well stocked with doves,' its rose garden and the lake on which young Thos. emulates Captain Flint, and Jeeves copes smoothly with a swan (*passim*)

Wooster: family name of the Earl of Yaxley, q.v.

Wooster (Wocestre) the Sieur de: (fl. 1415) is cited by his descendant Bertie Wooster as a notable combatant at the Battle of Agincourt (RHJ)

Wooster, Algernon: a key character for genealogists and for students of the Wodehouse opus, is the only established, specified blood link between the Wooster and Threepwood families. Mentioned as a guest at Blandings Castle, he is a cousin of Lord Stockheath, who is himself a cousin of the Threepwoods (LIP)

Wooster, Bertram Wilberforce: the pronunciation of Wooster and of Worcester is identical. *Chambers's World Gazetteer* (among others) states that the name of the Faithful City of Worcester is pronounced **Wooster.** Conversely, Bertie himself obliquely confirms that Wooster is pronounced **Worcester** when (as long ago as 1925 in COJ) he relates the confusion of one Kegworthy who, on hearing Bertie's surname, asks whether he spells it W-o-r-c-e-s-t-e-r. This seems conclusive, but if any have lingering doubts we may point to the no-English-nonsense rendering of Worcester in Ohio, U.S.A., where the capital of Wayne County is the city and township of Wooster.

The family is of some antiquity. Bertie (who is no snob) mentions the Sieur de Wocestre or Wooster who fought, apparently with distinction at Agincourt (1415). Elsewhere he states that the family not only came over with William of Normandy but were 'extremely pally with him'. This may have been so, but not, we imagine, under the name of Wooster. By the beginning of the present century, marriage connections had constrained the Woosters, in the then prevailing habit, to adopt hyphenations. When England blossomed with Heber-Percys, Cavendish-Bentincks, Maxwell-Hyslop-Maxwells, Ramsay-Fairfax-Lucys, Cave-Brown-Caves, Pelham-Clinton-

Hopes and Twisleton-Wykeham-Fiennes, the Woosters had prolif-
erated into Wooster-Mannering-Phipps. For a short period they
even dropped the Wooster and in MT (1917) were calling themselves Mannering-Phipps. With the rationalisation of English
society usage consequent on two wars and a social revolution, matters have become simplified. The Ramsay-Fairfax-Lucys of Charle-
cote have become Lucys once more. Heber-Percy has reverted to
Percy. The Twisleton-Wykeham-Fiennes of Broughton Castle call
themselves Fiennes, *tout court*, and the Wooster-Mannering-Phipps,
following the trend, have commendably retained only their oldest
patronymic, which is Wooster.

In WAW Richard Usborne (for whom I have the utmost respect)
states that 'the Wooster class is upper, without being of the county'.
I must demur. They are indeed not only of the gentry but of the
nobility. The Earldom of Yaxley, to which Bertie's uncle succeeds,
is heritable in the Wooster family. Bertie himself is in line of succession to it, as to the Wooster baronetcy merged in it.* The
Woosters' connection with the Earl of Emsworth's family, the
Threepwoods of Blandings, has already been shown. Several similar
alliances are deducible.

Bertram was country born, 'in the same village', he tells us, as
Bingo Little. As an infant he narrowly escaped asphyxia by swallowing his rubber comforter. Fortunately his Aunt Dahlia was at
hand to extricate it. Her regret for this rash act in later years is
forthright, frequent and poignant. His nurse was Nannie Hogg
(living now in retirement at Basingstoke) who suffered from flatu-
lence. At the age of six, 'when the blood ran hot', he once gave
Nannie Hogg 'a juicy one over the top-knot with a porringer'. He
remembers (JFS) being summoned by his mother to the drawing-
room to declaim 'The Charge of the Light Brigade' and Hood's
'Ben Battle' ('Bertie recites so nicely') for the edification of visitors,
and two years later attended the same dancing-class as the future
Hollywood screen star, Corky Pirbright, wearing 'a Little Lord
Fauntleroy suit and pimples'. About this time, it would seem, he
was orphaned. He rarely mentions his parents. That they were
well endowed is to be inferred by his own large fortune which (we
are to learn years later) has survived the war and supertax un-
impaired. At some time he was a choir-boy (he won the choirboys

* In that excellent book Usborne also touches on the autobiographical element
in the Wodehouse-Wooster *ens*. It should be mentioned, without undue emphasis,
that the Wodehouses are also of the nobility; that P.G.'s branch is a cadet of the
heritable Earldom of Kimberley, and that he is in line of succession to that title, as
well as to the still older baronetcy which it embraces. *Ed.*

bicycle race) and a Boy Scout. There followed the prep school period. Here he was known as 'Bungler Wooster', but the sole authority is the biased Upjohn. He also had, more plausibly, a habit of gaping at his mentors with open mouth. His boyhood seems to have been marked by normalcy in most respects. As a stripling he broke a valuable china vase with a catapult, earning thereby a castigation from Aunt Agatha which may even have equalled the classic reprobation administered by Aubrey Upjohn after the famous midnight biscuits episode, which he has 'always looked back upon as the last word in scholarly invective'. He introduced a white mouse into the English Literature class, too, and consequently made fifty consecutive explorations of a peak in Darien. To judge from his later proficiency (especially racquets) he must have had a good eye for a ball. He won a prize at Malvern House for the best holiday collection of wild flowers (since when, Aunt Agatha complains, he hasn't done a thing to advance the family name) and also won the much vaunted prize for Scripture knowledge. At 14 he wrote to Marie Lloyd for her autograph, but apart from that, he says, his private life can bear the strictest investigation. A year later he was discovered in the stable yard, smoking one of his uncle Percy Worplesdon's best cigars, and was chased for a mile across difficult country by the incensed nobleman, armed with a hunting crop. There are few references to his years at Eton, but, following the savage Malvern House days, perhaps no news may be taken as good news.

From Eton he went up to Magdalen. His memories are mainly confined to ragging, but he apparently played racquets for Oxford, partnered by Beefy Anstruther (MS). He also did some rowing, and still recalls some of the towing-path comments of Stilton Cheesewright, in the role of coach, about sticking his stomach out. At Bump Suppers and similar festivities he was known to take off all his clothes and ride round the quad on a bicycle, singing comic songs; on one occasion, insisting that he was a mermaid, he wanted to dive into the College fountain and play a harp. The episode raises doubts as to whether his college was in fact Magdalen (which has no fountain) or Christ Church. Years later, in JO, he is insistent that it was Magdalen. Besides Bingo Little (his exact contemporary), several other of his closest circle were at prep school, Eton and Oxford with him—Freddie Widgeon, Stilton Cheesewright, Catsmeat Pirbright, Lord Chuffnell and Kipper Herring among them.

It was during the formative school period that the famous Code, shared by almost all Drones, took its lifelong hold. As the Eton Boating Song reminds us, 'nothing in life can sever the chain that is round us now', and the bond voluntarily assumed by the Drones is just as real, just as artificial and just as eternal. You *must* stand by a friend when he needs, or appears to need, your help—however ridiculous the pretext; and you *must* honour a woman's professed devotion, even when you know, and she knows you know, that the true facts are as oompus-boompus as doodle gammon. Cervantes, Shakespeare, Goldsmith, Sheridan and many others have used these, or similar conceits as a matrix for comic situation; none have employed it more liberally or more uproariously than Wodehouse. The Code has landed his young men in more tureens than most of them would care to remember, and none more deeply than Bertie. How many times, to date, has he been saved from incompatible matrimony by the gong, or by sheer luck, or by the Jeeves lifeline? No other youngster in all Wodehouse has run things so fine. He once tried 'to marry into musical comedy' (a family occupation) but was 'dissuaded' by relations. He ardently wooed Corky Pirbright. He has several times proposed to Bobbie Wickham (she has held a perennial and near-fatal attraction for him) even after Jeeves has, at least twice, exposed her frivolity and 'larkiness'. Once he woke to find himself engaged to her without his knowledge. On three separate occasions he has got himself engaged at Brinkley, though 'no business resulted'. Even the barbed-wire-next-the-skin Aunt Agatha failed—resoundingly—to marry him off, after carefully selecting a prim, missionary type of girl who turned out to be a cracksman's moll. Tough intellectuals like Honoria Glossop and Florence Craye have tried repeatedly to 'mould' him, preparatory to marriage, only to find that his clay disintegrated into sand and slipped through their fingers. He has loved Cynthia Wickhammersley, but she was *sérieuse* and it petered out. He was smitten by Muriel Singer, who might have been a real menace had she not gone for bigger game. Gwladys Pendlebury and Beatrice Slingsby were the objects of his devotion for brief, but sensational, periods. He has all but sunk without trace in the soupy morass of Madeline Bassett's neo-Raphaelite goo and wilted in the gimlet gaze of Heloise Pringle. He was engaged to Pauline Stoker (for forty-eight hours only, during which he was in bed with a cold) in New York. Later he all but figured in a shotgun wedding at the hands of her father, after Pauline had found refuge in (the absent) Bertie's bed. His shock at this discovery was patent. He was the 'reputable bachelor whose licence had never been so much as endorsed'. It was clearly one up to Pauline, since the only other sensate beings ever discovered in Bertie's bed were a hedgehog and a lizard (up the left pyjama leg). More than forty years ago Bertie confided that 'Providence looks after the chumps of this world, and personally I'm all for it'. At that time he was growing from stage-dude beginnings into the most lovable young chump in fiction, and Providence, it seems, is still at work on the old stand.

Bertie's hobbies are: riding, swimming, racquets, shooting, squash, golf, tennis, darts, Big Squirting, Luminous Rabbiting, Cards-into-Top-Hat-Flipping. . . . His newspapers are the *Mail* and *Mirror* with occasional stabs at the crossword in Jeeves's copy of *The Times* or (JO) *Daily Telegraph*. His reading is exclusively whodunits and his collection must rival that of Freddie Threepwood. He's 'not much of a lad for the night-spots these days' but is still a member of about six nightclubs. His allergies (besides aunts) are old folk songs and violin solos, but he has a musical ear and (says Jeeves) a pleasant light baritone voice. His repertoire (bath or smoking-concert) includes 'Let's All Go Round to Maud's', 'The Yeoman's Wedding Song', 'A-Hunting We Will Go', 'Pale Hands', 'She Didn't Say Yes', 'Sonny Boy', 'Roll Out the Barrel', 'Ah, Sweet Mystery' and 'Every Morn I Bring Thee Violets'. Dogs like him ('the Wooster smell speaks to their deeps'), and cats also make for him with their tails up. His euphoria is remarkable. In his long career he has recorded only one cold (it covered the whole of his engagement to Pauline) and Jeeves (COJ) records one other. He is 'slim and willowy and tallish' (facts borne out by a Hyde Park orator and by Boko Fittleworth). Although his finances are still quite sound, he prudently attended an institution designed (to quote Jeeves) to teach the aristocracy to fend for itself, in case the social revolution should set in with even greater severity:

> 'Mr Wooster . . . I can hardly mention this without some display of emotion . . . is actually learning to darn his own socks. The course includes boot-cleaning, sock-darning, bed-making and primary grade cooking.'

In the event Bertie was awarded 1st prize for sock-darning and two pairs of his socks were exhibited on Speech Day. Then it was found he had used a crib—an old woman he had smuggled in—and was expelled in disgrace, to be immediately rejoined by Jeeves. His address for some years has been 3A Berkeley Mansions, W.1. Before that he was at 6A Crichton Mansions, Berkely St., W.1.

A concordance, however liberal, is not the place for a critical analysis even of this—the greatest of Wodehouse creations, though some attempt was begun under **Jeeves.** There is the sharpest distinction, critically, between Bertie's minimal and Jeeves's Olympian intellects. The farce characters (Wickhams and Ickenhams) ravage at will; Jeeves is but the august vehicle for divine reprobation the instrument of a loving justice; the amoral concept of the Bassetts and Spodes permits them to wreak havoc at no more cost than a salutary and enjoyable loss of dignity. But Bertie, like us, is subject to humanity's fallen nature and must, like ourselves, pay the price of pride or folly. In the realm of created character he is likest perhaps to the screen role of Charlie Chaplin. We share gloriously in his minute triumphs; we feels and ache for his humiliations; and we laugh as (and perhaps because) we are meant to laugh at ourselves. In Bertie we see Wodehouse the imperishable.

Wooster, Claude and Eustace: twin sons of the late Henry and of Emily Wooster, qq.v., and first cousins to Bertie, make a joint entrance in 'The Great Sermon Handicap'. Their subsequent departure from Oxford University, descent upon Bertie's flat, and occupation of the W.1. postal district, is a tour de force. It culminates in one of Jeeves's major tactical triumphs (IJ)

Wooster, Clive: gives harbourage in his Worcestershire home to his nephews Claude and Eustace when they are sent down (IJ)

Wooster, Emily: a member of the family who (one instinctively feels) would not rejoice at life's vicissitudes, as enjoined by Marcus Aurelius. Her appearances are invested with the need for urgent action and, too often, by the immediate execution therof by her sister-in-law Agatha. As wife of Henry and m. of those twin balls of fire Claude and Eustace, one perceives the truth of Agatha's 'poor' Emily (IJ)

Wooster, Sir George, Bart,: see **Yaxley. The Earl of,** He inherits the earldom at some point during the seven years between IJ and VGJ. As a Bart, he receives a severe shock (as a peer he specialises in administering them) when, toddling between the Devonshire Club and Boodles, he sees the wraith of his nephew Eustace, now supposedly en route for South Africa:

> 'You do think those two poor, dear boys are safe, Bertie?' said Aunt Agatha. 'They have not met with some horrible accident?'
>
> It made my mouth water to think of it. I thought Eustace *was* a horrible accident, and Claude about the same (IJ)

Wooster, the late Henry: remembered gratefully by Bertie, for his liberal tips but 'he did do some rather rummy things';

> notably keeping eleven pet rabbits in his bedroom. In fact, he wound up his career, happy to the last and completely surrounded by rabbits, in some sort of home (IJ)

Wooster, Willoughby: of Easeby Hall, Shropshire, an Oxford contemporary of Lord Worplesdon, writes his spirited reminiscences under the title of 'Recollections of a Long Life' for publication by Riggs and Ballinger. Bertie observes that Uncle Willoughby had been on the tabasco side as a young man about town, and might well turn out something pretty fruity if he started recollecting his long life. Florence Craye, currently engaged to Bertie, orders him to purloin the manuscript, and is shocked at its contents:

> 'If half of it is true,' she said, 'your uncle's youth must have been perfectly appalling. He plunges straight into a story of how he and my father were thrown out of a music-hall in 1887.'
> 'Why?'
> 'I decline to tell you why.' (COJ)

woozled: see **awash**

Wopple, Sir Oscar:
> 'How about that financier fellow who lives out Ditchingham way?'
> 'He shot himself last Friday, m'lord.'
> 'Oh, then we won't bother about him.' (RJ)

Words

If That's The Word I Want

AS THE FELLOW SAID, THE BURNED CHILD FEARS THE SPILLED MILK (JFS)

'Then what we have to do is to strain every nerve to see that he makes a hit. What are those things people have?'

'Sir?'
'Opera singers and people like that.'
'You mean a claque, sir?'
'That's right. The word was on the tip of my tongue' (MS)
'And another thing, Jeeves. It's all very well for her to say . . . glibly?'
'Or airily, sir. The words are synonymous.'
'It's all very well for her to say glibly or airily . . .' (SLJ)
'He's a mere uncouth Cossack,' she said.
A cossack, I knew, was one of those things clergymen wear, and I wondered why she thought Stilton was like one (JM)

I had seen him around the place, of course, but always in the company of a brace of assorted aunts, in each case looking Byronic. (Checking up with Jeeves, I find that that is the word, all right. Apparently it means looking like the late Lord Byron, who was a gloomy sort of bird, taking things the hard way) (MS)

Jeeves said it was something to do with inhibitions, if I caught the word correctly, and the suppression of, I think he said, the ego. What he meant, I gathered, was that Gussie had just completed a five years stretch of blameless seclusion among the newts, and all the goofiness which ought to have been spread out thin over those five years had been bottled up, and came to the surface on this occasion in a lump or—if you prefer it—a tidal wave (RHJ)

'So my errand was . . . what, Jeeves?'
'Bootless, sir.'
'Bootless? It doesn't sound right, but I suppose you know.' (SLJ)

'*Faute de* what?'
'*Mieux*, m'lord. A French expression. We should say "For want of anything better".'
'What asses these Frenchmen are. Why can't they talk English?'
'They are possibly more to be pitied than censured, m'lord. Early upbringing no doubt has a lot to do with it.' (RJ)

'What's that thing of Shakespeare's about someone having an eye like Mother's?'
' "An eye like Mars, to threaten and command", is possibly the quotation for which you are groping, sir' (MS)

When news reached me through well-informed channels that my Aunt Agatha, for many years a widow, or derelict, as I believe it is called, was about to take another pop at matrimony, my first emotion had been a gentle pity for the unfortunate goop slated to step up the aisle with her (JM)

'I see, sir. Most disturbing.'
I snorted a trifle.
'Oh?' I said. 'And I suppose, if you had been in San Francisco when the earthquake started, you would have just lifted up your finger and said "Tweet, tweet! Shush, shush! Now, now! Come, come!" The English language, they used to tell me at school, is the richest in the world, crammed full from end to end with about a million red-hot adjectives. Yet the only one you can find to describe this ghastly business is the adjective "disturbing". It is not disturbing, Jeeves. It is . . .'
'Cataclysmal, sir?'

'I shouldn't wonder' (VGJ)

Worple: valet to Alderman L. G. Trotter (whose Christian names are not the only secrets he would wish preserved) joins the Junior Ganymede Club and contributes his quota to the Club Book, with results most gratifying to the chatelaine of Brinkley Court, Worcs (JFS)

Worple, Alexander: after a lifetime's dexterous manipulation of the jute market, has the stuff in indecently large stacks, but believes that every young man should start at the bottom of the jute ladder (COJ)

Worplesdon, the Rt. Hon. the Earl of: Percival Craye, Southampton shipping magnate, principal owner of the Pink Funnel Line, is of Worcestershire origins. His family's links with the Woosters are of long standing; he himself was at Oxford with Bertie's uncle Willoughby and, later, affianced to Willoughby's sister Agatha. This was abruptly broken off after she read his press notices (see **Tottie**). A haughty and temperamental nobleman, Bertie observes that given the choice of a Worplesdon or a hippogriff as a walking companion he would choose the hippogriff every time. He cites the incident when, coming down to breakfast, the Earl gingerly lifted a few silver covers, remarked 'Eggs! Eggs! Damn all eggs!' and instantly legged it for the south of France, never to return to the bosom of his f. Given Lady Florence Craye and the Hon. Edwin as family, however, the peer had a point. He does, in effect, return years later, to contribute much of the sparkle to the superlative **JOY IN THE MORNING,** whose plot turns on his negotiations with the U.S. owner of the Clam Line. He is now married to the widowed Agatha Spenser Gregson and is in course of changing into a very different Earl. His relations with an ever-helpful Bertie are modified by seas of dance champagne, and from the bucko mate of a Western Ocean windjammer he is transmuted into a champion of jittery nephews against vindictive and overweening policemen. He now res. at Steeple Bumpleigh Hall, Hants (see also **Jeeves**):

'Don't make excuses for him, the man's a fool. And I should like to say,' said Uncle Percy, swelling like a balloon, 'that we have had far too much of late of these wild and irresponsible accusations. ... As long as I remain a Justice of the Peace I shall omit no word or act to express my strongest disapproval of it.'

'Quite all right, Uncle Percy.'

'It is not all right. It is outrageous. I advise you in future, officer, to be careful, very careful. And as for that warrant of yours, you can take it and stick it. . . . However, that is neither here nor there.' (COJ, JFS, JM)

Worplesdon, the Countess of: Agatha Wooster, sister of Bertie's late father, after a brief engagement to Percy Craye, m. Spenser Gregson, q.v. Is mother of young Thos., q.v. Widowed, she m. her former fiancé, now Lord Worplesdon, a union aptly summed up by Jeeves:

> 'You don't mean he's scared of Aunt Agatha? A tough bird like him? Practically a bucko mate of a tramp steamer.'
> 'Even bucko mates stand in awe of the captains of their vessels, sir.' (JM)

A pre-eminent do-gooder, imbued with the sense of responsibility which privilege bestows, Aunt Agatha has been Bertie's scourge since childhood:

> When I was a kid at school she was always able to turn me inside out with a single glance. There's about five-foot-nine of Aunt Agatha, topped off with a beaky nose, an eagle eye and a lot of grey hair, and the general effect is pretty formidable (IJ)

He betters the description in JM with the classic vignette, 'in appearance she resembles a well-bred vulture'. For a two-word-picture this is probably unexcelled. Agatha's methods are direct and draconic:

> The hotel which had had the bad luck to draw her custom was the Splendide, and by the time I got there there wasn't a member of the staff who didn't seem to be feeling it deeply. . . . Of course the real rough work was all over when I arrived, but I could tell by the way everyone grovelled before her that she had started by having her first room changed because it hadn't a southern exposure, and her next because it had a creaking wardrobe, and that she had said her say on the subject of the cooking, the waiting, the chambermaiding and everything else, with perfect freedom and candour. She had got the whole gang nicely under control by now. The manager, a whiskered cove who looked like a bandit, simply tied himself into knots whenever she looked at him (IJ)

Her assertion that Bertie is 'barely sentient' is as sincere as that he is virtually certifiable. She is accustomed to mark epochs by 'about the time Bertie lost that brooch', or 'just after Bertie made such an idiot of himself over Florence's birthday present'. The one advantage (he avers) in having such an aunt is that it makes one travel, thus broadening the mind. To him she is the aunt who eats broken bottles and kills rats with her teeth (MS), who wears barbed wire next the skin and conducts human sacrifices by the light of the full moon (JM), or who periodically turns into a were-wolf (JFS). That she 'devours her young' is to be doubted. Young Thos. is generally reckoned uneatable. It remains to record the one glorious occasion when Bertie, having at last 'got the hooks' on Aunt Agatha, summons up, instinctively and immediately, all the jargon of prefect- and magisterial-authority from which he has had to suffer through the years and gives Aunt Agatha her own Treatment A (IJ). But, though we are not privileged to assist at it, there is also the moment when, fortified by the sight of an Esmond Haddock quelling a whole nymphery of aunts, Bertie declines Jeeves's suggestion about the waterpipe and the milk train, but squares his shoulders:

> It would be deceiving my public to say that for an instant I did not quail. I quailed like billy-o. And then, suddenly, it was as if strength had descended upon me.
>
> 'Jeeves,' I said, 'I have just witnessed Esmond Haddock pound the stuffing out of five aunts. . . . It would ill beseem a Wooster to curl up before a single aunt. I shall now go down-stairs and pull an Esmond Haddock on Aunt Agatha.' And I strode to the door like Childe Roland about to fight the paynim (MS)

Wymondham-Wymondham, Algernon: comes in handy as a ratline, backstay or belaying-pin for Archie Mulliner to clutch at when, walking in Dover Street, they first catch sight of Aurelia Cammarleigh hailing a taxi.

Wyvern, Colonel Aubrey: Chief Constable of Southmoltonshire and f. of the attractive half-portion, Jill, q.v., res. at Wyvern Hall, near Southmolton. Like Vergil's Charon,

iam senior, sed cruda deo viridisque senectus

for when rumours reach him of certain nocturnal goings-on in the Henry VIII room at Rowcester Abbey, the gallant colonel takes forthright steps on his daughter's behalf with the supposedly errant

Earl of Rowcester, and even proposes to borrow the latter's own horsewhip to carry them out. (RJ)

Wyvern, Eustace: brother of Jill, wins a Littlewood's Pool and goes all high hat. Now moves on a different plane (RJ)

Wyvern, Jill, M.R.C.V.S.: d. of Southmoltonshire's Chief Constable, is well up in the attractive young prunes class of Wodehouse girl who, though half-pints in size, are more than equal to most exigencies. Not long ago a useful hockey outside-right, Jill is now an equally useful veterinary surgeon. Sought after doggedly by Bill Rowcester as his future Countess, she has anxious moments when watching the nocturnal movements of her lord to be, whether in or out of the Henry VIII room (RJ)

X

X ... and ... Q:

What made everything seem so sad and hopeless was the 'X.' As she emitted this, she drew her mouth back in a ghastly grin until the muscles of her neck stood out like ropes. And she went on and on and on. She refrained from Q-ing the 'Q' only to X the 'X', and when she wasn't X-ing to beat the band she was Q-ing away like a two-year-old. This pottiness was probably catching. Quite likely it would be coming out in himself, too. And a nice thing it would be for Aurelia if, as they stood side by side in the sacred edifice and the clergyman said 'Wilt thou, Archibald?' he were to reply 'Q ... X ...' or, worse, pant like a dog with his tongue out (YMS)

Xyrids and Squali, the: it is observable that rabbits which may turn at will into gnomes, stars doing a solo act, ducks getting theirs among the pondweed, the choreographic efforts of elves, or sharks transmuted to flatfish are among the many stimuli which may cause the eyes of Madeline Bassett to take on an appearance of flowers of the botanical order Xyridaceae (irises to you) drenched with evening dew. For those unlucky enough to be near by, the process is preceded by a sigh sounding like the wind going out of a rubber duck (RHJ)

Yaxley, the Rt. Hon. the Earl of: titular head of the Wooster family. We meet him first as Sir George Wooster, Bart., though he lives in the lively memory of Maudie Wilberforce (ornament of the old Cri. bar) as 'Piggy' Wooster. A festive old egg and an over-prominent landmark in St. James's Street, S.W., on most fine mornings, Bertie's Uncle George discovered (in advance of modern medical science) that alcohol is a food, and devotes his life to proving it. Periodically his system registers a mild protest, and he departs for Harrogate to get fined down. A well-known clubman, it is while on his way from the Devonshire to Boodle's that he is shocked by seeing the wraith of his nephew Eustace:

> 'Has it ever occurred to you, Bertie,' said Aunt Agatha, 'that your Uncle George may be psychic? Do you think it is possible he might see things not visible to the normal eye?'
> I thought it dashed possible, if not probable. (IJ)

It is when George, who has now inherited the earldom, contemplates matrimony with Rhoda Platt, a waitress at one of his clubs, that Aunt Agatha really extends herself:

> 'It is not unusual, sir,' said Jeeves, 'to find gentlemen of a certain age yielding to what might be described as a sentimental urge. They appear to experience what I may term a sort of Indian summer, a kind of temporarily renewed youth. The phenomenon is particularly noticeable, I am given to understand, among the wealthier inhabitants of the city of Pittsburg'. (VGJ)

Neither Agatha nor Lord Yaxley are allowed to learn that the Earl's subsequent marriage, not to Rhoda, but to her aunt (his old flame of Criterion days) is smoothly engineered by Jeeves. The chronicles do not inform us whether the title stems from the village of Yaxley in Suffolk or from its sister village of the same name in Hunts. Res. Jermyn St., W. (IJ, VGJ)

(Other students may, like myself, have been visited by strange and stimulating presentiments concerning this Yaxley earldom. The present peer is elderly and childless. Who is the heir? Claude or Eustace? Unthinkable. Everything points to Bertram Wilberforce Wooster as the senior nephew. If so, the long-term effects on the destinies of Britain and indeed of the world at large are quite incalculable. For Jeeves will surely persuade the young master that it is his duty to take his seat in the Upper House. And the

latent potentialities of a House of Lords ruled and directed in all
its policies by an Eminence Grise such as the master-mind of
Jeeves are as immeasurable—and a great deal farther reaching—
than in a previous period when both political parties were
dominated by the Fairy Queen—*Ed.*)

Yaxley, the Countess of: see **Wilberforce, Maudie**

Yoga: The Bwana performs his nightly, and with it, communion
with the Jivatma or soul (RJ)

Yoicks!: int. 1774, reports the S.E.D. charily (sim. **Yoi**, 1826;
app. rel. to **Hike**) is 'a foxhunting cry urging on the hounds', and
as such was frequent in the repertoire of Dahlia Travers in her
Quorn and Pytchley days. The hounds to which she applies this,
or similar epithets, now are usually human. It is also used by
Esmond Haddock, associated with such terms as 'Hark for'rard',
'Tally ho' and 'Loo-loo-loo-loo-loo' after his spiritual rebirth at
the village concert.

YOUNG MEN IN SPATS: first published 1936, is a coruscant
collection of Drones stories containing such classics as **'The
Amazing Hat Mystery'**, **'Tried In The Furnace'** and the
immortal **'Uncle Fred Flits By'**.

York and Ainsty Hunt Ball, the: of the year 1921, was (declares
Aunt Dahlia) the last occasion on which she experienced a tender,
sentimental approach from a stranger:

> 'What is this joint?' she was demanding heatedly. 'A looney-
> bin? First I meet Spink-Bottle racing down the corridor like
> a mustang, then you try to walk through me as if I were
> thistle-down, and now the gentleman in the burnous has
> started tickling my ankle—a thing that hasn't happened to
> me since the York and Ainsty Hunt Ball of the year 1921' (CW)

Z

Zachariah: there is something about evening service in a village
church in the summer time that affects the most hard-boiled, and

as Barmy Phipps drinks in the first lesson, and applies it to his own policy with Pongo Twistleton, he wonders whether Abimelech would have behaved like that to Jazzbo or—for the matter of that—Jazzbo to Zachariah (YMS)

Zambesi River: a Wooster is eaten by a crocodile on, (SLJ)

Zarietchayna: and Medvienko, the cock-eyed goings-on of, (JO)

Zend Avesta of Zoroaster: Rory Carmyle confesses that he has not read the, and is therefore not conversant with the mystical Ninth House:

> 'By Agatha Christie, isn't it?' (RJ)

zoom off: hearing Uncle Percy working through the concluding stanzas of his chanty, Bertie and Jeeves decide to, forthwith (JM)

Zoroaster: the dualistic religious system of, see **Zend Avesta** (RJ)

Zulu: Major Plank a firm believer in the efficiency of a Zulu knobkerrie in dealing with characters like Alpine Joe (SLJ); Boko's suggestion that Bertie should strip to the buff, smear himself with boot polish and attend the East Wibley revels as a Zulu chief, meets with a *nolle prosequi* (JM); Horace Davenport graces the Marlborough St. dock, and later the Drones Club, as a Zulu warrior (UFS)

Zutphen: and the pie-faced Bertie; see **Sidney, Sir Philip** (MS)

P. G. WODEHOUSE

JEEVES AND THE FEUDAL SPIRIT

Jeeves did not approve of Bertie Wooster's new moustache and expressed himself in such terms on the matter that some feeling of coolness between him and his employer could not fail to result.

Then the thunder-clouds began to gather from another direction, and Wooster thought that he might have to face the impending crisis alone. But Jeeves was not the man to allow a domestic tiff to come between him and their common enemy. The feudal spirit burned bright within him and he rallied to his master's cause as resourcefully and imperturbably as ever before.

CORONET BOOKS

P. G. WODEHOUSE

JOY IN THE MORNING

'Mr Wodehouse's idyllic world can never stale. He will continue to release future generations from captivity that may be more irksome than our own. He has made a world for us to live and delight in.'

Evelyn Waugh in a BBC broadcast

Bertie Wooster was trapped in Steeple Bumpleigh.

With him were Florence Craye to whom he had once been engaged; 'Stilton' Cheesewright to whom Florence was now promised and who regarded Bertie as a snake in the grass; Zenobia Hopwood and her guardian Lord Worpledon; and, biggest blot of all on the landscape, Edwin the Boy Scout, doing acts of kindness out of sheer malevolence.

Complete disaster could only be averted by the genius of Jeeves who, at the moment of crisis, extricated the young master with a stratagem as smoothly executed as it was brilliantly conceived.

CORONET BOOKS

ALSO AVAILABLE IN CORONET BOOKS

P. G. WODEHOUSE

☐	21789 8	Jeeves and the Feudal Spirit	60p
☐	21788 X	Joy In The Morning	70p
☐	21790 1	Thank You, Jeeves	60p
☐	22694 3	Plum Pie	75p
☐	22695 1	A Few Quick Ones	75p
☐	22696 X	Mr. Mulliner Speaking	75p

NICHOLAS MEYER

☐	21843 6	The West End Horror	80p
☐	20453 2	The Seven Per Cent Solution	75p

LESLIE CHARTERIS

☐	02287 6	Trust the Saint	75p
☐	01729 5	The Saint to the Rescue	75p
☐	17319 X	The Saint Abroad	75p

All these books are available at your local bookshop or newsagent, or can be ordered direct from the publisher. Just tick the titles you want and fill in the form below.

Prices and availability subject to change without notice.

CORONET BOOKS, P.O. Box 11, Falmouth, Cornwall.
Please send cheque or postal order, and allow the following for postage and packing:

U.K. — One book 22p plus 10p per copy for each additional book ordered, up to a maximum of 82p.

B.F.P.O. and **Eire** — 22p for the first book plus 10p per copy for the next six books, thereafter 4p per book.

OTHER OVERSEAS CUSTOMERS — 30p for the first book and 10p per copy for each additional book.

Name ....

Address ....

....